Mercy
immense and free

Mercy Immense and Free

Essays on Wesley and Wesleyan Theology

REVISED EDITION

Victor A. Shepherd

www.bpsbooks.com

MERCY IMMENSE AND FREE
Copyright © 2016, 2010 by Victor Shepherd

All rights reserved. No part of this publication may be reproduced, stored in a retrieval system, or transmitted, in any form or by any means, electronic, mechanical, photocopying, recording or otherwise, without the prior written permission of the publisher.

Published in 2016 by
BPS BOOKS
A division of Bastian Publishing Services Ltd.
Toronto, Canada
www.bpsbooks.com

First published in 2010 by Clements Academic, as volume 1 of Tyndale Seminary's *Tyndale Studies in Wesleyan History and Theology*.

Scripture quotations, unless otherwise noted, are taken from the Revised Standard Version of the Bible, copyright 1952 [second edition, 1971] by the Division of Christian Education of the National Council of the Churches of Christ in the United States of America. Used by permission. All rights reserved.

ISBN 978-1-72236-035-6

Cataloguing in Publication data available from Library and Archives Canada.

Cover portrait by Eric Jennings, Salisbury, England, to mark Wesley 250th anniversary celebrations by Salisbury Methodist Church.

Cover design: Daniel Crack, www.kdbooks.ca

In gratitude for

W. Raymond Cummins

*Scientist, Professor and Friend
whose discernment of evil
has never eclipsed his love of life*

Contents

Introduction 11

PART ONE: THE LIFE AND THOUGHT OF JOHN WESLEY

1. An Introduction to John Wesley 15
2. The Spirituality of John Wesley 29
3. Wesley and the Witness of the Spirit 45
4. Wesley's Understanding of the Law of God 59
5. Wesley on Reason, Gospel and Catholicity 85
6. Wesley and Small Group Ministry 95
7. Wesley's Understanding of Christian Perfection 101

PART TWO: THE WESLEYAN TRADITION

8. The Methodist Tradition in Canada 137
9. The Arminian Aspect of Wesleyan Theology 143
10. Charles Wesley and the Methodist Tradition 153
11. Egerton Ryerson and Public Education in Canada .. 171
12. New Connexion Methodism and William Booth 183
13. Thomas Oden, Exemplar of the Methodist Ethos ... 203
14. Neither Mist nor Mud 213

PART THREE: SERMONS

15. Susanna Annesley, a Mother's Day Sermon 225
16. "Our Doctrines," on Wesley Day 233
17. Holiness of Heart and Life (at Hay Bay) 243
18. "The Duty of Constant Communion" 253

Conclusion / John Wesley: A Gift to the Universal Church 261

Index 281

John Wesley, 1703–1791

INTRODUCTION

For centuries John Wesley was regarded as an itinerant evangelist, open-air preacher, translator (chiefly of German hymns from the Pietist tradition into English), poet, brother to Charles (the finest hymnwriter in English-speaking Church), founder of Methodism (although he was ordained, ministered and died an Anglican)—and yet, regrettably, theologically effete. The last forty years, however, have seen a major shift in the church's assessment: Wesley, to say the least, is recognized as the most significant Anglican theologian of the eighteenth century.

In light of the extensive and intensive Wesley Studies that the late Albert Outler precipitated forty years ago, however, Wesley's contribution is now seen to transcend Anglicanism; the man from Epworth is esteemed at present a major theologian of the church catholic. Any doubt on this score is dispelled by the plethora of books mining Wesley's writings. In addition the papers delivered at the Oxford Institute of Methodist Theological Studies, meeting at the University of Oxford every five years, continue to underscore Wesley's role in the ever-deepening tradition of the church's missional engagement with a world that God so loves as never to forsake.

The notion that Wesley's thought is relatively insubstantial because he did not write systematic theology in the vein of Aquinas, Melanchthon, Calvin or Barth is indefensible in light of the theological worthies whose substance no one questions yet who also did not write systematic theology; e.g., Luther, Edwards and Newman. Wesley's theology remains a lode that, once unearthed and refined, will continue to form and inform not only the many denominations claiming the title "Methodist," and not only the Holiness and Pentecostal Churches that own him as progenitor, but also Christian communions of every sort. The hymns of John and Charles, for instance, are now sung by worshippers in every denomination.

* * *

John Wesley's thought converged on the cross; his ministry radiated from it. Reflecting this conviction Charles Wesley's hymns extol the atonement above all else. (One need only think of Charles' Christmas carol, "Hark! The Herald Angels sing!" with its "Peace on earth and mercy mild, God and sinners reconciled.") The primordiality of the cross, it must be noted, forever renders God's effectual mercy the dominant feature of Wesley's thinking, preaching and counseling. Mercy triumphs over judgment. Mercy can be mercy only if it is pressed not only upon all without condition but also upon all without exception. The atonement wrought at Calvary, according to Wesley, renders insupportable any notion of "limited atonement," any suggestion that Jesus has died only for the "elect" but not for the entire creation. For this reason to hear Charles exult, "'Tis mercy all, immense and free" is to know that "mercy immense and free" gathers up the Wesleyan ethos as no other four-word summation can. Eschewing theological speculation (Wesley claimed to write only "practical divinity"), Wesley avoids fruitless conjecture on the incarnation or the self-emptying of the Son of God; instead he exalts atonement—and therefore atonement-wrought faith in addition—as the only purpose of incarnation and kenosis that needs to concern the troubled sinner .

Troubled? Any sinner in the grip of Spirit-wrought conviction will be troubled affectively. Yet contrary to much popular opinion that Wesley

INTRODUCTION

wrote what amounts to little more than religious psychology, he never deviated from—and his characteristic evangelism presupposes—his iron-fast certainty that unrepentant sinners live already under God's condemnation and can only perish, unless they make that grace-quickened "about-turn" Scripture calls repentance and cast themselves in faith upon a mercy they do not deserve and have not fashioned. Such mercy, both relieving them of sin's guilt and releasing them from sin's grip, will ever constrain them to adore and serve their Saviour until that day when, "Changed from glory into glory," they are "Lost in wonder, love and praise."

According to Wesley mercy immense and free is the beginning and the end of all the ways, works and words of God,

* * * *

Mercy Immense and Free unfolds in three sections. The first examines the work and witness of John Wesley. The second discusses the amplification and application of the Wesleyan tradition, including its expansion in the New World. The third consists of sermons that articulate Wesley's theology and ethos. Agreeing with the sixteenth-century Reformers, Wesley believed that preaching inhered the gospel; i.e., "gospel" means gospel preached. Everywhere his work confirms Heinrich Bullinger's pronouncement, *Praedicatio verbi Dei verbum Dei est*—"the preaching of the Word of God is itself 'Word of God.'" It is fitting to include sermons on Wesley in light of Wesley's tireless preaching ministry in fair weather and foul, in sickness and in health, until death parted him from his commission.

New to this edition is a conclusion that shows John Wesley as uniquely positioned to graft the western and eastern branches of Christendom into a new and more flourishing church in the twenty-first century. This piece was originally published in *Canadian Theological Review*, Winter 2012.

PART I

THE LIFE AND THOUGHT OF JOHN WESLEY

1

AN INTRODUCTION TO JOHN WESLEY

The Man, His Times and His Faith

John Wesley captured hearts, heads and hands as few other Christian leaders have been able to do. For this reason the movement bearing his name flared rapidly into a fire like that of Pentecost—warming, cheering, illuminating, purifying, and above all igniting whatever it touched as he and his descendants embodied the Good News wherever they went. The United Church of Canada could never have come forth without him; Methodists predominated in the 1925 union that created the church.

The public good in Canada is unthinkable without him. His spiritual descendants—Egerton Ryerson, for example—gave birth to public education in Canada, a huge advance on Britain's class-system with its invisible ceilings condemning most people to material bleakness. The benefits Canadians sometimes take for granted—like assistance for impoverished immigrants, public health programs and universal medical care—are the legacy of Prairie Methodists like James S. Woodsworth and Dolly McGuire. Our debt is colossal.

We came perilously close to being deprived of him. In 1709, the rectory in which he lived with his family—Wesley was the fifteenth of nineteen children—caught fire. A human pyramid lifted the six-year-old to safety seconds before the second-storey balcony on which he had been huddling collapsed. Thereafter he always referred to himself as "a brand plucked from the fire" (Zech. 3:2).

In his lifetime he would travel 400,000 km on horseback and preach 40,000 times. Having declared, "I love the poor," he would also pour himself out for the people whom he championed zealously.

See him at age 81. He has been trudging from door to door for four days straight, begging money. It is wintertime, his diary tells us, and his feet have been immersed from morning to night in slush. He stops begging at the end of the fourth day, not because he has managed to raise 200 pounds but because he has been overtaken by a "violent flux." (Today we'd say diarrhea.) Only his own sickness stops him "wasting" himself for those needier still.

He expected as much from his people in the New World, and they gave it gladly. Of the first 737 Methodist preachers in North America, fifty percent died before they were thirty years of age. Two-thirds didn't live long enough to serve twelve years. Hardship? His people were trailblazers as surely as was Jesus Christ before them, "the pioneer and perfecter of our faith" (Hebrews 12:2).

Methodism began as a renewal movement within the Anglican Church. After Wesley's death, a denomination emerged. In Canada, Methodists subsequently merged with Presbyterians and Congregationalists. How will it all end? The answer has everything to do with what "it" is now.

Wesley's preoccupation with love was intimately tied to his understanding of the Christian life. Christian existence, he insisted, is a life of self-forgetful love for God and neighbour as Christ's people abandon themselves to serve those who suffer atrociously, are customarily forsaken, and too often are near-friendless.

Here his eschatological approach differed from Roman Catholicism, for instance, whose people traditionally emphasize sight: in the eschaton we shall see God in a beatific vision that finally brings into focus all we've found fuzzy.

John Calvin's descendants emphasize knowledge: while we know but in part throughout our earthly sojourn, in the eschaton we shall know God in a way that dispels all doubt and corrects all misapprehension.

While embracing truth wherever he found it, Wesley nonetheless insisted that our vision of God and our knowledge of God would be gathered up and crowned eschatologically in our love for God as finally we were "lost in wonder, love and praise." For this reason he cherished John's first epistle just because it tolled relentlessly the love wherewith God loves us and the love whereby we must love one another.

In his famous tract, "The Almost Christian," Wesley explores what unbelievers lack specifically when they lack faith generally. You expect him to say right off that believers are marked chiefly by faith in God. Instead he says that believers are those who love God.

Of course, Wesley believed that faith marks the "faithful," binds us to Jesus Christ. Yet he was always leery of those who claimed to serve God and obey God without ever loving God. For this reason he insisted that there is no faith in God without a simultaneous love for God, and equally no love for God without faith in God.

"No love without faith." Faith is a matter of trusting the provision God has made in the cross for rebel sinners. Our estrangement from God disappears only as God absorbs it in the cross and thereby opens the way to our homecoming.

"No faith without love." All around him in eighteenth-century England, Wesley saw serious, sincere people whose theology was orthodox even as no warmth had ever thawed their icy hearts or unlocked their frozen lives. Wesley dismissed such so-called faith as self-congratulatory.

For Wesley, faith in God and love for God penetrated, implied and interpreted each other. His preoccupation with love admitted that while faith would give way to sight, and hope to hope's fulfilment, love would give way to nothing—except more love, forever and ever.

Of all the misunderstandings that falsify Wesley and his spiritual descendants, none is more defamatory than the assumption that the Methodist tradition doesn't think. While it is readily acknowledged that the Lutheran, Reformed, Roman Catholic and Eastern Orthodox families within the church catholic think and have always thought, Methodism, it is sometimes said, merely emotes.

Wesley contradicts this. Having insisted that his lay preachers study five hours per day, he studied more himself. He authored grammar textbooks in seven of the eight foreign languages he knew.

He deplored as narrow, ignorant and foolish the suggestion that preachers need read only one book. Such fanaticism meant that reading only the Bible guaranteed misreading it. Those who complained of having "no taste for reading" he rebuked on the spot: "Contract a taste for it by use, or return to your trade"—and watched more than a few preachers move back to farm, shop or mine.

His reading was as broad as it was deep. No area of intellectual endeavour escaped him. All his life he kept abreast of contemporary explorations in natural science. Schooled in classical philosophy at Oxford, he probed the contemporary empiricist thinking of John Locke. Aware that history is a theatre both of God's activity and of the church's response, he wrote a world history.

All his life Wesley eschewed mental laziness as he eschewed little else. Sleeping no more than six hours per night and arising each morning at four, he spent the freshest hours of the day expanding his mind, expecting all Methodists, but preachers especially, to follow him. To this end he brought together fifty books in his Christian Library, regarding them essential to the intellectual formation of his people. Methodism loves God with the mind.

After May 24, 1738, when he "felt my heart strangely warmed" in the course of hearing Luther's Commentary on Romans read at worship, he knew that justification by faith—free forgiveness of sins, rooted in God's mercy, without consideration for human merit—is the beginning and the stable basis of the Christian life. Unhesitatingly he announced that where justification isn't upheld, the church doesn't exist. In 1766 he was still declaring, "I believe justification by faith alone as much as I believe there is a God."

Still, he did not take church tradition lightly. He saw it as a storehouse of wisdom from which sorely pressed and perplexed Christians could draw. Wesley knew that a church that disdains Christian memory resembles a sailing ship without a keel. Without one, a ship can only be driven before the prevailing wind. With a keel, the boat can sail across the wind or even against it. Wesley knew that his movement, opposed by magistrates, merchants, and ecclesiastical officialdom, had to be able to use unfavourable winds if it was going to make headway.

In the same theological spirit, Wesley bridged West and East. For instance, the Western church, both Reformed and Roman, had understood original sin largely in terms of a massive original guilt that was somehow transmitted to posterity. The Orthodox churches understood it as the introduction of death, inward corruption, and loss of the Holy Spirit. Wesley preferred the latter without denying everything of the former.

Wesley remains the figure in the Protestant orbit who can "dance" with virtually anyone in the Christian family. Appreciating the East (especially the Eastern Fathers, whose luminary, Athanasius, Wesley always preferred to the West's Augustine), he also included in his Christian Library eight works by Roman Catholic mystics from the Counter Reformation. While the sixteenth-century Reformers had denied fasting as a means of grace (Zwingli, the leader of the Reformation in Zurich, had eaten sausages in Lent to publicize his disavowal of fasting), Wesley unambiguously declared it to be a means of grace, fasting weekly himself and urging his people to follow him.

Wesley's assertion that "the world is my parish" was no exaggeration. His theology was as wide as the world he knew God to love, and as deep as the sin he knew God to redeem.

Glad to identify himself with the wider church, Wesley characteristically moved his people to "holiness of heart and life." Always suspicious of a Christian understanding of forgiveness that relieved people of sin's guilt but left them in its grip, he judiciously matched "relief" with "release." The habituated (all sin is addictive) could know deliverance.

The habituation was not imagined. By 1750 England's annual per capita (children included) consumption of gin stood at more than ten litres.[1] Intoxicated children, even children with delerium tremens, were a common sight. The infant death rate, already high due to disease, skyrocketed on account of neglect. Of the 2,000 houses in St. Giles, London, 506 were gin shops.

Parliament often foreshortened its debates "because the honourable members were too drunk to continue the affairs of state." Gambling took down rich and poor alike. The degeneration accompanying all of this need not be detailed. Its dimensions are sufficiently attested in one advertisement, "Champagne, Dice, Music, or your Neighbour's Spouse." Wesley knew that something more than forgiveness was needed. It was his conviction, and soon his people's experience, that God could do something with sin beyond forgiving it.

"Holiness of heart and life," then, was yet another of the balances that Wesley maintained judiciously. Holiness of heart is release from inner evil tempers or dispositions. Holiness of life is release from evil conduct—believers, now freed, "do the truth." Both are needed. Holiness of life alone is self-serving legalism wherein a reputation is gained that is not deserved. Holiness of heart alone is self-indulgent, religious romanticism.

In Wesley's era all Christians agreed that "without holiness no one will see the Lord" (Hebrews 12:14). All Christians similarly agreed that Christ's people would be delivered "in the instant of death." Since Christ's people are going to be delivered in the moment of transition, Wesley contended, why not in this life? Why not now? To say that we are not going to be delivered until the "instant" is to doom the habituated to lifelong addiction.

Aware that God's commands are all "covered promises," and noticing that the root command in Scripture is "You shall be holy; for I the Lord your God am holy" (Leviticus 19:2), Wesley discerned that the "uncovered" promise of God was the unblemished, perfected holi-

---

1. Statistics and quotations in the following paragraphs are taken from J. W. Bready, *England: Before and After Wesley* (London: Hodder and Stoughton, 1938).

ness of God's people. Such a deliverance was the grand, overarching promise that guaranteed the fulfilment of all other promises. For this reason Wesley was fond of saying that all of Scripture was "one grand promise" that remedied all the ravages of the Fall and rendered God's people resplendent.

Unlike many of his successors, Wesley insisted that the promise of the Gospel had to be announced in the spirit of the Gospel. People were to be drawn, not driven, to the Gospel. God's promise had to be heard not as a threat, not even as an announcement, but as winsome, attractive, comely. This "Christian Perfection" was nothing less than perfection in love. People would forget their self-preoccupation in the immensity of God's love and the immediacy of their neighbour's need.

Without the experience of deliverance now—known, enjoyed, commended to others—Wesleyanism would have been stillborn.

Wesley's efforts on behalf of disadvantaged people are almost the stuff of legend. His heart convulsed at the spectacle of the poor people won to the Methodist movement. Poor people, he knew, are more frequently ill and more wretchedly ill than the socially advantaged, and have less access to treatment. Quickly Wesley gathered to himself a surgeon and an apothecary. He paid for their services by scrounging money wherever he could. In the first five months of his program, the apothecary distributed free drugs to 500 people. By 1746 Wesley had established London's first free pharmacy.

He acquainted himself with the latest in pharmaceutics, and recorded his findings in the aptly titled *Primitive Physic* (1747). In a pre-analgesic era, his trademark cure for headache was: "Pour upon the palm of the hand a little brandy and a zest of lemon, and hold it to the forehead." His remedy for the relief of protracted psychotic depression was a crude form of electro-convulsive therapy. Wesley placed an electrode on either side of a patient's head, and then cranked a handle to shock sufferers with static electricity. At least he had recognized that non-situational depression was rooted neither in defective faith nor in demonic possession.

Wesley was distressed by the predicament of aged widows, most of whom had survived scarcity while their husbands were alive, only to stare at the spectre of death by starvation, exposure or loneliness in their widowhood. He purchased houses for these women and refurbished them "so as to be warm and clean." So that the widows who lived in them did not feel demeaned as charity cases, Wesley often ate the food they ate, from the tables at which they sat. He also informed his preachers that if they wanted to avoid dismissal they should do the same.

When bankers refused to lend money to Methodists who wanted to start up small businesses, Wesley scrabbled fifty pounds and dispensed small loans. Later, those who had borrowed were themselves able to lend money to his "bank" so that the next wave could be helped. In the first year he helped 250 people make a fresh financial start.

Aware that education admits people to a world otherwise inaccessible, Wesley developed the Kingswood School. Early on, it educated the children of coal miners and straitened Methodist preachers; it operates to this day.

Yet Wesley's zeal for social betterment didn't come from British radicals who wanted to destroy social order. The "Levellers," as reformers rooted in the seventeenth century were labeled, had never persuaded Wesley, a Tory, that their agenda was sound. Instead, the Kingdom of God—present, operative, crying out for visibility—was the corrective lens through which Wesley saw creation transfigured as "new heavens and a new earth in which righteousness dwells" (2 Peter 3:13).

Tirelessly, Wesley urged his people, "Earn all you can; save all you can; give all you can."[2] When he drew thirty pounds per year as an Anglican priest, he lived on twenty-eight and gave away two. When book royalties boosted his income to 120 pounds, he lived on twenty-eight and gave away ninety-two. Wesley never understood hoarding. While he agreed

---

2. At age 86, Wesley lamented that his people were wonderfully adept at the first two yet pathetically indifferent to the third. In his frustration he fumed, "And yet nothing can be more plain than that all who observe the first two rules without the third will be twofold more the children of hell than they were before" (Wesley, *The Works of John Wesley* (Bicennial Ed.); (Nashville: Abingdon, 1984), vol. 4, p. 91. Hereafter cited as *WJW*, 4.91.

that the scriptural text pronounced the love of money to be the root of all evil, he maintained that no one could hang on to superfluous cash without coming to love it—and perpetrate the evil it guaranteed.

In all of this he was aware that it's always difficult to help without degrading those helped. Wanting to assist poor women by means of something other than "cold charity," he purchased yards of the fine black cloth that people normally bought to cover church windows for their funerals. Then he informed his assistants that they were to have the cloth sewn into elegant dresses and given to women who would otherwise never be able to afford a good outfit.

Small group nurture was the heart of the Methodist movement. While Wesley is often associated with huge outdoor gatherings, he spoke far more frequently to smaller congregations that provided a setting for mutual confrontation, correction and encouragement.

The "Society," the largest grouping, consisted of all the Methodists in a city or town or village. In the "Class," people were gathered into "twelves" according to their geographical proximity to each other. The "Band" was the smallest of all.

"Classes" were the most comprehensive. Mothers and miners met each other, shopkeepers and soldiers, the learned and the unlettered, young and old, prominent and penurious. Each class met once a week under the supervision of a leader. The only condition for membership was "a desire to flee from the wrath to come, and to be saved from their sins. But wherever this is really fixed in the soul it will be shown by its fruits."[3]

The first fruit was "doing no harm, and avoiding evil of every kind"—including "the using of many words in buying or selling" and "softness, and needless self-indulgence."

The second fruit was "doing good"—feeding the hungry, clothing the ill-clad, visiting the sick and imprisoned. Not to be overlooked, however,

---

3. For the details of the nature, purpose and rules of the classes and bands see Wesley, *WJW*, vol. 9, "The Methodist Societies: History, Nature and Design," ch. 3 and 4.

was "submitting to bear the reproach of Christ, to be as the filth and offscouring of the world."

The third fruit was "attending upon all the ordinances of God"—public worship, private prayer, and fasting every Friday.

"Bands" differed significantly. They were made up of only four or five people organized according to occupation (sailors, seamstresses, labourers, for example); or organized according to desperate need (alcoholics, gamblers, "whoremongers.") The bands had to be gender-segregated in light of the frank confession essential to them. The purpose was to "Confess your faults to one another, and pray for one another that you may be healed." (James 5:16) The rules of the bands, drawn up on Christmas Day, 1738, suggest a self-disclosure that couldn't be cloaked. For example:

> Rule 7: "Do you desire to be told of all your faults, and that plain and home?"
>
> Rule 9: "Consider! Do you desire we should tell you whatsoever we think, whatsoever we fear, whatsoever we hear, concerning you?"
>
> Rule 11: "Is it your desire and design to be on this and all other occasions entirely open, so as to speak everything that is in your heart, without exception, without disguise and without reserve?"

And then there was the question that Wesley insisted be put to every band-member at every meeting: "Have you nothing you desire to keep secret?"

The confrontation was severe. Yet Wesley knew that love worthy of the name has to scorch, or else it is nothing more than a polite indulgence which finally profits no one.

While public worship was essential to the spiritual health of his people, Wesley, unlike most evangelists, insisted especially on Holy Communion. It was nothing less than God's command. All who neglected it were disobedient or foolish. When some people complained that they weren't worthy, Wesley told them that Christ's mercy eclipsed all considerations

of merit. When others returned from the communion rail complaining that they didn't feel any different, he was quick with five benefits:
- we are strengthened "insensibly";
- we are made more fit for the service of God;
- we are made more constant in the service of God;
- we are kept from backsliding;
- we are spared many temptations.

For Wesley, to receive Holy Communion was to receive Christ himself.

The small man (5'4," 120 pounds) had feet of clay. All his life he lacked self-knowledge, particularly in his relations with women. He was autocratic. Often he irked his brother Charles. He could spew sarcasm. Still, he was wonderfully used of God. He was living proof of Luther's dictum: "God can draw a straight line with a crooked stick." In fair days and foul he never ceased having a heart as big as a house for sinning, suffering, sorrowing humankind.

Wesley was evidence of two miracles: first, that someone of his social and educational station could communicate with the disadvantaged. Second—and the greater miracle—was that he wanted to.

It is little wonder, then, that when the 86-year-old visited Falmouth and was showered with gratitude and love by mobs who had abused him forty years earlier, he jotted in his journal: "High and low now lined the street... out of stark love and kindness, gaping and staring as if the King were going by."[4]

He was not the king. He was, however, a very great ambassador.

---

4. Wesley, *WJW*, Vol. 24: Journals and Diaries VII (1787–1791), p. 151: Aug. 17, 1789.

2

THE SPIRITUALITY OF JOHN WESLEY

"If we are going to have two kings then we are going to have two beds," Samuel Wesley fumed in anger at his wife's intransigence. He had "heard" her silence when she ought to have voiced her "Amen" at his suppertime prayer for King William. "He is no king; he is but a prince," Susannah said of William of Orange, the Dutchman now married to Mary. Feted for his military prowess at the Battle of the Boyne (July 12, 1690), William had defeated James II, thereby ensuring the " Orange " or Protestant colour of Britain and its far-flung empire. Susannah, however, remained a "Non-Juror" who refused to swear loyalty to a foreign interloper.

Connubially deprived now, the woman who had already had fourteen children petitioned the Archbishop of York, complaining that her husband had reneged on his marriage vow. The archbishop declined to adjudicate the dispute. Meanwhile her husband, absent from the home for months on account of his attendance in London at Convocation, the highest court of the Church of England, returned home. They reconciled. John was conceived that night.

John's brother, Charles, was to be the eighteenth. One more daughter would complete the family. (Susannah had been the last of twenty-five, all born to Dr Samuel Annesley, a Puritan minister whose spacious London living room accommodated weekly meetings of ministers where everyone profited from Annesley's acclaimed sophistication in philosophy and theology.)

John and Charles would eventually become household names throughout the English-speaking world. John would dominate the theological, ecclesiastical and social landscape of the eighteenth century. Charles, possessed of consummate poetical gifts in a family where everyone could write poetry, would become not only the most able hymnwriter in English, but because of this, the vehicle whereby the truth and reality of the gospel migrated from head to heart to hands—in fact right into the bloodstream of the Methodist people. For as preaching quickened faith in hearers throughout the Evangelical Awakening, hymnody became the means whereby those who now loved Christ "with love undying" (Eph. 6:24) found themselves humming unforgettable tunes whose Scripture-laden words seeped so very deeply into them as to effervesce for the rest of their lives.

As a result of John's dramatic deliverance from the rectory fire (see previous chapter) Susannah deemed John to be appointed to a special work. Home-schooling all her children (at least from age three to six), she took particular pains with John, finding him precocious in a family where she expected all children to be reading by four. At eleven he left home for Charterhouse School, beginning each day with the breakfast nourishment of bread, cheese and beer. (Susannah had always brewed the family's supply.)

At Oxford University John landed in an environment that was socially privileged, academically indifferent and blissfully frivolous. Deploring the shallowness and silliness, he and a handful of serious scholars formed a group that mockers quickly labelled the "Holy Club." It survived their contempt, and in fact was marked by many profundities.

For instance, the group zealously consumed the classics, the classics being a carryover from Renaissance humanism. It cherished the Church

Fathers, Christian thinkers from the close of the apostolic era to the early Middle Ages whose writing was second only to Scripture in the theological and devotional formation of the church. "Christian Antiquity," as Wesley spoke of Patristics, could be mined at this time at Oxford since the university was in the twilight of exemplary Patristic scholarship.

The group was equally ardent at recovering the liturgy of the Church of England. Throughout his life John would recognize and honour other "modes of worship," as he called them, but would never abate in esteeming the Book of Common Prayer as the finest in Christendom and its liturgy as without peer. Whereas attendance at Holy Communion had declined until three times per year only (Christmas, Easter and Pentecost) was most common, Wesley and his friends insisted on a minimum of weekly Eucharist. (Over his life he would average 4.5 times per week.) Their recovery of the eucharistic dimension of worship, together with their zeal for the Fathers, was evident in Wesley's insistence that not wine only but wine and water be used. The latter point, in "High Church" worship, was an effectual reminder of the blood and water that had flowed from the Redeemer's side in God's recovery of the creation.

Lest their "Holy Club" become self-absorbed, the students visited the poor, attended the sick, and befriended the imprisoned. (Prisons at this time were one large room, its floor straw-covered and its "toilets" a bucket or two. They housed men and women together, young and old, deranged and perverse, social victim and hardened criminal. Years later it was the Methodists who campaigned to reform prisons, insisting on the segregation of male and female convicts in order to protect the latter against sexual molestation.)[1]

Upon graduating from Oxford, and following both ordination and several years' university teaching, Wesley departed England for the New World. Ostensibly he was going as a clergyman to the colonies in Georgia and a missionary to First Peoples. In fact he was pursuing a spiritual quest

---

1. See David Lyle Jeffrey, ed. *English Spirituality in the Age of Wesley* (Grand Rapids: Eerdmans, 1994), p. 21.

wherein he hoped to satisfy a nameless ache and longing within himself. Disembarking after the months-long voyage, he remained haunted by the spiritual certitude he had witnessed among the Moravian Christians on board, even amidst North Atlantic storms that saw Germans composed and the English panicked.

In Georgia he showed himself obnoxious: inflexible, autocratic, unreasonable, insensitive. Knowing that the infant mortality rate was fifty percent, he insisted nonetheless on immersing day-old babies. Yet the non-credibility he earned through his rigidity was slight compared to the opprobrium that deluged him following his mishandling of the Sophia Hopkey matter. Attracted to the 18-year-old woman (Wesley was now 34) Wesley was first frustrated then angry and finally vindictive when she resisted his amorous approaches. Soon she was engaged to another man, Mr. Williamson. Wesley's judgment eroded in proportion to his swelling decompensation. Helpless and hapless now, he "retaliated" by withholding Holy Communion from Sophia at Sunday worship. Since such withholding was a means of disciplining a serious offender, according to Anglicanism, Wesley had in effect publicly announced that the young woman was guilty of an offence without specifying it. He didn't have to. What would any congregation surmise to be the "offence" that a marriageable woman had committed? Williamson, outraged that his fiancée had been slandered by innuendo, mobilized the politically powerful to convene a Grand Jury, The Jury indicted Wesley. He boarded the next ship for England in order to escape a lawsuit. His spiritual quest was no more frustrated than everything else in his life.

And then on Sunday evening, May 24th, 1738, the disconsolate man stepped into a Moravian service in London. Someone was reading from the preface to Luther's commentary on Romans. As the Wittenberger's words fell on Wesley's ears, the Word resounded in his heart.

> About a quarter before nine, while he was describing the change which God works in the heart through faith in Christ, I felt my heart strangely warmed. I felt I did trust in Christ, Christ alone for

salvation, and an assurance was given me that he had taken away *my* sin, even *mine,* and had saved *me* from the law of sin and death.²

If he now trusted Christ, what had he been trusting? For thirteen years, following a religious "turn" in 1725, Wesley had relied on a not-uncommon compend of mysticism and moralism.

The mysticism he would hereafter execrate was non-Christological; it substituted psycho-religious inner cultivation for faith in God's provision, provision and faith alike given to us; it denied the depravity of the human heart, content to speak of a less-than-disastrous deprivation or deficit; it advanced absorption of the human into God instead of communion with God; it grounded one's standing with God on an internal works-righteousness rather than on the foundation of justification by faith; it spoke of Jesus Christ as ethical and spiritual exemplar but not as the sole, sufficient Saviour.

The moralism he now rejected was the ever-enervating attempt at gaining favour with God by pleading one's "obedience" (naively misunderstood, of course), as meriting such favour.

The Aldersgate Street episode was the turning point in Wesley's life and ministry. He never looked back. The difference in his self-understanding, his theology, his work and his approach to people is undeniable.

Earlier, in agreement with so very many of the mystics, Wesley had regarded humanly-wrought humility as the basis of one's life in Christ. Now he exalted faith, faith forged by Jesus Christ, the object and author of faith, as this One surged over people solely in his longing to bless them. (Never denying faith to be a human event and activity, following Aldersgate Wesley consistently denied it to be a human creation. In his sermon "Salvation by Faith"—the first in his "Sermons On Several Occasions"—Wesley writes, "Of yourselves cometh neither your faith nor your salvation.... That ye believe is one instance of his grace; that believing, ye are saved, another."³) Freed from the self-righteousness that the

---

2. Wesley, *WJW,* Vol. 18, pp. 249–250, emphasis Wesley's.
3. Wesley, *WJW,* Vol. 1, p. 126.

mystic/moralist had recently espoused, Wesley saw, in agreement with the sixteenth-century Reformers, that Christ (alone) is our righteousness just because he (alone) is the rightly-related covenant keeper who now defines those who are "clothed" with him by faith. Undeterred in his insistence on the rigour of the Christian life, he nonetheless made the seemingly small but actually huge shift from moralism as conformity to a code to the believing person's grateful, from-the-heart obedience to the Person whose Spirit infused and inspired it all. In the same way he changed from inward-looking self-assessment to outward-looking evangelism. And of course his self-preoccupation with religious performance (and putative superiority) gave way to self-forgetfulness in the service of others.

While some Methodists have recently entertained protracted discussion over the nature, scope and significance of "Aldersgate," on balance the event appears to be a watershed. Prior to it he was a seeker; after it he knew himself found. Prior to it had had no objection to the semi-Pelagianism that marked eighteenth-century Anglican soteriology; after it he endorsed the Reformation insistence that faith is a knowledge of God that arises as grace alone includes us in God's self-knowing. Prior to it he evinced little interest in evangelism; after it he travelled 400,000 km on horseback to visit good news upon those who either hadn't heard or hadn't responded.

Perhaps the most telling evidence of Aldersgate's watershed concerns the place he gave to justification by faith. Prior to 1738 he regularly speaks of humility as our bond with Christ where the Reformation speaks of faith. After Aldersgate, however, he never departs from the material principle of the Reformation. Justification by faith is "the very foundation of our Church [i.e., Anglican]...and indeed the fundamental [doctrine] of the Reformed Churches."[4] Always suspicious of the Society of Friends for what he perceived to be their waffling on this issue, he

---

4. Wesley, *WJW*, Vol. 4, p.395. Plainly Wesley understood justification by faith to be the fundamental doctrine of the Church of England (Anglican), and he understood said church to be "Reformed."

writes, "I have not known ten Quakers in my life whose experience went so far as justification."[5] Indeed, where justification isn't upheld, the church doesn't exist.[6] Wesley believed in justification by faith from the day of his conversion. "I believe justification by faith alone as much as I believe there is a God.... I have never varied from it, no, not an hair's breadth from 1738 to this day."

Wesley's emphasis here was "book-ended" by the doctrines of original sin and sanctification. These three were non-negotiable. Without them the "faith once for all delivered to the saints' (Jude 3) would be unrecognizable. Always eschewing the theologically novel as heretical (for Wesley the theologically sound had to be locatable in both Scripture and Patristics), he upheld the "Vincentian Canon":

> Moreover, in the catholic church itself, all possible care must be taken that we hold that which has been believed everywhere, always, by all; for that is truly and in the strictest sense catholic which, as the name itself and the reason of the thing declare, comprehends all universally.[7]

Whereas society in any era tends to be soft on central issues but inflexible on the peripheral, Wesley's approach to Christian understanding and life, like that of apostles before him, was opposite: unyielding at the centre while accommodating on the periphery.

Original sin he regarded as glaringly undeniable. His single largest tract explored it from every angle and adduced evidence for it that rendered indisputable the church catholic's profundity in maintaining that the root human predicament is its "control centre" now gone

---

5. See Thomas Jackson, ed. *Works of John Wesley* (1872; reprint, Grand Rapids: Zondervan, 1958–1959). "A Letter to a Person Lately Joined with the People Called Quakers," Vol. X, pp. 177–188.

6. "Minutes," 1745; John Rylands University Library of Manchester.

7. Vincent of Lerins: *Commonitorium*, Caput. II [A General Rule for Distinguishing the Truth of the Catholic Faith From the Falsehood of Heretical Perversity], par. 3.

awry. Wesley maintained that while he was "but a hair's breadth from Mr. Calvin" on several issues (e.g., predestination and the atonement as formal cause rather than instrumental cause of justification), concerning the doctrine of Total Depravity there wasn't so much as a hair's breadth. Wesley's laconic pronouncement here was that those who upheld the doctrine of Total Depravity might be Christians, while those who didn't most certainly weren't.[8] To deny the fact, nature and reach of original sin, he maintained, would render all Christian doctrine incoherent.[9] Wesley knew that when the doctrine of the Fall is compromised then the human condition—deep-dyed sinnership, a systemic infection like blood poisoning which warps everything about us and of which we cannot rid ourselves—is denied. The human condition in turn is reduced to a bland if not benign human situation where people fancy themselves limitlessly plastic, able to re-mould themselves however misshapen they might appear at present, thereby remedying whatever might seem unsightly in the light of social convention.

In one sermon alone Wesley brings forward five words that attest his conviction here. First is "supine," without exertion or energy. Next is "indolent," culpable sloth. The third is "stupid." Here he has in mind the eighteenth-century understanding of the adjective arising from "stupor," abysmal unawareness of the fact that sin has eroded reason's integrity (without, of course, eroding the structure of reason, apart from which the sinner would no longer be human), even as reason lends itself to endless rationalization. The fourth is "insensible [of his real condition"], for the worst consequence of humankind's sinnership is its blindness to its condition (and hence the impossibility of any repentance except that born of grace.) What the "natural" person can do, then, in the wake of the Fall is merely perpetuate its rebellion against God and perpetrate its self-destruction. "Full of disease" rounds out Wesley's diagnosis on

---

8. "Allow this, and you are so far a Christian. Deny it, and you are but an heathen still." *WJW*, Vol. 2. p.184.

9. Wesley makes this point repeatedly in his tract, "The Doctrine of Original Sin, according to Scripture, Reason, and Experience" (Jackson, *Works*, Vol. IX).

page one of one sermon alone.[10] Everywhere in his work "disease" implies not only pathology but putrefaction; the human condition is not only a sickness-unto-death but repugnantly so as God finds sin nothing less than loathsome.

Justification by faith, the middle item between the two "book-ends," restored believers to God's favour. After Aldersgate Wesley always regarded justification by faith as the inception of the Christian life and the stable basis for it. He agreed with Calvin, "Justification is the hinge on which religion turns"[11] and with Loescher, "Justification is the article on which the church stands or falls."[12]

Still, Wesley's overwhelming emphasis falls on sanctification or holiness or "perfection." Tirelessly he insisted that God could do something with sin beyond forgiving it; namely, God could deliver people from its power. Justification relieved people of sin's guilt; sanctification released them from sin's grip. Wesley knew that justification or forgiveness, undeniably glorious, would be little more than a counsel of despair, leaving people pardoned yet imprisoned, unless a grace-wrought, faith-affirmed sanctification or new birth released them from the habituations that haunted them in light of sin's characteristic addictiveness.

Sanctification or holiness, then, was their possession (albeit not their property) just because they "clothed" themselves by faith with the Ruler whose rightful reign broke the power of the "usurper"[13] who held them in thrall.

While the Protestant Reformation had contended for relief, Wesley took this up and contended for release. Without deliverance from sin's grip Methodism would have appeared stillborn as degraded people despaired. Wesley's gospel galloped ahead not (merely) because it told

---

10. Wesley, *WJW*, Vol. 3, p. 142.

11. Calvin, *Institutes of the Christian Religion* (Philadelphia: Westminster, 1960), 3.11.1.

12. Valentius Loescher (1673–1749), "Timotheus Venius," quoted in *First Things* (New York: 1995), August/September, p. 80.

13. Wesley, *WJW*, Vol. 1, p. 331.

imprisoned people they had been pardoned; more to the point, it opened prison doors and told them they now could and must walk out and never look back. His gospel introduced people to a future under God and in God, such a future alone being genuine, all other "futures" remaining no more than a disguised repetition of a dreary past.

In all of this it must be remembered that Wesley, an English Protestant and therefore undeniably a son of the Western Church, positioned himself as a westerner more attuned to the Eastern Church than anyone else in Christendom.

Wesley had come to know the Eastern Church through his reading of Patristics, always preferring the East to the West. The West's giants had been Ambrose, Jerome, Gregory the Great, and the favourite of both Thomas Aquinas and the Protestant Reformers, Augustine of Hippo. The East's notables had been Basil the Great, Chrysostom, Gregory of Nazianzus, and Athanasisus (the thinker whose gospel-preserving *homoousion*—the Father and the Son are of the same nature not merely similar nature— Karl Barth would later pronounce as the most important theological assertion since the apostles.)

Always upholding the doctrine of original sin, as was seen above, Wesley nevertheless distances himself from the West's characteristic emphasis on original guilt and its transmission to posterity (thanks to Augustine.) He prefers the East's emphasis on original sin as the introduction of death and corruption, together with the loss of the Spirit's immediate presence. Wesley maintains that Augustine's insistence on original guilt and its transmission has fostered fruitless dispute as to how such transmission occurs (not to mention the unfruitful Augustinian disdain for sex), the preoccupation here obscuring what is much more soteriologically and evangelically significant for Wesley; namely, the innermost spiritual distortion that gives rise to outermost disfigurement.

While the West, especially since the Reformation, had accented juridical concerns in the work of Christ for us, left-handedly giving rise to internecine disputes over the doctrine of justification, the Reformational and Roman Catholic Churches of the West had had virtually no disagreement over the doctrine of sanctification, content to subordinate it to their concern for the former. In the relation, then, of transaction and transformation, the churches of the West had massively highlighted transaction (What Christ has done *extra nos, pro nobis*, "outside us, for us") while admitting transformation (what Christ must do *in nobis*, "within us.") The churches of the East had always maintained the opposite: transaction exists for the sake of transformation, every aspect and activity of grace subserving God's ultimate purpose for God's people: their appointment to stand before God restored to that glory in which they were created, now relieved of the tarnish and defacements that the Fall had brought even as the Fall had never been able to efface the splendour. Sanctification, Wesley insisted everywhere, was nothing more and nothing less than the restoration of God's image. Here Wesley continues to be the figure who singularly bridges East and West ecclesially, the one Christian thinker whose work can be the substance of conversations that may yet lead to the healing of the East/West fissure of 1054.

Still reflecting the spirit of the East Wesley remained suspicious of all talk about a "state of grace." For centuries the church had spoken of believers as those who were living in a "state of grace," to which state they were admitted either by baptism or by the implementation of a decree of election, depending on one's place on the theological spectrum. Wesley objected to "state of grace" in that it exudes the mechanical rather than the personal, grace being the possession (but never the property) of believers as they continue to embrace the One who has first embraced them. Furthermore, "state of grace" suggested the static, when the Christian life is inherently dynamic. As Protestant Scholasticism ascended after the Reformation and displaced the Reformation's characteristic emphasis on Christology, intellectual apprehension of doctrine became the mark of Christian existence instead of that "heart seizure" at the hands of the One to whom doctrine points and of whom it speaks. The result was that "formalism" which Wesley came to execrate as the polar opposite of "fanaticism" or "enthusiasm." While the latter was a mindless subjectivism that disdained truth in favour of emotional self-indulgence, the former was an intellectual abstraction that re-shuffled mental furniture and forfeited the concreteness of person-with-Person encounter.

This is not to say that Wesley was indifferent to doctrine. Indifference to doctrine merely advertised those who were "of a muddy understanding" because their "mind was all in a mist."[14] Exalting neither mist nor mud, Wesley insisted on the place of doctrine but not its pre-eminence. The latter belonged to the One who filled the horizon of Wesley's life, reflected in his comments on his preaching at day's end, "I offered them Christ."

When early-day Methodists sang, "Moment by moment I'm kept in His love," their understanding of "moment" was never spasmodic or episodic or spastic or fitful or ephemeral. Wesley had simply schooled them in the fact that grace's self-giving was a boon for which they could only stammer their gratitude even as they knew that grace was the gracious presence of Jesus Christ rather than something which they could domesticate or control, let alone trade on or trifle with. Wesley always knew that where faith is concerned the reality isn't a doctrine of faith or the vocabulary of faith or the concept of faith; the reality is relationship. The relationship was not at risk. Believers were kept by the power of God, not having to rely on their own resources to remain bound to Jesus Christ. At the same time, since the relationship could erode as surely as any marriage can, faith ever remained a future-oriented venture that precluded cavalier or self-serving indulgence.

Yet there remained one issue, money, where Wesley was utterly out of step with the rising affluence the Industrial Revolution had brought Britain, even out of step with his own people. Wesley remained stymied by the seemingly built-in, self-destructive mechanism of the gospel. It was the gospel that brought dissolute people to faith. Newly sobered, chaste and industrious, they earned an adequate income, misspent none of it, and invariably saved much of it. Soon their swelling monetary fortunes facilitated social elevation. Their social elevation moved them into the orbit of people whose preoccupation was anything but the gospel and the mission inherent in the gospel. As their social position rose their

---

14. Wesley, *WJW*, Vol. 2, p. 93.

spiritual ardour fell. The gospel alone had moved them beyond dissolution and disgrace. And now it was their "improved" living that left their zeal for social preferment intact but drained it away for the gospel alone.

Wesley concluded that only as the Methodist people adopted something closely allied to the Roman Catholic notion of "evangelical poverty" could they spare themselves that spiritual unravelling that wouldn't even stop short of outright apostasy. Unlike so many others who maintained that how money was used determined whether it was a spiritual threat, Wesley insisted it was the fact that money was retained. Soon his three-fold "Earn all you can, save all you can, give all you can" became a household aphorism among his people—even as he concluded sadly that many of his people were commendably good at the first two and lamentably deficient concerning the last.

Still, he pressed ahead, ceaselessly warning his people of their spiritual vulnerability in this regard. He told his people that money was the talent that "contains all other talents."[15] (Does not what we do with our money gather up and express what we have done with our education or our natural talents by which we have acquired our money?) It is the temptation that fosters and foments all other temptations. It is the snare, "a steel trap that crushes the bones." It is the poison whose lethal toxicity kills our discipleship.

To hoard money rendered the hoarder "vain," for who possesses more than most without feeling superior and therein becoming prideful? To be sure Wesley's people, now grace-equipped to avoid gluttony and drunkenness, would invariably succumb to that "elegant epicureanism" which, he insisted, "does not immediately disorder the stomach, nor (sensibly, at least) impair the understanding." Wesley knew, however, that it disordered one's heart and vitiated one's understanding. For the erstwhile gluttonous drunkard, now savouring the dainties of the cof-

---

15. For the source of quotations in the next several paragraphs see *WJW*, "The Use of Money" (Vol. 2) and "The Danger of Riches" (Vol. 3).

feehouse echelon, cherished his inclusion among the socially enviable more than his inclusion in "the household of faith" (Gal. 6:10).

Wesley's perception was remarkable. For he correctly noted that as we become more affluent we acquire self-importance. In turn we become more easily affronted, supersensitivity being related to snobbishness. The more prone we are to being affronted, he noted with aching heart, the more prone we are to revenge.

Wesley was aware, in his tracing of spiritual decline, that increasing affluence spelled decreasing zeal for "works of mercy." He reminded his people that when they were newly quickened and recovering from horrific habituations they had never hesitated to head out, at any hour and in any weather, to bring the relief and release of the gospel to fellow-sufferers whose pain they knew only too well. Now, however, in their new-found frippery they didn't want to inconvenience themselves, especially in inclement weather. "What hinders?" cried the 78-year-old man bitingly in the wake of forty years' frustration on this issue, "Do you fear spoiling your silken coat?"[16] The caustic irony, meant to burn its way into his readers, was that it was the gospel that had ultimately brought them a silken coat when they had had no coat of any sort. Protecting it now threatened them with ultimate spiritual loss, for "Gold hath steeled your hearts."[17] Spiritual vitality (including self-forgetful service of others) and hoarded money were mutually exclusive. Only "give all you can" would keep faith throbbing.

Even before the Aldersgate awakening of 1738 he had taken to heart his oft-repeated text, "that holiness without which no one will see the Lord" (Hebrews 12:14). According to him holiness or "Christian perfection" wasn't neurotic perfectionism or fussy trivialism; it was simply love, self-forgetful love of God and neighbour. Such self-forgetful love of God and neighbour was God's fulfilment of God's earlier promise, "You shall be holy as I the Lord your God am holy" (Lev. 19:2). While

---

16. Wesley, *WJW*, Vol. 3, p. 244.
17. Ibid., p. 245.

justification, he had always insisted, gave us the right to heaven, holiness alone made us fit for heaven. Right and fitness were not the same. A ticket to a symphony concert gives us the right to attend, but only our musical ear makes us fit to attend. (Plainly apart from fitness, right would issue in torment.) Everything Wesley had proposed and proved concerning the Christian life pertained to spiritual fitness. He knew there was nothing arbitrary about Christ's promise that only the pure in heart will see God. For Wesley was aware that only the pure in heart want to, their aspiration being qualification enough.

3

JOHN WESLEY AND THE WITNESS OF THE SPIRIT

Abingdon Press's thirty-five-volume annotated edition of Wesley's *Works* (sixteen of which have been completed) begins with four volumes of sermons. Yet as soon as newly interested readers open Volume I of *Sermons On Several Occasions* they know that the form of these "sermons" has to differ from the form of Wesley's marketplace utterances. The crowds of thousands who heard Wesley preach included many who were minimally literate, more than a few who were not even that, and scarcely anyone who possessed Wesley's sophistication in theology, philosophy and literature. The published sermons, on the other hand, are replete with references that presuppose no little erudition. In addition the published sermons are devoid of the illustrations and the rhetorical devices that preachers employ to retain the attention of those unaccustomed to the relatively abstract medium of an oral address lacking the advantage of repeated examination. Plainly the form of the printed sermon is better suited to discussion in the classroom or perusal in the study.

In fact for the most part the sermons are the unillustrated distillate of Wesley's daily pronouncements; unillustrated, that is, compared to the sort of preaching necessary to attract and hold throngs. The sermons, then, were essentially tracts written for people who needed a compendium of the doctrines which underlay the Revival. In addition the sermons attempted to defuse the hostile attacks of those who misunderstood Wesley and his movement, falsely accusing them of theological dilution, social destabilization, psychological exploitation, and even sedition.

While the sermons were not preached verbatim as they appear in Wesley's *Works*, they were yet "preached" inasmuch as Wesley's ceaseless itinerating found him constantly expanding, illustrating, repeating and subtly reshaping them. (According to his *Journal*, for instance, he preached on Ephesians 2:8—"For by grace you have been saved through faith"—no fewer than sixty times.)

There is another sense in which some sermons were "preached": the theological substance of the sermon was found in Wesley's public proclamation while the sermon itself was never preached on any one occasion. In other words the sermon was made public only in written form, even though its content leavened Wesley's oral pronouncements on assorted topics. The two sermons, "The Witness of the Spirit (I and II)" belong to this latter category. Today we should simply designate them essays.

As is evident from even a casual reading of the *Works*, Wesley had to contend on several fronts throughout his ministry. One front was the Scylla/Charybdis of "formality" and "enthusiasm." Formalism was an intellectual frigidity that confined itself to doctrinal refinement (or speculation) without impact on life. Enthusiasm (which Wesley defined as the elevation of experience above Scripture) was a superheated emotionalism that disdained doctrine only to gush and gurgle in a mindless sentimentality devoid of morality and a religious romanticism devoid of righteousness. Head and heart were always to complement one another.

Wesley refers to these two pitfalls in his Preface as he states once again the purpose of his work:

> And herein it is more especially my desire, first to guard those
> who are just setting their faces toward heaven...from formality,
> from mere outside religion, which has almost driven heart-religion

JOHN WESLEY AND THE WITNESS OF THE SPIRIT

[Wesley's Journal entry of 2nd August, 1771, speaks of heart-religion as "righteousness and joy in the Holy Ghost ... the gate of it, justification ... the life of God in the soul of man."] out of the world; and secondly, to warn those who know the religion of the heart ... lest at any time they make void the law through faith, and so fall back into the snare of the devil.[1]

When Christians of Methodist conviction spoke of the witness of the Spirit they were instantly accused of an enthusiasm amounting to fanaticism. Wesley, however, steadfastly refused to be stampeded. He knew that the indefensible vagaries found in those who valued heat above light did not discredit the gospel-quickened faith of those who cherished Paul's legacy: God's children are permitted and privileged to know themselves such. Wesley steadfastly maintained that the witness of God's Spirit, assuring believers of their standing in Christ, had everything to do with their salvation, their comfort, their holiness (and therefore their temporal and eternal happiness, since he consistently linked holiness and happiness—"None but the holy are finally happy"); everything as well to do with an undeviating discipleship that eschews both formalism and fanaticism; everything to do, for preachers especially, with urgency and zeal in the fulfilment of their vocation.

Wesley always regarded the *Sermons On Several Occasions* as his major theological statement. At the same time the major statement never precluded many minor. He supplemented the *Sermons* with other treatises as situations arose, in the unfolding of the eighteenth-century Evangelical Revival, that required additional comment. (One thinks immediately of *A Plain Account of Christian Perfection* [1777] bracketed by two sermons, "Christian Perfection" [1741] and "On Perfection" [1784]. Rather oddly, then, the *Sermons On Several Occasions* were considerably less "occasional" than the supplementary materials, the sermons functioning as the theological primer of Wesleyan Methodism. At the same time they were a theological grid that provided the interpretative

---

1. Wesley, *WJW*, Vol. 1, p. 106.

framework needed to prevent Methodist Christians—and preachers especially—from suffering doctrinal disorientation. (In this regard the Sermons functioned much as Calvin's *Institutes* had in the sixteenth-century Reformation in Geneva, even as Calvin continued to write occasional pieces in response to crises.)

THE WITNESS OF THE SPIRIT

"... it is the Spirit himself bearing witness with our spirit that we are children of God."

(Romans 8:16)

The inclusion of the "The Witness of the Spirit" (I & II) in *Sermons on Several Occasions* indicates the place Wesley gave to assurance in his understanding of the Christian life. For several years his critics had insisted that the Revival merely fanned the "enthusiasm" that the eighteen-century Enlightenment despised. While the same critics regarded assurance as merely one more aspect of the despicable, Wesley himself insisted that the spiritually needy who looked to the gospel yet were devoid of assurance had therein had their everyday anxiety exacerbated by a peculiarly religious anxiety. At the same time he admitted that those who prattled cavalierly of assurance even as they undervalued the specificity of gospel-truth plainly were enthusiasts and merited being exposed as such. He wanted to help his people along the fine line between the two distortions. He knew that failure to identify and walk the fine line would leave his people meandering and flip-flopping.

In the first paragraph of Part I Wesley identifies the pitfall of subjectivism. "How many have mistaken the voice of their own imagination" for the witness of God's Spirit, only to assume they were children of God when in fact they continued to behave in conformity to their actual father, the evil one.[2] This lack of self-perception (born of presumption) is "truly

---

2. All quotations in this chapter are from Wesley, *WJW*, Vol. 1, sermons 10, 11 and 12.

and properly" enthusiasm. As lack of self-perception is protracted it sets like concrete. In addition to their initial mistake the enthusiasts confuse their vehemence and impetuosity and intractability with obedience to the command of God to "contend for the faith" (Jude 3).

In view of the widespread abuse of such a "witness" Wesley concedes that nervous observers might wish to dismiss the contemporary application of the doctrine, relegating the "testimony" to those extraordinary gifts that were said to cease with the close of the apostolic age. His reading of Scripture, however, does not permit this facile evasion—even though he will have to spend the rest of his life disowning the distortions surrounding this one theological conviction. Wesley could never deny that the "testimony of the Spirit" looms large in Scripture, "a truth revealed therein not once only, not obscurely, not incidentally, but frequently, and that in express terms ... as denoting one of the peculiar privileges of the children of God."

In discussing the relation of the Spirit's testimony to our spirit's, Wesley carefully avoids collapsing one into the other. The text (not to mention the corroborating experience of believers) speaks of both the testimony of God's Spirit and the testimony of ours concerning our adoption.

With respect to the testimony of our spirit Wesley maintains that Scripture is unambiguous. It states repeatedly, for instance, that the children of God keep the commandments of God (1 John 2:5) even as they love fellow-children of God (1 John 3:14). Upon examining themselves believers conclude that they do keep the commandments of God and love fellow-Christians, and therefore rightly conclude that they are indeed God's children. Wesley admits that "this is no other than rational evidence: the 'witness of our spirit', our reason or understanding."

If self-doubt besets believers and they ask themselves how they know whether they truly love fellow-Christians or keep God's commandments, Wesley attempts to succour them by resorting to an intuitionist epistemology, as valid in the realm of Christian existence as it is in the realm of sense-experience.

> How does it appear to you that you are alive? And that you are now in ease and not in pain? Are you not immediately conscious of it? By the same immediate consciousness you will know if your soul is alive to God; if you are saved from the pain of proud wrath .... By the same means you cannot but perceive if you love, rejoice, and delight in God.... Your conscience informs you from day to day if you do not take the name of God within your lips unless with seriousness and devotion, with reason and godly fear.

The foregoing is the testimony of our spirit. "It is a consciousness of having received, in and by the Spirit of adoption, the tempers mentioned in the Word of God as belonging to his adopted children."

Plainly, the testimony of our spirit is an inference-following-reflection. Self-examination concerning our conformity to the command of God leaves our conscience unaroused; we conclude that the Spirit of God has effected such transmutation within us as to give rise to those marks that constrain us to thank God for his self-evidencing work of grace.

Admittedly, Wesley is placing no little emphasis on the assumption that self-examination yields self-perception. He did not deny the submerged currents of sin in humankind, as his unqualified endorsement of the sixteenth-century Reformers' doctrines of Original Sin and Total Depravity attests. At the same time, he always insisted on holding out hope for those discouraged by the submerged currents (which, sorry to say, are never merely submerged). He knew that hope, in order to be biblical hope and not natural wishful thinking, had to be grounded in the actuality of deliverance. Throughout his ministry Wesley reminded his people that God could do something with sin beyond forgiving it. (According to Wesley, deliverance from the power of sin was confirmation that one had been pardoned from the guilt of sin.) The blaspheming substance-abuser, now possessed of God-fearing sobriety and social usefulness, could legitimately conclude that by the grace of God he was a child of God.

Having discussed briefly the testimony of our spirit so as to distinguish it from the testimony of God's Spirit, Wesley proceeds to consider the latter.

Wesley knows he is probing mystery in this matter. Mystery, it is commonly acknowledged, is not something bizarre or Hallowe'enish or occultish. Mystery is an everyday phenomenon (e.g., being in love) that is therefore ordinary or commonplace even as it is profound. It is inexpressibly profound; no vocabulary can do justice to it. Mystery may be described but never explained, let alone explained away. Mystery may be pointed to, commended, urged upon others, above all experienced. Yet before it language can finally only stammer. Definition and explanation are impossible; description is inadequate, description being the inarticulate attempt at having others undergo the same experience even as everyone recognizes the poverty of the words which have to be employed.

Wesley knows there are unfathomably mysterious depths to our encounter with God that leave our speech halting. The fact of the Spirit's testimony does not leave Wesley tongue-tied at all; yet when he attempts to describe the how of it he first cautions us, "It is hard to find words in the language of men to explain 'the deep things of God'. Indeed there are none that will adequately express what the children of God experience." Nonetheless, since the alternative to semi-functional articulation is non-communication born of silence, Wesley steps forward. His initial assertion is unambiguous.

> The testimony of the Spirit is an inward impression on the soul whereby the Spirit of God directly 'witnesses to my spirit that I am a child of God'; that Jesus Christ hath loved me and given himself for me; that all my sins are blotted out, and I, even I, am reconciled to God.

The substance of the Spirit's testimony is readily understood: believers have been reconciled to God through the love of that God who sacrificed himself in his Son, with the result that their condemnation is rescinded. The "how" of the Spirit's testimony, says Wesley, requires much greater explication even as adequate explanation is finally impossible.

In his initial statement Wesley's use of "inward impression on the soul" and "directly" indicates clearly where the Spirit's testimony differs from our spirit's. Whereas the latter is inference-following-reflection, the former is entirely non-inferential—at the same time as it is necessarily related to the gospel. The testimony of the Spirit is an idiogenic "mediated immediacy." The immediacy of the Spirit is not the immediacy that Kierkegaard rightly denounced. ("Immediacy is paganism," since immediacy disdains the particularity and historicity of the incarnate one, whereas the immediacy of the Spirit is always "mediated" through the gospel.) At the same time, the testimony of the Spirit is not a conclusion drawn from premises. It is that "stamp" of the Spirit who presses and impresses himself upon us in such wise that he authenticates himself, and does so indisputably. In other words, the self-authentication of the Spirit is necessary (there being nothing outside of God that is able to authenticate him) and sufficient (there being nothing outside of God that is needed to authenticate him).

Next Wesley is careful to remind us that while he discussed the testimony of our spirit before that of God's Spirit, in fact the latter precedes the former. "We must be holy of heart and holy in life before we can be conscious that we are so.... But we must love God before we can be holy at all; this being the root of all holiness. Now we cannot love till we know he loves us.... And we cannot know his pardoning love till his Spirit witnesses to our spirit."

Several matters invite comment here. Wesley's "know" is plainly more than "have correct information about." He refers here not to the "head-knowledge" of an intellectual (doctrinal) apprehension of the meaning of "God is love," but rather to "heart-knowledge," the "inward impression on the soul," the innermost conviction and assurance that the theological assertion concerning God's love adequately describes the reality of the cosmocrator's benevolent seizure of the believer.

The subtlety of Wesley's dialectic in this discussion is profound. While the testimony of God's Spirit plainly has to do with the "heartfelt-ness" of immediacy, Wesley judiciously directs believers away from themselves, away from a preoccupation with introspection. Evidently he fears fostering an introspection amounting to obsession, an obsession wherein believers think they can discern the testimony of God's Spirit by ransacking themselves. First we must love God; we are directed away from ourselves to God, only then to find that God so honours our looking to him as to vouchsafe to us the assurance that he has pardoned us. In other words, reality always precedes apprehension of reality. At the same time, it is the nature of this reality (God) to forge within humankind an apprehension of the reality. The logical priority of the Spirit (i.e., the logical priority of God) does not entail divine remoteness. In fact the proximity (proximity of such a nature as to generate an "impression on the soul") of God simultaneously facilitates the categories for apprehending the selfsame proximity. It is not the case that an impression is made on the soul even as beneficiaries of it are left puzzled as to its nature, origin and meaning. (Much as primitive people might be aware of the phenomena of a thunderstorm yet remain ignorant as to its origin and significance.) Wesley has carefully distinguished the transcendence of God from the testimony of God's Spirit, and these in turn from a projection or fantasy that would leave him defenceless against the charge of enthusiasm.

The logical order of his discussion is inviolable: we must be reconciled to God through becoming the recipients of God's pardon before we can be conscious of this.

So very concerned is Wesley to minimize misunderstanding on this matter that he looks at the topic now from this angle, now from another, much as a gemmologist observes scintillations reflecting off a precious stone as the stone is viewed from several different angles. Succinctly he comments, "It is he [i.e., the Holy Spirit] that not only worketh in us every manner of thing that is good, but also shines upon his own work, and clearly shows what he has wrought." God enlightens us as to what God is doing in us. Were God to effect his salvific work in us and not enlighten us concerning this work within us, Wesley reminds us, we should then be left without awareness of "the things which are freely given to us of God" (1 Corinthians 2:12), and to this extent the testimony of our spirit would be enfeebled, in fact rendered impossible. Because God illumines us with respect to his work within us through the testimony of his Spirit, we are never left (i) wondering incessantly whether we are "in the boat" with Jesus or have missed it, (ii) attempting to impart an ersatz "assurance" by means of "enthusiasm." The testimony of God's Spirit, in concert with the testimony of our spirit, obviates both anguished insecurity and groundless bravado.

Once again Wesley turns the gem over in his hand. Anticipating a query from someone who is afflicted with doubt concerning her adoption, Wesley reverts to his intuitionist epistemology. When, in the normal course of our lives, we delight in something creaturely that pleases us, the immediacy of our delight is as much assurance as we need (or can have) as to the actuality of our delight. In the same way, he adds, someone in pain needs no argument to persuade her she is in pain. To love God, delight in God, rejoice in God is to know incontrovertibly that one loves, delights, and rejoices. And to know that God is the author and object of all this is to know that one is a child of God.

Then, in his sermon, "The Witness of the Spirit," Wesley advances for our consideration what seems only a redundant instance of his oft-illustrated assertion, "A Christian…has as full an assurance [of his being a child of God] as he has that the Scriptures are of God"—when in fact he has reached back into Calvin's doctrine of Scripture and borrowed its logic concerning the work of the Spirit. In a pregnant passage much cherished throughout the Reformed tradition Calvin writes, "…Scripture exhibits fully as clear evidence of its own truth as white and black things do of their colour, or sweet and bitter things do of their taste" (*Institutes*, 1.7.2). Just as Scripture needs no external authentication of its truth, so believers need no external authentication of their standing in Christ. Calvin's point is this: to the extent that the Spirit is used of God to bind us to Jesus Christ (i.e., to the extent that the Spirit authenticates Jesus Christ and our inclusion in him), the Spirit by that fact also authenticates the means by which our Lord and we became fused. Wesley's point is that as the gospel-truth concerning the Spirit's witness is promulgated, the Spirit confirms the adoption of believers so as to leave them no doubt concerning the truth that is now "impressed" upon their heart. Since God alone authenticates himself to believers (the sixteenth-century Reformers were fond of saying, "God is the only fit witness to himself"), the demand for the criteria of such authentication Wesley pronounces an "idle demand."

Wesley concludes his overview of the Spirit's testimony by reminding readers that the mystery surrounding this unique work of the Spirit precludes definition and explication.

> The manner how the divine testimony is manifested to the heart I do not take upon myself to explain.... But the fact we know: namely, that the Spirit of God does give a believer such a testimony of his adoption that while it is present to the soul he can no more doubt the reality of his sonship than he can doubt the shining of the sun while he stands in the full blaze of his (sic) glory.

In Part II of "The Witness of the Spirit" Wesley amplifies this point, arguing that the moment Paul heard the voice of God on the Damascus road he knew it to be such, even though the apostle himself could never have proposed criteria by which to deem any one "voice" to be the voice of God. Wesley simply states, "But how he knew this who is able to explain?" In the same way, when God speaks forgiveness to believers of any era they know themselves pardoned beyond refutation or extrinsic confirmation.

Yet lest any "enthusiast" claim hallucination or any other species of subjectivism to be the word of God Wesley carefully distinguishes once more between the joint testimony (of Spirit and spirit) and presumption or delusion. The unrepentant sinner, upon hearing of this "privilege of true Christians, ... is prone to work himself up into a persuasion that he is already possessed" of it. Nonetheless, Scripture consistently points out that conviction of sin always precedes assurance of pardon. Drawing on his experience as spiritual director, Wesley notes that humility is one concomitant of the testimony of the Spirit, while the presumptuous invariably exalt themselves. In the same vein the presumptuous are cavalier concerning the commandments of God, especially the command enjoining self-denial or cross-bearing, the presumptuous loftily announcing that they have "found an easier path to heaven." Moreover, those who have deluded themselves in the matter of the Spirit's testimony undervalue Scripture's insistence on the joint testimony; their "discipleship" fails to display the fruits of the Spirit. In any case the vehemence of the self-deluded's expostulations does not obviate the veridicality of the Spirit's work in others, just "as a madman's imagining himself a king does not prove that there are no real kings."

Calvin had said that when even the children of God look into their own heart what they find there is enough to horrify them; they find pathetically little evidence of their renewal at God's hand. Is Calvin correct? Is Wesley naive where the Genevan may have been realistic? In Part II, written in the light of twenty years' pondering Part I and twenty years' evaluating the spiritual condition of the Methodist people, Wesley concurs with Calvin's assessment. There are episodes in the Christian's life when the residues of sin becloud the testimony of our spirit. At such times only divine testimony can attest that we are a child of God in the face of our inner whisperings to the contrary. For this reason Wesley now states as a spiritual director of greater maturity, "we contend that the direct witness may shine clear, even while the indirect one is under a cloud." (It is noteworthy that while Calvin doesn't use the vocabulary of "the testimony of our spirit" he does recognize the effect of believers' residual sin upon their assurance of their standing in Christ. In his commentaries on Hebrews 10:22 and 2 Corinthians 1:21 Calvin speaks of the subordinate assurance of faith that the love engendered in believers lends them. However, Calvin strictly understands such assurance—born of the fact that the "good tree" is now producing "good fruit"—to be subordinate. It can never be the ground of assurance. Love is defective even in believers, he reminds us in his commentary on 1 John 4:13, and the good deeds of even believers ever remain sin-tainted.) Commensurate with his greater maturity Wesley shifts his emphasis so as to link the testimony of the Spirit explicitly to justification: assurance chiefly confirms believers in their forgiveness at God's hand and their acceptance with God despite the arrears of their sin. Indeed, since we cannot believe ourselves justified, on account of our lingering proclivity to sin, apart from the witness of the Spirit, to deny the testimony is "in effect to deny justification by faith." This, of course, Wesley will never do, thoroughgoing son of the Reformation that he is. As if to remind his readers of his confessional standing he borrows the vocabulary of this seventeenth-century Puritan forebears: the Spirit attests the "imputation" of Christ's righteousness.

Even so, episodes of the sort mentioned above do not last forever. The clouds that becloud the indirect witness part, and Wesley returns to his characteristic insistence that the testimony which assures believers is finally a joint testimony as the fruits of the Spirit appear, however slenderly, in Christ's people.

For as long as breath remained in him Wesley rejoiced that "this great evangelical truth has been recovered, which had been for many years wellnigh lost and forgotten."

Who had recovered it? And who has been mandated to safeguard it? Wesley's conviction here was ironfast.

> It more clearly concerns the Methodists, so called, clearly to understand, explain, and defend this doctrine, because it is one grand part of the testimony which God has given them to bear to all mankind.

The mandate has never been revoked.

4

WESLEY'S UNDERSTANDING OF THE LAW OF GOD

In his *Notes on the New Testament* Wesley mentions, in his introduction to Romans, that when Paul is writing to churches that he has planted or visited he exemplifies a "familiarity" with them that is either "loving or sharp" depending on their deportment.[1] When he writes to congregations that he has never seen, on the other hand, he "proposes the pure, unmixed gospel in a more general manner."[2] Plainly Wesley's sustained exposition of the law of God, a major motif in Romans and a crucial ingredient in the gospel, pertains to the "pure, unmixed gospel." For Wesley, then, the gospel includes the law, and Romans singularly identifies and amplifies this inclusion.

In order to grasp Wesley's understanding of gospel and law and the manner of their relationship, however, we must look chiefly not to the *Notes* but to his *Sermons on Several Occasions*. Admittedly, Wesley's single, sustained exposition of Romans is found in his *Notes on the*

---

1. Wesley, *Notes on the New Testament* (Wakefield: William Nicholson and Sons, 1872); p. 355. (Hereinafter cited as *NT Notes*.)
2. *op.cit*

New Testament[3]. However the entire exposition here uses only forty-four pages, half of which merely reproduce the English text, leaving but twenty-two pages to probe the sixteen chapters of Paul's major work. Wesley's texts for his three major tracts on the law of God are Romans 7:12 and 3:31: "Wherefore the law is holy, and the commandment holy, and just, and good," as well as "Do we then make void the law through faith? God forbid! Yea, we establish the law."[4] Wesley's exposition of Romans 3:31 in the *Sermons* requires twenty-four pages of text, while his comment in the *Notes* is concluded in two lines. Similarly he uses nineteen pages in the *Sermons* to expound Romans 7:12, but only twenty-six words in the *Notes*.

Obviously his New Testament *Notes* are not a major source of his thought concerning the epistle.

Then will ransacking the Romans references throughout the *Sermons* yield, albeit compositely, Wesley's convictions concerning this epistle? I submit that it won't, for at least two reasons. While there are scores of references to Romans in the *Sermons*, there are only twice as many as there are references to 1st John, one of the briefest New Testament epistles. (This fact alone informs us that Romans doesn't occupy the place in Wesley that it occupied, for instance, in the sixteenth-century Protestant Reformers.) Secondly, despite the profusion of references to Romans, many of these references are deployed not exegetically but rather illustratively; i.e., they are adduced to illustrate or support a theological point that Wesley is making apart from the Romans text. In short, ransacking the references to Romans in the *Sermons* will yield not the singularity of Wesley's approach to this epistle but rather the singularity of his theology as a whole.

Still, his insistence that the gospel is the substance of the law, together with his insistence that the law is indispensable for the Christian life; his tenacity here is generated by his understanding that two texts in

---

3. *loc.cit.*
4. Wesley, *WJW*, Vol. 2, pp. 4,20,23. Hereinafter cited as *WJW* 2:4,20,23.

particular (Romans 7:12 and 3:31) go a long way in comprehending the totality of the gospel.

The work of Martin Luther was instrumental in the spiritual awakening of both John and Charles Wesley. Faith in the saving person and work of Jesus Christ was born in Charles as he read Luther's *Commentary on Galatians* (21st May 1738), and in John three days later as John heard read the preface to Luther's *Commentary on Romans*. Thereupon both men repudiated and forsook the blend of moralism and mysticism they had theretofore regarded as faith. They never looked back from their new understanding and conviction; namely, that Christians are distinguished from unbelievers not by humility, for instance (John had insisted in his pre-Aldersgate sermon, "The Circumcision of the Heart," that humility gives us "a title" to the praise of God[5]), but by that faith which grace alone quickens and which embraces Jesus Christ, its author and object. Believers cannot take any credit for faith's commencement or its continuation. Reflecting Calvin's "What can a dead man do to attain life?"[6] Wesley adds, "Of yourselves cometh neither your faith nor your salvation. 'It is the gift of God,' the free, undeserved gift—the faith through which ye are saved, as well as the salvation which he of his own good pleasure, his mere favour, annexes thereto. That ye believe is one instance of his grace; that believing, ye are saved, another."[7]

Initially claiming Luther as an ally, Wesley subsequently thought that the German Reformer's understanding of the relation of law and gospel fostered a cavalier attitude to the specific, concrete obedience that gospel-quickened people are to render God. Thereafter Wesley insisted on the most delicate balance between faith alone and holy living, without thereby turning the former into a pretext for antinomianism (in this having "faith alone" cut the nerve of faith) or turning the latter into moralism (in this depriving "holy living" of the holy.)

---

5. *WJW* 1:409.
6. Calvin, *Commentary* John 11:26.
7. *WJW* 1:126.

The line here, like all the lines in both theology and discipleship, is finer than a hair and harder than diamond. Never cavilling that "the imputed righteousness of Christ" was synonymous with justification, Wesley was dubious when he heard eighteenth-century Calvinists speak of sanctification as "the imputed obedience of Christ,"[8] regarding "imputed obedience" as dangerous to Christian integrity if not simply self-contradictory. At the same time he denied any claim to "inherent righteousness," the notion that whatever righteousness believers possess in themselves, however slight, is the *ground* of their justification. He knew that confused Christians could correctly recognize and repudiate an outer "works righteousness" (we are deemed righteous on account of what we do) and in the same instant endorse an inner "works righteousness" wherein we are deemed righteous on account of a (so-called) godly disposition. In the "stillness controversy" that threatened the nascent Methodist movement, Moravian dissidents maintained that those who lacked assurance of faith were to gain it by remaining "still" in a deliberate inertia wherein they did nothing, attending upon neither Scripture nor sermon nor sacrament nor service. In other words, they disdained both the ordinances of God and the concrete obedience that distinguishes genuine faith (in Jesus Christ) from mere "beliefism." Concerning these people Charles Wesley wrote, "They speak largely and well against expecting to be accepted of God for our virtuous actions; and then teach that we are to be accepted for our virtuous habits or tempers. Still the ground of acceptance is placed in ourselves.... Neither our own inward nor outward righteousness is the ground of our justification."[9]

Wesley saw that his people had to be led to see that the law is to be affirmed not as a moral code (such notions he labelled "heathen") but rather as an implicate of Jesus Christ and therefore of faith in Christ. Neglect of the law would entail antinomianism, and antinomianism

---

8. See Randy Maddox, *Responsible Grace: John Wesley's Practical Theology* (Nashville: Abingdon, 1994), ch. 7.

9. Charles Wesley, "Preface" to *Hymns and Sacred Poems, 1739*. Quoted in Tyson, J.; *Charles Wesley: A Reader*; Oxford: Oxford University Press, 1989.

would collapse faith. (Wesley, unlike the Calvinists around him in the Church of England, always maintained that believers could "make shipwreck of faith.") As early as 17th November 1739 his *Journal* reads

> I left Bristol, and on Saturday came to London. The first person I met with there was one whom I had left strong in faith and zealous of good works. But now she told me Mr. Molther had fully convinced her that she *'never had any faith at all'*, and had advised her, till she received faith, 'to be *still*, ceasing from outward works', which she had accordingly done and did not doubt but in a short time she should find the advantage of it. In the evening Mr. Bray also was highly commending 'the being *still* before the Lord'. He likewise spoke largely of 'the great danger that attended the doing of outward works'....[10]

The "stillness" controversy, of course, was one aspect of a twofold problem with respect to the relation of law to faith, the two aspects of the problem belonging to "enthusiasts" and "formalists" in turn. Wesley customarily described those with a defective attitude to the gospel as "enthusiasts" who elevated their experience or opinion above Scripture, while "formalists" were those who claimed to be possessed of saving faith but possessed only a theological ideation. Antinomians clearly belonged among the enthusiasts, and moralists among the formalists. Wesley knew from the outset of the awakening that he would have to address both parties.

While Wesley continued to preach and teach with respect to the dangers of the misuse of the law, he didn't pen a tract on the topic until 1750. From 1748 to 1750, however, he had published thirteen sermons, "Upon our Lord's Sermon on the Mount." He subsequently insisted that the aim of these thirteen was "to assert and prove every branch of *gospel obedience* as indispensably necessary to gospel salvation."[11] Now he reckoned it necessary to develop an argument on the relation of

---

10. *WJW*, 19:119 (emphasis his).
11. Letter, Nov. 17, 1759 (emphasis his), *WJW* 1:466.

law and gospel as a sequel lest the latter suggest either antinomianism to those who thought gospel and faith to eclipse the law or moralism to those who thought the law to be a code against which people measured themselves and preened themselves, aided and abetted in this by the dominant Arian Christology and semi-Pelagian soteriology of eighteenth-century Anglicanism.

Wesley wrote the three tracts, "The Original, Nature, Properties and Use of the Law," "The Law Established through Faith (I)," and "The Law Established through Faith (II)" in the way Luther had written his "occasional" theology; namely, tracts produced to provide immediate assistance for people whom the gospel had brought to faith and whose discipleship was threatened by theological distortions that claimed to reflect "the faith once for all delivered to the saints" (Jude 3) but in fact contradicted it, and contradicted it so as to imperil those whom the Wesleyan movement's evangelism had "brought to the birth" and thereby nullify a grace-wrought testimony through ensuing disgrace. Wesley knew precisely what was at stake here: nothing less than the spiritual well-being of the Methodist converts, the public reputation of the Societies, and the future of the movement. Antinomianism would derail the movement through outer degradation; moralism would derail it as surely through inner enervation.

While Wesley would certainly have preached and taught on these matters between 1738 and 1750, there is no record that the three homilies were ever preached. He wrote the three to be printed, distributed and read.

Without thinking himself at all overstated, Luther had maintained that theologians are defined by their ability to distinguish between law and gospel.[12] Wesley begins his exposition with a statement similarly global: "Perhaps there are few subjects within the whole compass of religion

---

12. See Gerhard Ebeling, *Luther: An Introduction to his Thought* (London: Collins, 1994), p. 111.

so little understood as this."[13] Immediately he highlights the nature of the misunderstanding: readers of the Romans epistle assume that the apostle's reference to the law pertains either to the Jewish law or the old Roman law. As Gentiles they dismiss the law inasmuch as they aren't Jewish; as moderns they dismiss it inasmuch as they aren't ancients.

The Mosaic law "inflamed" sin, "showed" sin, but couldn't remedy sin, and therefore bore fruit unto death as it incited believers to an obedience they couldn't attain.[14] Believers (i.e., Christians) are wedded to the "body of Christ" (i.e., to Christ himself), and this law is expected to be fruitful unto life. Believers, wedded to Christ, are delivered from "that whole moral as well as ceremonial economy,"[15] since Christ's death has slain this economy and it subsequently has as little claim upon believers as a dead marriage-partner has upon the survivor. The result is that believers are to serve "him who died for us and rose again";[16] i.e., believers are to serve Jesus Christ as present, living person. Implicitly he is asserting the Mosaic economy to be the Torah abstracted from the gospel, from Christ himself; explicitly he evinces his (mis)understanding when he states that the service believers render the living person of Jesus Christ "in a new spiritual dispensation" is contrasted with the "bare outward service" rendered the Mosaic economy.[17] While the Mosaic dispensation has been set aside, the law as such has not been and cannot be, just because (as will be made plain later) Jesus Christ is the substance of the law. In this regard Wesley's understanding and Calvin's are identical.

---

13. *WJW* 2:4.

14. Wesley's understanding of the logic of Torah is now recognized as highly questionable.

15. *WJW* 2:5.

16. Ibid.

17. Ibid. Wesley failed to see that the Torah never enjoins "bare outward service."

"MORAL" LAW

Like the Magisterial Reformers before him, Wesley first identifies the moral law as that law which antedates Moses[18]; antedates, in fact, the creation of the terrestrial world, but not the creation as such, since the "morning stars" of the creation were angelic intelligences with a capacity to know God.[19] These angelic intelligences were created with understanding to discern truth from falsehood and goodness from evil, and "as necessary result of this, with liberty, a capacity of choosing the one and refusing the other."[20]

Several matters call for comment here. While Wesley's vocabulary might suggest he is adopting the moralism he eschews, it must be understood that liberty isn't that freedom wherewith only Jesus Christ can set us free. Liberty is the pre-fallen creature's uncoerced response to the truth and reality and goodness of God. In mentioning "liberty" Wesley wishes to emphasize that these intelligences are agents, not automatons, and neither an aspect of God nor an emanation from God. Their uncoerced affirmation of God is essential to them as creatures. Freedom, to be distinguished from liberty, will be the Christ-wrought capacity to obey Jesus Christ as believers, now redeemed and reconciled, find restored in them that *imago Dei* that the Fall has defaced. In the second place Wesley maintains that the end of "moral" law, for these unfallen intelligences, is knowing God. Then plainly "moral" isn't the word he wants in his discussion of "moral law." In the third place, moral law is that by which these creatures could serve God and therein find their service "rewardable in itself."[21] The service of *God* (by means of the "moral" law) is such a delight, a fulfilment, that it is inconceivable because inherently inappropriate that "something" be granted as the

---

18. J.T. McNeill, "Natural Law in the Teaching of the Reformers," *Journal of Religion*, #26 (1946), pp. 168–82.
19. *WJW*, 2:6.
20. Ibid.
21. Ibid.

law's reward. In other words, the moral law (plainly mis-named) is that by which the living God invites creatures to know him and enjoy him. Their knowledge of God, indistinguishable from their service of God (here the force of *law* is retained), is inherently the reward of God. In saying that the law which gave these intelligences is "a complete model of all truth so far as was intelligible to a finite being"[22] Wesley is plainly borrowing from his coming pronouncements concerning Jesus Christ as the substance of the law.

When God created humankind he gave it the same law, inscribed on humankind's heart as on angels', "to the intent that it might never be far off, never hard to be understood; but always at hand, and always shining with clear light...."[23] While the law was "well-nigh" (i.e., almost) effaced in the Fall, it was never obliterated. Undeniably, then, the law of God inscribed on the heart is identical with the *imago Dei* in Wesley's understanding. In the wake of the Fall the *imago* is defaced but never effaced, or else the sinner wouldn't be human. For exactly the same reason Wesley maintains that the inscribed law can't be obliterated. Law as the *imago Dei* is the irreducible, indefeasible humanness in which we are created, regardless of the extent to which we contradict it as fallen creatures.

Then Wesley adds that through the reconciliation which God fashioned "through the Son of his love" God "in some measure re-inscribed the law on the heart of his dark, sinful creature."[24] "In some measure" indicates that Wesley doesn't want to predicate of the atonement as such what the church catholic reserves for incorporation in Christ; namely, that the *imago Dei* is restored only as we "put on" Christ through faith, as he is "formed" in us. On the other hand, Wesley insists on a Christological determination of that work of God whereby God gives up on no one, abandons no one, but rather re-asserts his blessing and claim. The "re-inscription" of the law, effected through the atonement, is of course a work of Christ. Wesley isn't speaking here of the person united

---

22. *WJW*, 2:6.
23. *WJW*, 2:7.
24. Ibid.

to Christ in faith; he is insisting, nevertheless, that in the act of God *extra nos, pro nobis*, but not yet *in nobis*, there has been re-engraved that which the Fall had well-nigh effaced. The question can always be asked, "If 'well-nigh' means 'not entirely,' then is re-inscription necessary?" Wesley would argue, in sound theological fashion, that we ought always to argue from actuality to necessity (i.e., God's act forestalls all speculation as to its necessity.) Re-inscription, then, is the claim of Jesus Christ specifically, the reassertion of *his ownership* in the reclamation of the sinner. The re-inscription effected through the atonement means that what is re-inscribed (the law) is nothing less than the claim of the Son who has come to fallen creatures as Salvager. This action of the Salvager upon *all* humankind entails the following:

[1] His claim, while admittedly authoritative (or else his claim is hollow), is never authoritarian, authoritarianism meaning here the assertion of a demand which is arbitrary since the demander isn't entitled to it, and compliance with which demand is therefore coerced. Instead, because the claim is one with God's mercy ("the *Son* of God's love") rather than extraneous to that mercy and unrelated to it, the claim is an implicate of this mercy and therefore not alien to the fallen creature.

[2] This claim pertains to the essence of humankind's humanness. To be human is to be made by the Son for the Son, and, in the wake of the Fall, to be cherished by the Son, sought by him, and reconfirmed as the one upon whom the Son's mercy-wrought ownership is restated.

[3] The grace that is God's action and provision in his Son is also that grace now at work preveniently in all people everywhere, preparing them for the day when their hearing the gospel of grace resonates within them on account of the grace with which they are graced now unknowingly. In other words, while it appears that Wesley never speaks formally of Jesus Christ as the substance of prevenient grace, plainly "the Son of his love" *is* this as he forges himself within all men and women everywhere, apart from which the explicit declaration of the gospel would be pointless. While Wesley agrees entirely with the Magisterial Reformers in their

understanding of "total depravity"[25], and therefore agrees that in the wake of the Fall humankind is dead of itself *coram Deo*, he insists that all fallen people are beneficiaries of that re-inscription which is nothing less and nothing other than the action of the crucified upon them.

[4] A corollary of the foregoing is the truth that no human is God-forsaken. God's act of reconciliation, the heart of which is the Son's utter and *actual* forsakenness at the hands of the Father, means that *for the Son's sake* no one is God-forsaken now or can be.

[5] Since only by grace can grace be discerned, and since only by grace can anyone respond to grace, then the action of the Son in the cross is an instance of a visitation of God's grace vouchsafed to all humankind apart from which fallen people would be neither response-able nor response-ible. In a word, apart from the re-inscription of the law (the substance of which the is the atonement wrought in the Son), fallen humankind would find the gospel of grace inherently incomprehensible.

[6] Since the re-inscription of the law arises from the cross, the crown and climax of God's work, and presupposes incarnation and atonement, the (so-called) natural law is never merely natural but is always graced, such grace always being constitutive of humankind. This grace, it must be noted, is not an outer structure whose inner content is human achievement. Wesley bears no resemblance to Gabriel Biel and other medieval scholastics akin to Biel. This grace, rather, means that those who hear the gospel do not add to or bring to the proclamation of the gospel a "faith" which is their self-fashioned "contribution" (as it were.) Faith ever remains God's gift.[26] At the same time, the gift has to be exercised; faith is always a human affirmation and activity or else it isn't a human who responds. Here Wesley is strong where the Magisterial Reformers were weak in their insufficient recognition that faith, even as God's gift, must ever be a human activity. Wesley's understanding of re-inscription (i.e., tantamount to prevenient grace) means that what God wills for people

---

25. *WJW* 1:118.
26. *WJW* 1:126.

(faith in Jesus Christ) God must also will in them, or else faith is a human invention; at the same time, what God wills in them God must will in them not so as to coerce them but rather so as to have them now *will for themselves* in a genuinely *human* act what he has already willed for them and in them—or else they simply haven't responded. The so-called natural law is thoroughly Christological.

Notwithstanding the discussion just concluded Wesley maintains that humankind's flight from God finds God choosing a "peculiar people" (Genesis 6:12) "to whom he gave a more perfect knowledge of his law."[27] What is the force of "more perfect?" Does Wesley mean here a psycho-religious intensity—i.e., Israel's awareness of the law of God is extraordinarily vivid? Or does he mean not increased vividness but rather greater subtlety and specificity concerning the details of the law? He indicates that he has neither in mind in view of the fact that the Ten Commandments are but the "heads" of the law, the law being much more extensive than the heads. Moreover, these "heads" were given to Israel because the people were "slow of understanding"; i.e., they lacked familiarity with subtle details. I submit he means a deeper understanding of God's self-sacrificing love for his people. Since it is the Son's sacrifice that re-inscribes the law, a "more perfect" knowledge of the law must pertain to that sacrifice willed and enacted by the Godhead in concert on behalf of sinners. In virtue of God's election Israel is made aware of God's self-sacrificing love (albeit by anticipation of the death of the Nazarene.) Gentiles, on the other hand, who are taught the Ten Commandments, have only the "heads" of the law.

Wesley's conclusion to his discussion in this part of his tract—"And thus it is that the law of God made known to them that know not God"—may appear to contradict the argument I have advanced. After all, if they know the law of God without knowing God, what do they know? A moral code? They know something other than a moral code, however, for "moral code" operates in the orbit of an ethic rooted in

---

27. *WJW*, 2:7.

metaphysics; Wesley's insistence that they are aware of a *claim* upon them operates in the orbit of the presence and power of the living God. In short, they are aware of a claim upon them without knowing precisely *who* has claimed them. For this reason, says Wesley, their knowing the law of God "does not suffice."[28] Why not? He adds, "They cannot by this means comprehend the height and length and breadth thereof."[29] Thereof? Of what? Obviously of the law. Yet the indisputable reference to Ephesians 3:18 speaks of Christ's love for us. Wesley's next sentence, "Plainly God alone can reveal this by his Spirit,"[30] grants readers a greater glimpse of what he has in mind as he renders "this" explicit by quoting Jeremiah 31:31-33, where God promises to write the law on the hearts of his people. It can only be concluded that for Wesley *the law of God written on the heart* and *the love of Christ* are identical.

Earlier Wesley had said that knowing the law of God doesn't suffice. It is evident now that what doesn't suffice is that love of Christ which is *pro nobis* but not yet *in nobis* in the absence of faith. As Jesus Christ is embraced in faith the love of Christ takes root in us; as this occurs the law of God comes to be written on the heart. Plainly Jesus Christ, the gospel, and the substance of the law are the same.

THE NATURE OF THE LAW

Having discussed the "original" of the law at length, and having hinted many times over at the nature of the law in its Christological substance, Wesley now discusses the nature of the law in terms that permit no other interpretation than that Christ is Torah incarnate.

The law is "an incorruptible picture of the high and holy One that inhabiteth eternity."[31] Here, it must be noted, "picture" doesn't mean "illustration only" in the sense that a picture of an object isn't the object

---

28. *WJW*, 2:8.
29. Ibid.
30. Ibid.
31. *WJW*, 2:9.

itself. The language Wesley uses throughout his discussion of the nature of the law indicates that by "picture" he means exactly what Calvin means by "mirror." Mirror, for Calvin, is never mirror only or mirror-image only in the sense that the reflection lacks the ontic status of what is reflected. When Calvin says that Jesus Christ mirrors the Father or the Son mirrors our election, he means that Jesus Christ is our effectual election, *is* the electing God electing us, and this truth and reality is both operative and known to be operative in Christ alone. "Mirror" for Calvin never implies that "image" lacks substance. For Calvin the purpose of the mirror is to render substance accessible and knowable.

In the same vein "picture" for Wesley is the effectual presence of substance. This is evident when he speaks in the same paragraph of the *law* as "the face of God unveiled."[32] Admittedly, in his homily on the law Wesley doesn't link explicitly the law as the face of God unveiled with 2nd Corinthians 4:3-6 (where Jesus Christ is spoken of in this manner.) Still, in his New Testament *Notes* on 2nd Corinthians 4 he does, and his exegetical comments are as profound as they are subtle. In commenting on "But if our gospel also is veiled" Wesley adds parenthetically, "As well as the law of Moses," and then goes on to say, "The gospel is clear, open and simple, except to the wilfully blind and unbelievers…[the gospel itself] has no veil upon it,"[33] and by implication, neither has the law of Moses. Wesley avers that there was a veil on the face of Moses, while the law of Moses is as transparent as the gospel of Christ. Lest anyone think the foregoing comment strained Wesley underlines it in his discussion of 2nd Corinthians 4:6. Here he states that the glory of God (which shines in the face of Christ) is God's glorious love and God's glorious image, and the face of Christ reflects this glory "more resplendently than the face of Moses."[34] Once again, however, "more" is predicated of the face of Christ compared to the face of Moses, but not compared to the law of Moses. In his *Notes* Wesley points out by way of illustration that God

---

32. Ibid.
33. *NT Notes*, 2nd Cor. 4:3–6.
34. Ibid.

is not merely the author of light but *is* light itself,[35] and this light shines in the face of Christ; i.e., God manifests *himself* in the face of Christ.

To recapitulate: Wesley says that the law is the face of God unveiled. Paul says Jesus Christ is this. For Wesley, Jesus Christ is plainly the substance of the law.

My interpretation of Wesley here is supported by his remark (still in the same paragraph of his homily) that the law is "God manifested to his creatures as they are able to bear it."[36] Wesley's unqualified assertion here must be allowed its full weight: the law isn't a message from God or truth of God but is rather God himself disclosing himself; i.e., God is both the author and object of revelation, and all of this in such a manner as to preserve us, as Wesley once again echoes John Calvin's ubiquitous notion that God "accommodates" himself to us finite, frail creatures lest his glorious self-disclosure annihilate us.[37] Wesley then adds with limpid simplicity, "[The law] is the heart of God disclosed to man,"[38] when the heart of God, in light of the incarnation, can only be the gospel. Temporarily puzzling, then, is Wesley's comment, "Yea, in some sense we may apply to the law what the Apostle says of his [i.e., God's] Son—it is the 'streaming forth' or the outbeaming 'of his glory', the express image of his person."[39] Does "in some sense" mean that Wesley is now retracting what he has stated concerning the relationship of the law to Christ? Bewilderment vanishes, however, with Wesley's commentary on Hebrews 1:3. Here he declares without qualification that glory is "the nature of God revealed in its brightness"[40]; i.e., the law can only be God's nature shining compellingly. Concerning Hebrews' "the express image of his [God's] person" Wesley adds, "Whatever the Father is, is

---

35. Ibid.
36. *WJW*, 2:9.
37. See Ford Lewis Battles, "God was Accommodating Himself to Human Capacity" in *Interpreting John Calvin* (Grand Rapids: Baker Books, 1996).
38. *WJW*, 2:9.
39. Ibid.
40. *NT Notes*, Hebrews 1:3.

exhibited in the Son."[41] Insisting in his commentary that "person" and "substance" are synonyms, Wesley states that the Son as express image of God's person means that the Son is possessed of "the unchangeable perpetuity of divine life and power."[42]

Clearly Wesley is predicating of the law what has been predicated of the Son. This is possible only if the Son is the substance of the law. Then what does he mean by his caution, "in some sense"? He gives no indication. In light of his understanding of the relation of law to God and to the gospel, it appears he hesitated with the same hesitation that dogged Calvin before him; *viz.*, if gospel and law are identical in essence, wherein do they differ? Calvin resorted to such expressions as "less clear," "more brightly," etc.[43] Wesley reflects Calvin's vocabulary in the speaking of the law as "these faint pictures to shadow out the deep things of God."[44]

Still expounding the first of his three homilies on the law (Romans 7:12), Wesley circles back to 2nd Corinthians 4:3-6, referring once again to the "unveiled face" of God, albeit this time through a seemingly circuitous reference to Cicero. Cicero had said, "If virtue could assume such a shape as that we could behold her with our eyes, what wonderful love she would excite in us."[45] Wesley immediately adds, "It is done already. The law of God is all virtues in one, in such a shape as to be beheld with open face by all those whose eyes God hath enlightened."[46] His summary comment here is "What is the law except divine virtue and wisdom assuming a visible form?"[47] Does "virtue" take Wesley back to the moralism he seeks to avoid? It might if "virtue" were to be understood in a classical sense. The context of Wesley's reference to Cicero,

---

41. Ibid.

42. Ibid.

43. See Victor A. Shepherd, *The Nature and Function of Faith in the Theology of John Calvin* (Macon: Mercer University Press, 1983), pp. 129–178.

44. *WJW*, 2:10.

45. *WJW*, 2:9.

46. Ibid.

47. Ibid.

however, makes it plain that "virtue" here *with respect to the law* is the claim of God. And the claim of God, whose unveiled face is seen in the Son, reinterprets all such expressions as "virtue." Additionally, lying behind the Ciceronian reference to "virtue" is Wesley's insistence on the substantial identity of Christ and the law. His point in the reference to Cicero (virtue, once beheld, quickens love in the beholder) is amplified in his 1745 tract, *A Farther Appeal to Men of Reason and Religion, Part II*. Here he speaks of God's opening the eyes of our understanding, only to add that the immediate consequence of such "seeing" is loving God.[48] And we can't love God, he continues, without "a tender love to the whole of human kind."[49] The law of God, then, is "virtue" only in the sense that the law grants us understanding of the nature of God in such wise that our understanding unfailingly gives rise to love for God and neighbour. The (perhaps dubious) reference to Cicero, then, merely highlights Wesley's insistence that to "see" the law (i.e., understand it) is invariably to love it; better, love him whose face and heart the law is. Wesley's Christological understanding of the law contradicts any putative moralism, however dangerous it may have been for him to adduce a reference to Cicero when eighteenth-century Anglicanism was only too ready to think of law in terms of moralism.

Wesley knows that no language is adequate to the wonder, glory and magnificence of the law, aware as he is of the "shortness, even impropriety, there is in these and all other human expressions."[50] Still, he resorts to them just because they are the only expressions humans have. Therefore he circles around the law again, approaching it now from a different angle of vision, declaring it to be "supreme, unchangeable reason; it is unalterable rectitude; it is the everlasting fitness of all things are or ever were created." It must be noted once more that by "unchangeable reason" and "everlasting fitness" Wesley is not departing from Christology and migrating towards moralism. As early as 1733 in *The Circumcision of*

---

48. *WJW*, 11:269.
49. Ibid.
50. *WJW*, 2:10.

the Heart he deplored all attempts at "grounding religion in 'the eternal *fitness* of things', or 'the intrinsic *excellence* of virtue', and the *beauty* of actions flowing from it—on the *reasons*, as they term them, of good and evil, and the relations of beings to each other."[51] Wesley denounces all efforts at grounding "religion" in moralism of any sort, even moralism supplemented by rationalism and aesthetics, all such moralism aiming at a righteousness other than that which believers receive through faith in Christ. It must be noted that Wesley penned even this criticism before the Aldersgate episode of 1738, after which he never failed to declare justification by faith.

If, then, the foregoing is what Wesley can't mean by "unchanging reason" and "everlasting fitness," what does he mean? It appears that "reason" has to be understood as *logos*, where *logos* means "word, reason, rationality, intelligibility." The *logos* of God is unchangeable in that God is unchangeable. The *logos* of God is the outer expression of God's "innerness," now imprinted indelibly on creaturely actuality in its entirety. In other words, since the Son of God is the *logos* of God, and since the Son of God and the law of God are substantially identical, then the law of God is the *logos* of God now rendered incarnate in Jesus of Nazareth.

And the "fitness of all things?" Wesley appears to have in mind here the "fitting-ness" of all things in the sense of Colossians 1:17: "In him [i.e., Christ] all things hold together." In his commentary on this text Wesley writes, "*And by him all things consist*—the original expression not only implies that he sustains all things in being, but more directly, *All things were and are compacted in him, into one system.* He is the cement and support of the universe. And is he less than the supreme God?"[52]

In fact Wesley's *Notes* on Colossians 1:15-18 predicate of Christ what his homilies on the law predicate of the law; e.g., "the glorious pre-eminence of Christ over the highest angels" means that Christ is "begotten before every creature; subsisting before all worlds, before all

---

51. *WJW*, 1:410 (emphasis Wesley's).
52. *NT Notes,* Colossians 1:17 (emphasis Wesley's).

time, from all eternity."⁵³ This is precisely how he spoke of the law in the early part of his homily. Now in the same homily Wesley brings forward a concatenation of English expressions even as, regrettably, he doesn't supply the Greek he has in mind. He describes the law as "a copy of the eternal mind," "a transcript of the divine nature," "the fairest offspring of the everlasting Father," "the brightest efflux of his eternal wisdom," and "the visible beauty of the most high."⁵⁴

Once again, then, while some expressions Wesley uses concerning the law might be read, at first sight, as turning obedience to Christ into moralism, "first sight" can never be "last word": Wesley's anti-moralistic rigour remains undiluted.

In his final comment on the nature of the law Wesley says that the angels delight in the law and marvel at it, as will "every wise believer, every well-instructed child of God upon earth."⁵⁵ Surely angels and humans, recognizing the Christoform nature of the law, marvel at it because it is the God-authored vehicle of God himself; they delight in it because God himself is their consummate blessing. It is little wonder Wesley pronounces the law *"ever* blessed,"⁵⁶ "ever" denying any suggesting that the law of God might be provisional only, to be honoured in one era but not in another. "Ever" suggests instead "eternal," pertaining to the Godhead itself.

THE PROPERTIES OF THE LAW

A: Holy

Having discussed the nature of God's law Wesley attends to its properties, first among which, following Romans 7:12, the text of his homily,

---

53. *op.cit.*, Colossians 1:15.
54. *WJW*, 2.10. Note here the similarity with respect to the reference in Cicero, where Wesley discussed the force of "beauty" and "visible."
55. *WJW*, 2.10.
56. Ibid. (emphasis mine.)

the law is holy; even "...internally and essentially holy."[57] By "internally" Wesley intends "inherently."[58] Since God alone is inherently holy, Wesley understands the law of God to be God himself in his inherent holiness, fostering in his people the holiness he purposes for them. When the law is "transcribed"[59] into "life" and into "the soul," the result is the "pure, clean, unpolluted worship of God," when by "worship" Wesley characteristically has in mind a godliness that is the sanctification of all of life.[60]

Wesley maintains that the law must be holy, otherwise "it could not be the immediate offspring, and much less the express resemblance of God, who is essential holiness."[61] This statement is rich. Plainly the law can be holy only because it is substantially identical with the God who is essentially holy. To forfend any suggestion of subordinationism or even Arianism, Wesley maintains that the law isn't merely the immediate offspring of God (allowing the interpretation "made not begotten") but is rather the "express resemblance." Again, without citing either the Scripture passage or the Greek word he has in mind, he evidently means "eikon," identity not similarity. The law as holy is the "eikon" or image of God who is essentially holy; i.e., the law isn't merely functionally holy, an instrument or tool that God deploys to effect holiness (of some sort) in his people. ("Of some sort" must be added, since only if the law is one with the God who is essentially holy is God-in-his-holiness forging holiness in his people by means of the law.) Since the law is essentially holy, Wesley reminds us, it is blasphemous to speak of it as sin or the cause of sin, even though the law, upon meeting sin, exposes sin.[62]

B: Just

---

57. *WJW*, 2:11

58. See footnote # 30, *WJW* 2:11 where the editor comments on this meaning throughout all the editions of this homily in Wesley's lifetime.

59. See above where Wesley speaks of the law as "transcript."

60. *WJW*, 2:11.

61. Ibid.

62. Ibid.

The law is also just: "It renders all their due. It prescribes exactly what is right, precisely what ought to be done, said or thought, both with regard to the author of our being, with regard to ourselves, and with regard to every creature which he has made. It is adapted in all respects to the nature of things, of the whole universe and every individual. It is suited to all the circumstances of each, and to all their mutual relations, whether such as have existed from the beginning, or such as commenced in any following period. It is exactly agreeable to the fitness of things, whether essential or accidental. It clashes with none of these in any degree, nor is ever unconnected with them. If the word be taken in that sense, there is nothing *arbitrary* in the law of God: although still the whole and every part thereof is totally dependent on his will, so that 'Thy will be done' is the supreme universal law in earth and heaven."[63]

Many aspects of this extended passage invite comment.

[a] God's law is equated with God's will, and God's will is God himself in the act of willing.[64]

[b] God's law is his intention for every aspect of the creation.

[c] The law pertains to the creature as created or the creature as found, to the creature as intended or the creature as instantiated, in the wake of the distortions of the Fall and the complexities of world-occurrence.

[d] The law befits "exactly" all things, whether essential or accidental; i.e., the law of God comprehends the totality of the creaturely order: original, fallen, essential, accidental. There is nothing, no one, no situation, development or circumstance that is law-exempt. The ground of this, of course, is that there is nothing that hasn't been made through the Son for the Son.

[e] The law cannot clash with "any of these" for the same reason that it cannot be unconnected with them: the "connection" and the "fit" are rooted in the fact that the law, characterized by God's essence, cannot

---

63. *WJW*, 2:12 (emphasis Wesley's).
64. "The will of God is God himself." *WJW*, 2:13.

be the contradiction of anything that has been made but can only be its "whence," its "whither," its fulfillment, its blessing.

[f] There is nothing arbitrary in the law of God. (i) There couldn't be, since the law is the "transcript" or "efflux" of God. (ii) No one can repudiate the law on the ground that the law is arbitrary and therein a surd element whose imposition on humankind renders human existence ultimately absurd. If the law were arbitrary it would never subserve the human good but would at best be "unconnected" with that good and at worst contradict it.

Wesley underlines once more that all things, together with their "essential relations to each other," are the work of God's hands; and for this reason there arises the "fitness" of all things. The law as "the immutable rule of right and wrong" depends on this "fitness."[65] All of this—the nature of all that exists, its interconnectedness or "fitted-ness," occurs through the will of God, by which they "are and were created."[66] With this last statement Wesley has adduced Revelation 4:11. While he doesn't amplify the scriptural text, he plainly has it in mind. Revelation 4:11 states that by God's will there has been created all that exists. The immediate context of the passage informs us that the seer looks into heaven and sees the throne and the exalted Lord Jesus seated upon the throne. Lightning, voices and peals of thunder issue from the throne—a reminder of Sinai, and an especially pointed reminder that the throne of God is essentially related to the promulgation of the law at Sinai, even as the Trisagion of the worshipper recognizes in God the holiness that characterizes God, throne and law.[67] And of course Revelation 11:15 insists that the one seated on the throne is none other than Christ, for to him there has passed sovereignty over the world. The antinomians, then, are without excuse: the law can no more cease to be good than can God. In the same way, antinomians who claim to have embraced Christ yet disdain the law have embraced only a chimera.

---

65. *WJW* 2:13.
66. Ibid.
67. See G.B. Caird, *The Revelation of St John the Divine* (London: Black, 1966).

WESLEY'S UNDERSTANDING OF THE LAW OF GOD

If the antinomians are self-contradicted, what about the moralists? Wesley immediately adds, "it may be granted...that in every particular case God wills this or this (suppose that men should honour their parents) because it is right, agreeable to the fitness of things, to the relation wherein they stand."[68] In other words, the law of God comprehends all of creaturely existence in its multidimensionality and its interconnectedness. Obviously the law can't be a moral code, notwithstanding the reference to the Fifth Commandment, since no code comprehends what Wesley says the law comprehends. The law comprehends what it does in that the substance of the law is Christ, through whom and for whom all things have been made and in whom all things hold together or "fit."

C: Good

Not only is the law holy and just, it is also good, and good in that it flows from the goodness of God, which goodness inclined God "to impart that divine copy of himself to the holy angels."[69] Here Wesley reinforces his point against the antinomians, that the law is good because a "copy" of God, only to strengthen the case for the law by adding that God's motive in supplying the law was his "tender love" in manifesting his will "afresh to fallen man."[70] In fact, Wesley insists, love alone moved God to publish the law in the wake of the Fall, to send prophets to declare the self-same law to the sin-hardened, and finally to send the only-begotten Son to "confirm every jot and tittle" of the law with a view to writing it in the hearts of all his children; and all of this with the eschatological result that the Son can deliver his "mediatorial function" to the Father.[71] Plainly Wesley sees the promulgation of the law comprehended in the one-and-only Mediator himself; i.e., the law is the Mediator claiming those whom he has visited and acted for in light of his "tender love." Not

---

68. *WJW* 2:13.
69. Ibid.
70. Ibid.
71. *WJW* 2:14.

surprisingly, then, Wesley climaxes the accolades he heaps upon the law (e.g., "sweeter than honey in the honeycomb") with "mild and kind" and "wherein are hid all the treasures of divine knowledge and love."[72] "Mild and kind" points unambiguously to Matthew 11:29-30 where Jesus insists that his yoke (a common metaphor for the Torah in the Old Testament) is "easy" and "light" just because he himself is gentle. The second reference is Colossians 2:3, a passage in which Paul refers to Christ alone. For Wesley, then, "law" and "Jesus Christ" imply each other.

The enthusiast-antinomians think they can be the beneficiaries of Christ while disdaining the law. The formalist-moralists, on the other hand, think they can benefit from the law while disdaining Christ. Both are wrong, and wrong not because the antinomians lack morals while the moralists lack religion. Morals added to antinominans and religion added to moralists would still leave both sunk alike in unbelief and condemnation. Both groups fail to understand that the law is good in itself because it is God-authored and Son (substance)-informed, and that it effects good (i.e., godliness) in those who honour it. Failing here, they fail to understand that a fruit of the law in believers is that righteousness of which Isaiah 32:17 ("And the effect of righteousness will be peace, and the result of righteousness, quietness and trust for ever" RSV) speaks. Their ignorance is only highlighted when Wesley, eschewing both antinomianism and moralism, maintains that righteousness isn't merely an effect of the law (this might lend itself to a moralistic misinterpretation); rather, "the law itself is righteousness," even as he glories in the truth that Christ alone is ever our righteousness.[73]

CONCLUSION

Many New Testament exegetes have maintained that "Christ our righteousness" is the central theme of Romans, while others have insisted chapters 9-11 are the pivot of the epistle, and with it the relation of

---

72. Ibid.
73. *WJW* 2:14.

Torah to Jesus Christ. Wesley would spend little time adjudicating this issue. For in the introduction to Romans found in his *New Testament Notes* Wesley maintains that in the Romans epistle in particular Paul "labours...to produce in those to whom he writes a deep sense of the excellency of the gospel, and [labours] to engage them to act suitably to it."[74] Wesley's exposition of the constellation of gospel, law, Christ, righteousness, faith; his exposition in the Sermons supports what he insists in the *Notes* is Paul's intention in Romans; viz., a magnification of the beauty, attractiveness, winsomeness of the gospel, and therein of believers' self-abandonment to its claim upon them, which of course is nothing other than their self-abandonment to the one who is their life, their comfort, and their eternal blessing.

---

74. *NT Notes*, 355.

5

REASON, THE GOSPEL AND CATHOLICITY

Following Wesley's "Aldersgate heartwarming" in 1738 no one was more surprised than he at the response that met his preaching, both indoors and out. While previously his theology had been an effete hybrid of mysticism and moralism, following the evening service in which he knew his sins forgiven his theology was thereafter built upon justification by faith (a synonym for forgiveness of sins, according to the sixteenth-century Reformers.) Wesley never sought any other foundation, and always thought ill of those who did.

Within months of his fresh understanding of the gospel of justification and his fresh attestation of it in his preaching, his forthright declaration of good news found more than a few hearers convulsing, or groaning, or screaming, or barking—or simply prostrate in a dead faint. At first Wesley was impressed positively, looking upon such phenomena as evidence of the Spirit's power. Soon, however, he was more discriminating, aware that in some cases bizarre behaviour was regrettably unaccompanied by any discernible transformation of character, while in other cases

---

*   Convocation Address, Roberts Wesleyan College, September, 1995.

intra-psychic vividness was sought as a spurious end in itself. His settled position reflected that of Jonathan Edwards, whose best-known book *Religious Affections* cautioned readers against two inaccurate assessments of the revival: that everything in it is of God, or that nothing in it is of God. The spirits would have to be tested, and Edwards' *Religious Affections* aimed at helping readers with the requisite assessment.

Schooled at Oxford University, steeped in the wisdom of the Church Fathers (Patristics), informed and formed by Anglican theology of the seventeenth- and eighteenth- centuries as well as by the English and Continental Reformers, and appreciating the insights of Counter-Reformation Roman Catholics, Wesley was never tempted to set aside reason, critical thinking, in favour of an uncritical effusiveness. All his life he insisted that "religion and reason go hand in hand."[1] Elsewhere he insisted "I would as soon put out my eyes to secure my faith, as lay aside my reason."[2] Unrestrained fantasy he unhesitatingly denounced as "a religious madness," which madness, he noted, caused (or occasioned) its victims to "despise and vilify" reason.[3]

Wesley knew, on the one hand, that the Holy Spirit of God could not be restricted to human expectation; on the other hand, that God's grace restores people to their "right mind" as surely as the Gadarene demoniac had been restored to his. Therefore no one could claim irrationality or mindlessness as a manifestation of the Spirit. Reason ever remains an essential feature of the *imago Dei*.

Wesley was always aware that the gospel supplies the substance of the Christian message; reason does not. While reason is not a source of our knowledge of God it remains a God-ordained tool for ordering and commending the knowledge of God we gain through grace-quickened faith that clings to the crucified One who has been given for us, given to us, and is at work within us.

---

1. Wesley, *WJW*, Vol. 9, p. 382.
2. Jackson, *Works*, "A Dialogue between an Antinomian and his Friend" (1745), Vol. 10, p. 267.
3. Wesley, *WJW*, Vol.2, pp. 50 and 587 respectively.

The Oxford don who treasured his own education always sought to improve the education of others. For this reason he insisted that his lay preachers, underprivileged in that they had been denied access to higher education, were nonetheless to study several hours per day. Methodist Christians have characteristically cherished educational opportunities, and for this reason have established schools, colleges and universities wherever they have gone. Commitment to higher education remains non-negotiable for all who claim to be descendants of the man from Epworth.

I: REASON

To know John Wesley is to know how nervous he was at the appearance of "enthusiasm" (or even at the mention of it). Enthusiasm, he insisted, was a form of fanaticism born of elevating experience above Scripture. He denounced it and ever sought to distance himself from it. Warning his people against it in *A Plain Account of Christian Perfection*[4] he unhesitatingly labelled it "a daughter of pride." "Give no place to a heated imagination," he added immediately. (We must be sure to underline "heated" since Wesley's appreciation of poetry would never find him disdaining imagination or the imaginative as such). He insisted on discernment with respect to "dreams, voices, impressions, visions, revelations," for while they could be from God, they could also be from nature or even from the devil.

In the same *Plain Account* paragraph Wesley insisted we are equally at risk if we "despise or lightly esteem reason, knowledge or human learning." If "enthusiasm" (fanaticism) was by definition the elevation of experience above Scripture, then "enthusiasm" was by extension the undervaluing of reason. "I advise you never to use the words 'wisdom,' 'reason,' or 'knowledge' by way of reproach. On the contrary, pray that you yourself may abound in them more and more. If you mean...false reasoning, say so; and throw away the chaff but not the wheat." (Wesley

---

4. All references in the next two paragraphs are from Wesley, *A Plain Account of Christian Perfection* (London: Epworth Press, 1952).

was characteristically intolerant of anything that appeared to be an instance of "false reasoning." In 1788, when he was 85 years old, his diary tells us he read logic on four consecutive mornings.) Words like "reason," "rational," "learned," "knowledgeable" must never be used pejoratively, must never even be lightly esteemed. Such words must be used only to compliment, extol, praise; only, in short, to denote genuine accomplishment and merit.

Wesley knew that Christians delight to hear and heed the command of God. And the command to love God with the mind is just that: a command. Unnecessary ignorance is not God-honouring; neither is cavalier stupidity nor the obscurantism born of intellectual laziness nor the silly notion that reason has to be suppressed in order to make room for faith. In a tract, "The Case of Reason Impartially Considered," Wesley denounced any and all who disparage reason: "Never more declaim in that wild, loose, ranting manner against this precious gift of God. Acknowledge 'the candle of the Lord,' which he hath fixed in our souls for excellent purposes."

We should remember that no Christian, and no Christian educational institution, is permitted to undervalue reason in view of the fact that the incarnation is the foundation of all things Christian. When the fourth gospel affirms that the Word became flesh, the word it uses for "Word," *logos*, also means rationality or intelligibility. The gospel-writer tells us that the entire creation has been fashioned through the Word, through the *logos*. Since the Word is God, the inner principle of God's own mind, the *logos*, has been imprinted indelibly on the creation.

Science is possible only because there is a correlation between patterns intrinsic to the scientist's mind and intelligible patterns in the physical world. Otherwise put, science is possible only because there is a correlation between the structure of human thought and the structure of the physical world, when the *logos* of God is the origin of this correlation.⁵ John Polkinghorne, a physicist and a Christian, writes, "The Word is God's agent in creation, impressing his rationality upon the world. That same Word is also the light of men (sic), giving us access thereby to the rationality that is in the world."⁶ Polkinghorne's statement is illustrated by the fact that when mathematicians and physicists have compared notes, they have seen that the relations purely within human thinking (mathematics) reflect the pattern and structures in nature that scientific investigation (physics) uncovers. In other words, there is a correlation between the rationality of human thinking and the rationality imprinted indelibly in nature. Of course. All things—the creation, as well as the mind of the scientist investigating the creation—have been made through the *logos*, through that Word become flesh in Jesus Christ.

No Christian, and no Christian educational institution, then, can "lightly esteem" reason and celebrate the obscurantism deemed "realistic" in some academic quarters today.

At the same time when Wesley rightly insisted on the place of reason in the economy of grace he was not countenancing rationalism. Christians are always to be rational, never rationalistic.

While reason is the "handmaid" of faith, rationalism is a philosophy that by its nature precludes faith. Rationalism assumes that ultimate reality is accessible to reason; i.e., reason gains admission to reality and apprehends it. This assumption renders revelation superfluous; more to the point, it renders revelation a non-category, since reason is adequate to grasp the totality of reality and reason alone can. In other words, there is nothing that needs to be revealed and nothing that can be. Here reason is no longer a servant of faith but rather that which similarly renders faith a non-category. (In short, the gospel reveals the essence of humankind to be spirit, while reason subserves spirit; rationalism, on the other hand, assumes the essence of humankind to be reason, while

---

5. In this paragraph I am indebted to Thomas F. Torrance, *The Christian Frame of Mind* (Colorado Springs: Helmers & Howard, 1989), chap. 2, "The Concept of Order in Theology and Science."

6. Quoted in Torrance, op. cit., pp. 33–34.

spirit is a non-category. Wesley unhesitatingly insisted that what reason could grasp was related to what spirit knew as "painted fire" was related to fire itself.)

Rationalism assumes, in the second place, that reason is unimpaired. Yet Freud showed how reason is prone to become rationalization; i.e., the logic of the reasoning process perdures while reason(ing) subserves a motive of which the reasoner is entirely unaware. Marx showed us as much in the sphere of economics. So have contemporary sociologists of knowledge with their focus on the place of the reasoner's social location. And before all of this so did the pastoral counsel of Patristic writers. And so did the apostle Paul with his insistence on fallen humankind's proclivity for "futile thinking," futile, that is, with respect to its capacity for apprehending the truth of God and the truth of the human condition before God. Reason, together with the rest of the creation, has not been spared the ravages of the Fall. Reason needs the corrective of the gospel if reason's integrity is to be restored.

II: THE GOSPEL

As was noted earlier, to speak of reason as fallen is not to say that reason is now illogical (if it were, reason would not be fallen reason so much as non-existent); the Fall finds reason's structure intact and reason's integrity devastated with respect to our knowledge of the divine and human); it is rather to know that reason has a Fall-induced bias to rationalization. G. K. Chesterton remarked that mad people are not those who have lost their reason; mad people are those who have lost everything except their reason. "Everything" includes the gospel.

Where the gospel is "lost" (as it were) human reasoning no longer reflects the truth of ultimate reality; spiritual psychosis has set in. Since psychosis, by definition, is the loss of reality-testing, spiritual psychosis is the loss of testing with respect to ultimate reality: God, his truth, our inclusion in it. Then the gospel is necessary lest rational people are left with nothing more than reason. To say the same thing differently, grace (grace-wrought faith) restores reason to reason's integrity. Grace frees reason from reason's diverse bondages to self-interest in the diverse contexts of race, class, money, gender, etc. To put it most concisely, the gospel releases reason from reason's captivity to idolatry. The Christian educational institution has a witness here to render the world of education. This witness must never be blunted or hidden or minimized.

While we are speaking of the role of the Christian educational institution with respect to the world of learning I should like to make a plea for the richest humanism that has been part of higher education ever since the Renaissance. For centuries humanism was seen in some quarters as an enemy of faith. It is an enemy of faith if humanism (that is, cultural riches and all that generates them) claims for itself humankind's ultimate trust, love and hope. At the same time, cultural riches—not to be rejected, according to 1 Timothy 4—are to be received with thanksgiving. In the same vein the book of Revelation maintains that the kings of the earth are going to bring their glory into the New Jerusalem (Rev. 21:24).

Ever since the eighteenth-century Enlightenment the glories of humanism have been regarded as somewhat less glorious. Humanism's glories were diminished yet again by turn-of-the-century thinkers such as Freud and Marx. These men maintained that statements put forward as truth-claims are not that at all but rather are mere reflections of one's psychological need to posit a benign world or of one's need to defend one's economic privilege. Perhaps the most telling tarnish arose through the philosophical postulate of positivism; namely, that the meaning of a statement was given by the process of verifying it (falsifying it) empirically. Any statement that could not be verified (falsified) empirically was deemed cognitively meaningless. Assertions arising from the humanities —e.g., ethics, aesthetics, metaphysics—were pronounced cognitively meaningless (because non-empirically testable), and then by extension simply meaningless. The acids of a positivistic outlook appeared to corrode the splendours of humanism yet again. I am persuaded that the church, through the church's educational institutions, has a major role to play in restoring the glories of the very humanism that has, in a different era, postured itself as a rival to the faith of the church.

We do well to remember that even as sixteenth-century Reformation thinkers and Renaissance thinkers came to see that they were in different orbits with respect to the human condition and the necessity, nature and means of the ultimate good, the giants of the Magisterial Reformation were educated first as humanists. We do well to remember that the clergy of that era who were not trained first as humanists were able to operate acceptably as ecclesiastical functionaries but were unable to generate any leadership for church or society.

In a word, a Christian college knows that unless reason is upheld and venerated God is not honoured; a Christian college knows too that if reason alone is upheld then reason is deprived of that gospel which alone frees reason for reason's integrity. And a Christian college has peculiar responsibility for preserving the humanities from the reductionisms and obscurantisms currently deemed "realistic" in some areas of academia.

"I offered them Christ," Wesley says over and over in summing up his daily ministry. The Christian college too must "offer them—the academic disciplines—Christ" as a crucial aspect of its mandate.

III: CATHOLICITY

Lastly, I should like to refer to Wesley's theological catholicity in urging a catholicity of education.

While Wesley was a lifelong Anglican (and never wanted to be anything else) he cherished the theological riches of the church catholic. As an Anglican he was informed immediately by the Anglican formularies: the Book of Common Prayer, the Thirty-Nine Articles, and the Edwardian Homilies. At the same time he was steeped in the literature of the Puritans. His love of the Puritans, however, did not impede his finding his eucharistic doctrine largely in the work of an Anglo-Catholic. And his appreciation of the latter never prevented him from positioning himself "but a hair's breadth" from John Calvin with respect to justification. It would seem a huge distance from Calvin and Calvin's emphasis on Reformed doctrine to Roman Catholic mystics of the Counter-Reformation, yet Wesley adopted eight Roman Catholic Counter-Reformation mystics for his Christian Library, the collection of readings he expected all Methodists to peruse. A child of the Western church, he nonetheless esteemed the Eastern Fathers. A child of modernity to the extent that he experimented with electro-convulsive treatments for severe depression, he yet knew Christian antiquity (Patristics) thoroughly. Always insisting on the need to expound Christian truth in the context of the thought-forms and social setting of his own era, he nevertheless judged novelty in theology to be heresy (as if the prophets and apostles could ever be improved upon).

This is not to say that he was uncritical with respect to the tradition of the church catholic. Far from it. Yet he recognized its wisdom, balance, depth, and riches even as the unnormed norm of the gospel impelled him to assess it. (In the same way he was a lifelong monarchist; his being such, however, did not render him an uncritical devotee of all things royal. Concerning Queen Elizabeth I he wrote with no little discrimination, "As just and merciful as Nero and as good a Christian as Mahomet.")

Today I am urging a comparable catholicity of learning; a catholicity of space (the literature of Latin America, philosophy from Germany, jazz from the U.S.A.), as well as a catholicity of time (C. S. Lewis pointed out that for every two modern books we read, we should read at least one from the medieval and ancient eras lest we come to think that the questions modernity poses are the only questions, or are even questions at all.)

Students can begin to appreciate all of this now; and if they do, they will find themselves profiting from it—and more importantly, relishing it and delighting in it long after their formal education is concluded.

I am not decrying specialization. Specialization is essential, both the specialization that selects an academic discipline for concentration as well as the intra-disciplinary specialization that focuses on a particular aspect. In an era of superficiality and mediocrity, no one can decry the specialization needed for academic and vocational sophistication, let alone mastery.

In all of this I remain grateful for those whose catholicity of learning has moved me and inspired me and encouraged me. Among such people I recall two exceedingly able American poets, Wallace Stevens and William Carlos Williams, the former an insurance company executive and the latter a physician to the dispossessed in slum-areas of New Jersey. We should aim at nothing less for ourselves.

Since a Christian college is called to attest the truth that in Jesus Christ "all things hold together" (Colossians 1:17), its sons and daughters ought never to reduce the scope of "all things."

In 1734 John Wesley penned a tract, "The One Thing Needful,"[7] in which he stated a theme that he would repeat tirelessly for the rest of his life: the one thing needful is "the renewal of our fallen nature." The tract is a sustained insistence upon the necessity "to re-exchange the image of Satan for the image of God, bondage for freedom, sickness for health." In the tract Wesley asserts that learning is "the fairest of the fruits of the earth." His assertion here must be given its full weight, especially in view of those unlearned commentators who continue to think that the Wesleyan tradition undervalues learning.

Yet in the light of that Kingdom which cannot be shaken Wesley is correct in rating learning, "the fairest of the fruits of the earth," as penultimate. While it "may sometimes be conducive to" the one thing needful, it is not the one thing needful itself. This lattermost will always be humankind's re-creation at God's hand.

The Christian college will ever acknowledge that the height of learning, while gloriously high (and deservedly so), is yet dwarfed by the fathomless depth of God's grace.

---

7. *WJW*, Vol. 4, #146.

6

WESLEY AND THE ROLE OF SMALL GROUP MINISTRY

I shall never forget the man who found the courage to pour out before me his heart-wrenching confession of sin. He was able to articulate it despite his shame and humiliation only because he trusted me to help him. Aware of his predicament and his fragility, I summoned up all the pastoral wisdom I could find within me and pressed upon him as persistently, patiently and convincingly as I could that forgiveness of God whose immensity comprehended the length and breadth, height and depth of human self-contradiction. After all, if God's people are to forgive "seventy times seven," would God himself ever do less? To my dismay the fellow remained unaffected. After a few seconds of anguished silence he blurted, heart-brokenly, "I don't want forgiveness; I want deliverance."

The man meant, of course, that he didn't want mere forgiveness. John Wesley would have concurred. For Wesley knew that the early-day Methodist communities thrived on a truth that had lain dormant too long in the church at large; namely, God can do something with sin beyond forgiving it (as glorious as forgiveness is.) Specifically, God can release people from its power over them. Forgiveness or pardon relieves us of sin's guilt, Wesley insisted; newness of life releases us from sin's grip. Wesley knew that to offer people relief now, only to tell them that release awaited them at life's end (all Christians agreed that release was guaranteed post-mortem) was to consign them to despair for this life. He insisted that there was no limit to the scope of God's deliverance in this life. Years later he noted that where this truth was upheld the Methodist communities flourished; where it was submerged they withered.

At the same time Wesley's people were anything but naïve concerning sin's grip. They knew that all sin is addictive. (If it were less than addictive wouldn't all sinners—which is to say, everyone—have long since given it up?) And they had in their midst people whose addiction was notorious: public, pronounced, undeniable and undisguisable. Either such people would find the gospel merely a pronouncement of pardon that meanwhile left them victims to their addiction or they would come to know that there is indeed One "who can break every fetter"—and do so now.

Since Wesley insisted there to be "no holiness but social holiness,"[1] he gathered his people into small groups or "bands" of four or five individuals; these bands were the context for and occasion of his people's deliverance. These bands were effective only if people were utterly honest at the weekly meeting, withholding nothing. For this reason, then, the bands were segregated by gender.

Since there were temptations and traps peculiar to people in particular jobs, there were bands for coalminers, bands for shopkeepers, bands for homemakers, bands for soldiers, and so on. In addition there were bands for those struggling with a particular habituation: bands for "drunkards," for "whoremongers," for abusers of drugs such as laudanum and opium. In addition there was a group for people who were afflicted with no notorious, besetting sin but whose spiritual maturity had brought them to see that darkness of every sort still lurked in them, and had brought

---

1. Wesley, *Works of John Wesley* [ed. Jackson] "Preface to 1739 Hymns and Sacred Poems," Vol. 14, p. 321. For Wesley's sustained polemic against those who disagree with him on this matter see *WJW*, Vol. 4, #122, "Causes of the Inefficiency of Christianity," *passim*.

them as well to crave deliverance from it as they single-mindedly craved nothing else.

In all of this Wesley had in mind the "root" commandment of Scripture: "You shall be holy as I the Lord your God am holy." (Leviticus 19:2) Yet in the wake of his Puritan ancestry (both his paternal and maternal grandfathers had been outstanding Puritan ministers) he knew that all God's commands are "covered promises": what God requires of his people God will unfailing work in his people. Linking the "root" commandment of Israel (and the church) with the "great commandment" of Jesus—"You shall love the Lord your God with all your heart, soul, mind and strength, and your neighbour as yourself"—Wesley's "band" aimed at ultimately, for everyone regardless of the expression of one's sin, deliverance from every impediment and inhibition right here. In other words, the bands aimed at a deliverance that began in release from one or another, more or less dramatic, addiction, only to end in release from a "selfism" that found someone self-abandoned in self-forgetful love of God and neighbour. Wesley knew this alone to be the "freedom" that the gospel promises.

Never naïve about the grip with which sin grips us, Wesley was aware that several things were essential if the bands were to operate effectively. (Needless to say, if the bands weren't effective they would disappear overnight.) In the first place, those who tentatively, tremblingly stepped into one had to know they were loved and would continue to be cherished. In the second place they had to know that those before whom they disburdened themselves could be trusted—trusted not to be affronted by what they heard, trusted not to ridicule the suffering of someone whose habituation was as painful as it was embarrassing, and above all trusted not to betray anyone by blabbing on the street what had to remain in the meeting. In the third place band-members themselves had to be without disguise and without dissimulation but rather transparent and truthful.

On Christmas Day, 1738, Wesley drew up the "Rules of the Band Societies."[2] He stated the band's purpose unambiguously: "The design

---

2. All references to the bands, etc. in this chapter are found in *WJW*, 4:67-79.

of our meeting is to obey that command of God, 'Confess your faults one to another, and pray for one another that ye may be healed." Then he specified the "rules." For instance,

> Rule #1: "To meet once a week, at the least."
> Rule #4: "To speak, each of us in order, freely and plainly the true state of our souls, with the faults we have committed in thought, word or deed, and the temptations we have felt since our last meeting."

Then Wesley wrote, "Some of the questions proposed to every one before he is admitted amongst us may be to this effect"—and proceeded to list some such questions. For instance,

> Question #6: "Do you desire to be told of your faults?"
> Question #7: "Do you desire to be told of all your faults, and that plain and home?"
> Question #11: "Is it your desire and design to be on this and all other occasions entirely open, so as to speak everything that is in your heart, without exception, without disguise, and without reserve?"

Wesley, however, wasn't finished. While the preceding questions "may" be asked, the "five following [must be asked] at every meeting." For instance,

> Question #4: "What have you thought, said or done of which you doubt whether it be sin or not?"
> Question #5: "Have you nothing you desire to keep secret?"

Plainly the self-disclosure asked of the band-members was stark and startling. Wesley knew, however, that only such searing honesty and accountability in a context of pledged support would suffice as the environment for the One who could and did "break every fetter."

The "small group movement" in the church today owes everything to Wesley. And so do the para-church groups, such as Alcoholics Anonymous. They thrive on the frankest self-disclosure, self-abandonment to the group and the group's "Higher Power," accountability that is near-brutal in its confrontation, and a willingness to endure any inconvenience at any hour for the sake of a fellow-sufferer whose pain has become unendurable and who cries out desperately for a deliverance whose alternative is despair.

At one point in my theological education I studied under a psychiatrist who related to the class a simple experiment that has been documented many times over. Ten people are placed in a room. Nine people have been "clued in" beforehand as to what's going on. The tenth, however, has been told nothing. A box is brought forward containing twenty marbles. Everyone is asked to count the marbles. Then each person is asked to state how many there are. One after the other says "Nineteen; exactly nineteen." The "not-clued" person, having carefully noted that there were twenty, begins to doubt himself. Soon he capitulates, admits he must have miscounted, and agrees: nineteen.

My psychiatrist-instructor pointed out that sooner or later everyone capitulates; we differ only in how long it takes different people to capitulate. Then the experiment is changed slightly: there are two people in the "game" who haven't been clued in. When they count the marbles and announce "Twenty" they hold out far longer in the face of those who insist "Nineteen." When a third person is added, the three together don't capitulate.

The experiment, of course, operates merely at the level of the natural. How much more is promised a group of sufferers when the power of "Our great God and Saviour" is added.

7

WESLEY'S UNDERSTANDING OF CHRISTIAN PERFECTION

Wesley's misgivings concerning the Lutherans' *simul totus peccator simul totus iustus* (believers are at the same time both totally sinful and totally justified) are a major feature in the background to his exposition of Christian perfection. As is so often the case, what is safe in the hands of the original articulator is safe in the hands of no one else. The Lutherans insisted that the alternative to *totus...totus* was *partim...partim*; we are partly sinful and partly justified, justified to the extent that we are not sinful (the position of the Council of Trent, 1545–1563). If *partim* had been accepted the Lutherans would have asked, "Which part of us is justified, and which sinful?" They knew there is no aspect, area, dimension or deed of believers' lives for which they are spared having to plead God's pardon. Two hundred years later, however, Wesley felt that the Lutherans' *totus simul* implied (i) resignation with respect to one's residual sinfulness, (ii) complacency in it, (iii) capitulation to it amounting to licence. Wesley was suspicious of

---

* This chapter was commissioned by the Oxford Institute of Methodist Theological Studies (1997) and appeared in *Papers of the Canadian Methodist Historical Society* (Toronto: CHMS, 1997), pp. 18–43.

a *totus simul* that could be regarded as a vehicle of antinomianism for the spiritually slack and a counsel of despair for the spiritually serious.

Wesley's insistence on the simultaneity of *sola fide* (by faith alone) and holy living is yet another prominent feature of the background to his understanding of Christian perfection. *Sola fide*, standing alone, had always precipitated a cavalier attitude toward godliness, the reduction of faith to doctrinal apprehension, and the jettisoning of the rigours of discipleship (e.g., crossbearing). Paradoxically, "faith alone" cut the nerve of faith. On the other hand, holy living, standing alone, had always precipitated moralism: rigorous conformity to a code devoid of the holy and devoid of life, with faith reduced to a compend of ethical striving, pelagianism, and a shallow view of the Fall that settled for deprivation while eschewing depravity. In *sola fide* and holy living, however, Wesley believed that what God had joined together no one should put asunder.

Aspects of the foregoing "marriage" are found in the four principal tracts related to his fullest statement, *A Plain Account of Christian Perfection* (1765–1777).[1]

For Wesley salvation is the restoration of the defaced image of God. It is the destiny of believers to be "*wholly* transformed into the image of him that created us"(1:351).[2] Perfection is this transformation.

In *Christian Perfection* (1741), his earliest tract on the subject, Wesley maintains that we *must* speak of the notion, since Scripture is not silent on the matter, and we must not be found silent where Scripture speaks (2:99).[3] Here Wesley carefully denies that Christian perfection implies freedom from error or from poor judgment or from "the infirmities of our creatureliness" (i.e., freedom from the limitations of our finitude).

---

1. Wesley, *A Plain Account of Christian Pefection* (London: Epworth Press, 1952).
2. All such references are to *WJW*.
3. Interestingly, Calvin uses the same argument exactly in explaining why the church must declare and cherish the doctrine of predestination in its two-fold form of election and reprobation. "For Scripture is the school of the Holy Spirit, in which, as nothing is omitted that is both necessary and useful to know, so nothing is taught but what is expedient to know" (*Institutes* 3.21.3).

Wesley denies as well that such perfection (synonymous with holiness) precludes "continual increase"(2:104). Even the "perfect" continue to grow in grace. Left-handedly he indicates the reason for his tenacity in speaking of Christian perfection: if we set limits *a priori* to the scope of God's grace in subduing our sinfulness in this life (a defect he thought he saw in the Reformed and Lutheran traditions) then we are making allowances for sin. To say that God does not deliver us from all sinning in this life is to say that we *must* continue to sin (2:112). But to say this is to deploy shabby excuses and undercut human responsibility. (Here Wesley has in mind such thinkers as John Gill, a contemporary whose hyper-Calvinism Wesley deplored not least because it appeared to render God the author of sin.) Wesley insists that we are freed not only from sins that are publicly observable (our deeds) but also "from evil thoughts and tempers" (on account of the heart's no longer being evil), as well as from "all the reasonings of pride and unbelief against the declarations, promises or gifts of God"(2:117). Believers should *expect* to be freed from all the qualifications the spiritually unexpectant invoke to condition the declarations, promises and gifts of God. Freed from the impediment of unexpectancy, believers find the aforementioned fulfilled in them. In support of his notion here Wesley quotes Charles' hymn-line, "Calmly to thee my soul looks up,/and waits thy promises to prove"(2:122). One such promise is the declaration that "No one born of God commits sin"(1 John 3:9). The exegetical commonplace—that the force of the text is that no one born of God "wilfully" or "habitually" commits sin—he dismisses curtly without any discussion of the syntactical subtleties in the Greek text (2:107). Finding no little support still in 1 John for his notion of perfection, Wesley moves on to 1 John 1:9: "If we confess our sins, he is faithful and just, and will forgive our sins and cleanse us from all unrighteousness." He reads "cleanses" not as "pardons" but as "purges." "Cleanse," he insists, cannot be reduced to "justifies"; "cleanse us from all unrighteousness does not appose "will forgive us our sins."(2:120)

As the debate between Reformed/Lutheran and Methodist convictions unfolded Wesley sought to curb what he regarded as the overstatement of people such as Thomas Maxfield; viz., that Christians are rendered incapable of sin—with the result that antinomianism appeared yet now could not be named "sin." Wesley wanted to repudiate that shallow view of sin which could only "booby-trap" those who held it, without suggesting there existed *any* sin beyond God's triumph.

In his *On Sin in Believers* (1763) Wesley maintains "'That there is no sin in believers' is quite new in the church. Such a notion was never heard of for 1700 years, never till it was discovered by Count Zinzendorf. I do not remember to have seen the least intimation of it in either ancient or modern writers, unless perhaps in some of the wild, ranting antinomians."(1:324) Forbearing to say that his 1741 statement itself must have been an overstatement, Wesley invokes the "testimony of antiquity" (i.e., Patristics) in support of his contention that believers have an "evil nature."(1:317) Plainly he does not want to say categorically that believers are sinless. The believer can be "a *new creature* and an *old creature* at once."(1:325) Such a person is "partly renewed"(1:326); by grace he may yet become not only "truly" but also "entirely" renewed(1:326), being "delivered from the guilt and power of sin but not from the being of sin."(1:328) Wesley's statement here is more nuanced than that of 1741, distinguishing as it does between the power of sin and the being of sin, even though he does not amplify the distinction. While never denying the Reformers' understanding of justification by faith (and never denying its place in the inception of the Christian life), Wesley consistently emphasizes the actuality of the regeneration and sanctification of the justified person. When he writes, "We allow that the state of a justified person is inexpressibly great"(1:320), the reader expects him to expand on the greatness of justification; instead he speaks immediately of the blessings of sanctification.[4] Wesley typically has "sanctification" stand for "justification plus sanctification"; i.e., for the *whole* of the Christian life. (Here he reverses Luther's "shorthand.") Plainly the doctrine of

---

4. Here Wesley complements dialectically his earlier advice: "When we are going to speak of entire sanctification, let us first describe the blessings of a justified state as strongly as possible." "Minutes of the Second Annual Conference; August 1, 1745." Quoted in Outler, *John Wesley*, 151.

sanctification is as luminous and illuminating for Wesley as justification was for Luther. It stands at the centre of and is the organizing principle for his theology; every aspect of the Christian economy converges upon it and radiates from it.

The sin from which sanctification delivers us is both "inward" and "outward." Outward sin is manifestly behavioural; inward is the attitudes and proclivities of the depraved heart. ("Pride, anger, self-will" are Wesley's unholy trinity that he mentions tirelessly throughout his work.) Resentment—one such "temper"—is a near-universal yet not insignificant instance of "inward" sin. "Resentment at an affront is sin," Wesley unselfconsciously confesses, "and I have been guilty of this a thousand times."(1:331) Believers have a heightened awareness both of the specific sins that dog them and of the sin whose "being" riddles them and all that they do—even as their heightened awareness does *not* collapse their assurance. (In other words, heightened awareness of one's depravity does not diminish, let alone overturn, the witness of the Spirit concerning one's standing in grace.)

In *On Sin in Believers*, written 22 years after *Christian Perfection* (and written after much scrutiny of both the blessings and the "enthusiasms" of the revival), Wesley adduces four arguments to support his contention concerning sin in believers. Any affirmation of believers' sinlessness (i) contradicts Scripture, (ii) contradicts the experience of God's people, (iii) is new-fangled and therefore merely a human invention (novelty in doctrine being, for Wesley, heresy by definition), (iv) has deleterious consequences. (The peril of the "perfection" imputed to Zinzendorf was that it "cuts off all watching against our evil nature."(1:328)) Yet while the "being" of sin remains, grace dethrones sin so that "the usurper...grows weaker and weaker."(1:331)

If relentless vigilance concerning sin is a sign of faith, so is the horror with which believers react when rationalization whispers to them that sin may be indulged (1:332).

Four years later Wesley penned *The Repentance of Believers* (1767). He begins his tract by reminding readers of the repentance that pertains to the *commencement* of faith and discipleship: a conviction of utter sinfulness (our very being is sin-vitiated) and guiltiness (we can plead nothing to extenuate our condemnation) and helplessness (we are unable to remedy or rectify ourselves in any way)(1:335). Then Wesley speaks of the *ongoing* repentance of *believers* that is as essential to their *growth* in grace as initial repentance was to their entering the kingdom. If spiritual rigour is relaxed even for a moment, such crudities as "lust" and non-crudities as "inordinate affections" will recrudesce—along with love of praise and fear of dispraise (1:339). All of these together will ensure that the work of grace within believers is undone.

We most note here Wesley's emphasis on singlemindedness (a matter to be amplified below). Either we fear God and therefore nothing else or we don't fear God and therefore everything else. With the insight of the wise spiritual director Wesley notes that spiritual peril attends even our obedience to God, since obedience may become the occasion of sin-fuelled superiority or self-congratulation—all of this on account of the depraved nature we continue to have (1:342). Believers, after all, are "but in part 'crucified to the world', since the evil root remains in their heart"(1:339).

Then Wesley abruptly makes the pronouncement with which the Wesleyan tradition has been more or less identified: "inbred" sin is destroyed as God grants to believers what they could never bestow on themselves and for which they could only wait upon God's good pleasure. Despite our utmost spiritual attentiveness and discipline "we cannot wholly cleanse either our hearts or our hands. Most sure we cannot, till it shall please our Lord to speak to our hearts again, to 'speak the second time, Be clean'"(1:346). Despite his insistence that such "cleansing" is *by faith* (and not by those self-purgations that the mystics prized) Wesley's insertion here is startling in view of everything he has insisted on to this point in order to support his contention that inbred sin is just that. *After* justification, however, he maintains that believers, now aware of even deeper recesses of their depravity ("the inbred monster's face"), are to repent of *these*—and believe the promise of God here too—this time not merely for the pardon of sin but for all "cleansing" (by which Wesley means, as was seen above, elimination or eradication) of "indwelling sin"(1:348). The result is nothing less than "entire sanctification"(1:351).

In the penultimate paragraph of his tract Wesley quotes a hymn-stanza of Charles' that begins, "Break off the yoke of inbred sin" yet concludes "Till I am wholly lost in thee!"(1:351) In his ultimate paragraph Wesley again quotes his brother, the stanza beginning, "I sin in every breath I draw" and goes on to say "But still the Fountain open stands,/Washes my feet, my heart, my hands," only to conclude, "Till I am perfected in love."(1:352) (In the final section of this paper the force of these two quotations—"*wholly* lost in Thee" and "perfected in *love*—will be expanded and put forward as what Wesley intends in his sometimes convoluted exposition of Christian perfection.)

Forty-three years after *Christian Perfection* Wesley added *On Perfection* (1784). Here he qualified "perfection" further as he insisted that no one, regardless of the degree of sanctification (including "entire"), is ever beyond needing the intercession of the "merit" of Christ (i.e., no one is sinless). In view of our proclivity to transgress, our "innumerable violations of the Adamic as well as the angelic law"(3:73), "...every living man needs the blood of the atonement or he could not stand before God."(3:74) In this tract Wesley now states unambiguously that "This is the sum of Christian perfection: it is all comprised in that one word, love." Christians are mandated to love God and neighbour; "'on these two commandments hang all the law and the prophets': these contain the whole of Christian perfection"(3:74). Furthermore, the command to be holy is identical to the command to love: "perfection is another name for universal holiness—inward and outward righteousness—holiness of life arising from holiness of heart"(3:75).

Adopting the Puritan tenet that all the commands of God are but "covered promises," Wesley maintains that God's commanding his people to be holy is but God's guaranteeing that they will be holy. "The command here is equivalent to a promise, and gives us full reason to expect that he will work in us what he requires of us"(3:77).

In view of all that Wesley has said so far there must be probed the nature of that sin from which believers may be wholly saved *now*. Wesley's well-known definition is, "a voluntary transgression of a known law." He vehemently insists that he has nowhere said we are delivered in this life from sin in any wider or deeper sense of the word. Moreover, "this is the sense wherein the word 'sin' is over and over taken in Scripture" (3:79). It is sin *in this sense* that is to be "rooted out" (3:79). And it is sin in this sense that Wesley has in mind when he wearily, if not somewhat sarcastically, says to those who continue to oppose his doctrine of perfection with their *simul...totus*, "so we will allow sin, a little sin, to remain in us till death"(3:79)—only to deny this explosively, expostulating that the "little" that is tolerated will invariably be the beachhead wherefrom a fresh invasion of sin vanquishes us (3:80).

Addressing objections to all of the foregoing Wesley adds, "What rational objection can you have to loving the Lord your God with all your heart?" (3:83)—only to pose the same question again—"Why should you be averse to universal holiness—the same thing by another name?...the being inwardly conformed to the whole image of God, or an outward behaviour in very point suited to that conformity? Can you conceive anything more amiable than this? Anything more desirable?" (3:84). Not surprisingly Wesley poses the question a third time: "Can anything be more desirable than this entire self-dedication to him [God]?" (3:85). (Plainly he is implying here that "entire sanctification" is entire dedication of oneself to God.) The question has an edge to it when he puts it the fourth time: "Do you then love sin [a line earlier he had repeated his definition of "a voluntary transgression of a known law], that you are so unwilling to part with it?...In God's name, why are you so fond of sin?" (3:86).

The constellation of the foregoing expressions yields a rich understanding: holiness, love of God and neighbour, conformity to the will and image of God and behaviour appropriate to this conformity, whole-souled self-dedication to God that entails disavowal of sin and desire to part with it. These were the "pearls" of Methodism that ought not to be cast before the unappreciative. For this reason such holiness should be taught only to those who are "pressing forward...always by way of promise, always drawing rather than driving."[5] Wesley's grasp of a grace-wrought, faith-facilitated self-offering to God that bleaches sin's allure and breaks sin's grip estops any suggestion that perfection is pelagian moralism at the same time that it highlights the dynamic of the doctrine. Furthermore, holiness as constellated by Wesley's nuanced affirmations and questions comports with the aspiration and conviction of the church catholic—his definition of sin excepted.

It is therefore all the more surprising to find in *On Patience* (also written in 1784) an exhortation to a perfection that amounts to utter sinlessness: "wholly delivered from every evil word, from every sinful thought; yea, from every evil desire, passion, temper, from all inbred corruption, from all remains of the carnal mind, *from the whole body of sin*" (3:179).[6] If this isn't sin*less* perfection, then what would sin-free perfection be? Such sanctification "is to be received by plain, simple faith" (3:178). Candidates for it are to "believe...that he [God] is not only able, but willing to do it *now!*"(3:179). Having interviewed 652 testifiers to this "experience," Wesley concluded, "as all change was wrought in a moment—I cannot but believe that sanctification is commonly, if not always, an *instantaneous* work"(3:178).

Wesley, it will be recalled from the beginning of this chapter, believed the Continental Reformers to have made their peace too readily with the "arrears" of sin. Having settled into the *simul totus* they offered, thought Wesley, little more than confirmation in one's residual sin for those who were not upset by it and despair for those who were. Even the English Puritan tradition, so dear to Wesley (thirty-two of the fifty books in his *Christian Library* were by Puritan divines) conceded too much to the "arrears." While Puritanism amplified sanctification enormously in terms of the "third use of the law" (a notion that the Puritans acquired from Melanchthon through Calvin), the "third use" being Christ's claim upon the obedience of believers whereby he conforms them to himself, Wesley

---

5. "Minutes of the Second Annual Conference; August 1, 1745." Quoted in Outler, *John Wesley*, 147.

6. Emphasis added.

thought that Puritanism held out too little concerning *deliverance* from the grip of sin upon people and by the same token too little of *present* restitution of its disfigurement. He was convinced that God could do more *now*, even as believers should wait on God for it and delight in it.

PLAIN ACCOUNT

The "more" that Wesley insisted God longed to do in his people, it must be repeated, was not the divine crowning of a more zealous moral endeavour. This much is evident from the formative thinkers who preceded Wesley and whose work Wesley cherished.

Jeremy Taylor (*Rules and Exercises of Holy Living and Holy Dying*) had stressed believers' intentional resolution to lifelong purity of heart; believers must dedicate themselves singlemindedly, wholly, to God.

Thomas à Kempis (*The Imitation of Christ*) similarly stressed "simplicity of intention" (singlemindedness) that was also a purity of affection: one loves but one thing.

William Law (*Christian Perfection, A Serious Call to the Devout and Holy Life*) insisted that *all* must be yielded to God.[7]

It is important for us to be aware of Wesley's reading in this regard, for our familiarity with it will be a major factor in our interpretation of his *A Plain Account of Christian Perfection* (1777).

The following are major aspects of *Plain Account*.

[1] Scripture points to discipleship as "a uniform following of Christ, an entire inward and outward conformity to our master"(*PA*, 6).[8] This inward and outward conformity is a matter of loving God with our utmost ardour: "the one perfect good shall be your ultimate end"(*PA*, 7). Not forbidden to love all else, we nonetheless love all things for God's

---

7. For the foregoing summary I am indebted to Thomas Oden, *John Wesley's Scriptural Christianity* (Grand Rapids: Zondervan, 1994), p. 312.

8. All such references are to John Wesley, *A Plain Account of Christian Perfection* (London: Epworth Press, 1991).

sake. In this we are to have a "pure intention of heart" and a "steadfast regard to [God's] glory"(*PA*, 8).

[2] In loving God whole-heartedly we recognize that God orders all things for our good (*PA*, 12).

[3] We are to love our neighbours, only to find that we can love even our enemy, since love banishes "evil tempers"(*PA*, 12).

[4] We eschew "laying up treasures on earth," since wealth is as spiritually deleterious as adultery (*PA*, 14).

[5] We are not freed from temptation; nevertheless, some temptations, at least, lose their fascination, "flying about" us but no longer "troubling" us (*PA*, 23).

[6] While justification gives us the right to heaven, holiness renders us fit for heaven (*PA*, 31).[9]

[7] *All* sanctification admits of growth; even the "perfect" grow in grace, in the knowledge of Christ, and in the love and image of God *after* their "entire" sanctification (*PA*, 33).

[8] The "perfect" continue to need Christ's atoning intercession (*PA*, 43).

[9] Perfection is not a state but a relationship: "Christ does not give life to the soul separate from, but in and with, Himself"(*PA*, 44).

[10] Perfection is a theological/spiritual category and is not to be understood as a psychological category. The mind may be distressed, sorrowful, perplexed, in pain, while "the heart cleaves to God by perfect love, and the will is wholly resigned to him" (*PA*, 49).

[11] Those dedicated to holiness (perfection) must ever guard against pride, enthusiasm ("pride's daughter") and antinomianism. (Here Wesley speaks of enthusiasm as expecting the end without the means, as well as disesteeming reason, knowledge, wisdom, or thinking oneself invul-

---

9. Wesley makes the same point in *On the Wedding Garment* (4:144). He expected this written sermon (March, 1790) to be his last, his pronouncement here concerning the relationship of justification to holiness being his final word to the Methodist people. (He lived another year and penned another five sermons.)

nerable to temptation. Wesley everywhere abhors antinomianism: while holiness is certainly more than ethical rigour it is never less.)(*PA*, 88).

[12] Affliction is the best aid in fostering growth in the perfect (*PA*, 98).

[13] God's perfecting us vindicates God's promises to us (*PA*, 31).

[14] The testimony of the Spirit is essential to our awareness that we are love-filled. (Merely feeling that we are is not adequate.) The sanctified "have as clear an inward witness that I am fully renewed, as that I am fully justified"(*PA*, 52, 56, 57).

CRITICAL COMMENTS

[1] Wesley's lattermost point is problematic. Justification, by definition, admits of no degrees. The forensic model precludes partial condemnation or partial acquittal. Sanctification, however, is not "all or nothing." A plethora of scriptural injunctions urge us to keep on growing, to remove impediments to growth, to pray daily for forgiveness (this can only mean that believers sin daily), to acknowledge we are "unprofitable servants," to own our Lord's left-handed assessment of his most intimate followers—"If you then, evil as you are...." Furthermore, it would seem that "fully renewed" must ultimately mean to be sinless with respect to the "being" of sin and therefore to be beyond needing the intercession of the atonement.

[2] Wesley's working definition of sin, *adopted for the purposes of discussing perfection* ("a voluntary transgression of a known law"), appears inadequate. To be sure, Wesley used "voluntary" and "known" so that believers could be encouraged by manifest victory over sin. At the same time, problems arise with respect to "known" when the human heart has limitless capacity to "forget" what it doesn't want to "remember" or know, when Scripture characteristically insists that ignorance of God is culpable, and when the force of general revelation (e.g., Romans 1) is to render humankind "without excuse."

Problems arise too concerning Wesley's use of "voluntary." In the Continental and English Reformers (whom he did not disesteem) "voluntary" meant "pertaining to the will" (*voluntas*), and "will" referred to

WESLEY'S UNDERSTANDING OF CHRISTIAN PERFECTION

one's capacity to act; voluntary never meant "conscious," "deliberate," "premeditated"—as Wesley means here.[10] To transgress, according to the Reformers, is to transgress "voluntarily," since transgression presupposes will. (Not to will is not to be human.) Pleading that one did not intend to do what one has done nor to sin in what one has done underestimates sin, presupposing as it does an undervaluing of the biblical witness to the complexity, subtlety and scope of the heart. However profoundly perfection may be expounded with respect to sin in Wesley's sense of "voluntary," too much remains unsaid for that corruption which is none the less culpable for its being *in*voluntary. All of this is puzzling in view of the fact that Wesley insists throughout his work that by "total depravity" he means nothing less than the Reformers meant. (He insisted that on the matter of total depravity he *wasn't* even a "hair's breadth" from John Calvin.)

[3] Wesley is aware of the contradiction in his discussion of "voluntary transgression," since in insisting that the perfect still need the atonement for their "mistakes" (where "mistake" means non-intentional sin in believers) he admits that all such "mistakes" are a transgression of the law of God—and therefore "sin" in the absolute sense of the word. Moreover, by referring to deep-dyed depravity (albeit in believers) as "mistake" Wesley is fostering spiritual naiveness, shallowness and self-victimization in his readers.

[4] Wesley's concluding, on the basis of interviewing several hundred people, from 1759 to 1762, that perfection is universally instantaneous (4:178), poses many questions. Has Wesley here elevated experience above Scripture? (Has he here displayed that "enthusiasm" he characteristically deplores?) Why has he atypically adduced something that contradicts his insistence everywhere that Scripture is the unnormed norm for Christian understanding?

---

10. See Outler's introduction to *John Wesley*, 32, where Outler interprets "voluntary" as "*so far as conscious will and deliberate action* are concerned." Outler makes the same point in his introduction to *On Perfection* where he highlights Wesley's "definition of sin as deliberate." (3:71)

[5] While Wesley was careful, in his discussion on faith, to uphold faith as dynamic rather than static (i.e., to uphold faith in terms of relationship), and while he maintained that perfection was received in faith and was not a state, the tenor of much of his discussion of sanctification suggests a state (e.g., the testimony of the Spirit that one is "fully renewed.") In *On Patience* Wesley maintains that unqualified humility is one feature of "entire sanctification"(3:176). Since self-forgetfulness is the essence of humility (self-disparagement being but a form of self-preoccupation), the believer requires the testimony of the Spirit that he is utterly humble. There appears to be a problem here, and the problem here may betoken a problematic aspect of Wesley's doctrine of Christian Perfection as a whole.

[6] Wesley disagrees vehemently with those who hold that the texts in 1 John (so dear to Wesley in his insistence that no *a priori* limit be placed on God's renewing his people *in love*) refer to the fact that believers no longer sin habitually or sin characteristically. ("No one born of God commits sin...." [1 John 3:9]). Yet exegetes maintain that the apostle's selection of verb tenses is crucial: the present indicative and infinitive (rather than the aorist) support the understanding not that the Christian never sins (this notion is contradicted elsewhere in the epistle) but that sin doesn't characterize the Christian (Christ's righteousness does), and while the Christian may be overtaken by sin, she doesn't sin "habitually"—this latter expression being the one that Wesley scorned. Again, it is surprising to see him dismiss (without any discussion) a point in Greek syntax when his Greek testament was never out of his hand.

STRENGTHS IN WESLEY'S EXPOSITION

[1] Wesley's discussion of "inordinate affections" (seen to be such only in the light of our "ordinate" love for God) points in the direction of what he was always struggling to say throughout his conversations on the doctrine dearest to him; namely, to love God above all else is *ipso facto* to order rightly those subordinate loves (which loves our love for God never negates). In loving God whole-heartedly we *abandon* ourselves to God's

will for us. Wesley knows that a massive work of grace is needed to free us from that self-preoccupation (inordinate self-love) which otherwise inhibits us from loving God and neighbour self-forgetfully. To say the same thing differently, the singular work of grace that frees us to love God and neighbour unselfconsciously frees us from addiction to self.

While Wesley does not use "self-forgetful" the word suggests itself repeatedly. Love that calculates, assesses risks, evaluates outcomes is no love at all. "Entire" is entirely appropriate when Wesley means that we are turned out of ourselves and our self-absorption, because turned toward God and neighbour in a self-abandonment that is impervious to slights, setbacks, barbs, apparent ineffectiveness. In all of this believers discover the "expulsive power of a new affection" (Thomas Chalmers) as self-forgetful love exorcises the leech-like "evil tempers" that otherwise leave us anaemic, self-absorbed, useless and ugly.

"Perfection *in love*" (owning "the one perfect good" as one's "ultimate end") leaves us singleminded and therefore non-fragmented. The key to integration is neither a psychological technique (modern) nor a religious technique (pre-modern) but rather whole-soulled, self-oblivious, "otherward-looking" love.

[2] Wesley's linking affluence with spiritual declension is entirely biblical—and entirely unacceptable to the church today. Jesus maintains that we serve—and give ourselves to—either God or mammon. These two are mutually exclusive and jointly exhaustive. Either our hand is open because giving or clenched because grasping. Wesley was dismayed, enraged, frantic—even contemptuous and derisory ("Do you fear spoiling your silken coat?"(3:244))—at the spectacle of Christians who preferred pennies to love-wrought, love-directed perfection-in-love.

[3] While we are never freed from all temptation, and while the temptation to pride lurks everywhere, Wesley encouraged believers who were struggling with temptation to the point of spiritual exhaustion (and therefore to the point of capitulation); he credibly pointed them to the relief that God's sanctifying grace afforded them. In short, they could be released from "effectual" temptation. If Wesley hadn't proffered this much the earliest Methodist communities would have lasted no longer

than an Alcoholics Anonymous group in which no one ever becomes "contentedly sober." Because grace denatured "effectual" temptation, God could do something with sin beyond forgiving it. While will and affection remain distinct they are nonetheless intimately related. Wesley was aware that we will most readily what we love (whether for good or ill.)We can always will (and do) what we don't love, which doing is popularly described as "by force of will"—an expression suggesting someone who is grim, tense, taut, about to falter if relaxed for a moment. The experience of Alcoholics Anonymous comes to mind once again. The alcoholic who is "contentedly sober" can continue to will his sobriety in that he profits from "the expulsive power of a new affection." (Thomas Chalmers) The "dry drunk," on the other hand, is someone whom AA members recognize (by virtue of their own experience) as chemically sober yet with the "tempers" (disposition) of the not-yet-sober, agitated rather than contented, and therefore someone who always appears strained, racked, self-wrenched. Wesley inadvertently indicates as much in a discussion having nothing to do with Christian Perfection when he insists that grace renders affections "more vigorous" and therein "assists" the will (2:489).[11]

Perhaps Wesley's most perceptive discussion of the aforementioned point is found in *On Patience*. The believer, *qua* believer, is justified and sanctified and therefore indisputably holy. Yet the believer's holiness remains "mixed"; e.g., such a person's humility is genuine but not unadulterated with pride (3:176). The new affection ("being filled with love") integrates all his passions, with the result that "all his passions flow in a continued stream, with an even tenor to God"(3:176). To the extent that there is "no mixture of contrary affections" the believer's holiness is no longer "mixed." By the same work of grace his will is now "wholly melted down into the will of God"(3:176). In other words, will and affect are no longer a contrary mixture. The integration of the

---

11. The grace described as "assisting" the will in 2:489 is prevenient grace. This point, however, does not overturn Wesley's understanding of the relation of grace and will.

affections *together with* the integration of affect and will are the fruit of the grace-wrought, faith-appropriated restoration of the *imago Dei* to its integrity. Rejoicing in a new affection that assisted the will was one of the glories of early-day Methodism.

[4]Wesley is oceans deeper than contemporary Christendom when he puts his finger on the difference between our "right" to eternal blessedness (justification) and our "fitness" for it (holiness). The tone-deaf can always be given the right to a symphony concert; but what would be the point of their going? Musicality alone makes anyone "fit" for the concert. Wesley makes this point again when he comments, "There is a difference between one that is *perfect* and one that is *perfected*. The one is fitted for the races; the other, ready to receive the prize" (*Notes*, Phil. 3:12).[12] Holiness, it seems, has too often been discussed narrowly in terms of intra-psychic elevation (an experience) or in terms of moral reinvigoration (an achievement). Wesley more profoundly discusses it in terms of God. ("Holy," in the Hebrew bible, is that which characterizes God as uniquely God.) Wesley knows that the sanctifying work of grace is God himself forging himself within us as he forms us and fits us for the unimaginable intensity of utmost intimacy with him. C.S. Lewis has remarked, "It is safe to say that only the pure in heart shall see God; only the pure in heart will ever want to"—Wesley's point exactly. In his discussion of Christian perfection Wesley amplifies the truth that the all-consuming fixation of the Christian's life is God.

---

12. All such references are to Wesley's *Explanatory Notes upon the New Testament*. In his exegetical discussions of the "perfect" word-group (*teleios, teleo, teleios, teleiotes*) Wesley rarely amplifies the notion of Christian perfection that preoccupies him elsewhere. Most surprisingly, the text he quotes tirelessly, "the holiness without which no one will see the Lord"(Heb. 12:14), he doesn't expand in the *Notes*. Similarly he says nothing about Christian perfection in "let us go on to perfection" (Heb. 6:1). Elsewhere in the *Notes* he treats "perfect" as "a state of spiritual manhood in understanding and strength" (Eph. 4:13), "experienced Christians"(1 Cor. 2:6), "endued with every Christian grace" (Col. 4:12), "a real Christian" (Matt. 19:1). "Not perfect" he deems to mean "weak in faith" (Phil. 3:15).

[5] Wesley is hauntingly profound when he comments that affliction is the best aid to spiritual growth. (Compare C.H. Spurgeon: "Affliction is the best book in a minister's library.")[13] Wesley knew that the Son of God, Son though he was, "learned obedience through what he suffered." (Hebrews 5:8) Affliction visits itself on Christians just because they are Christians, even as it visited itself on their Lord on account of who he is. There is nothing in Wesley of the North American "Prosperity Gospel." We must recall Wesley's dictum that prosperity is a spiritual threat more dangerous than adultery, even as we recall his dismay at those whose new-found affluence (the product of discipleship, Wesley noted with perplexity) had blunted their zeal and their sacrifice. Even the "perfect" need affliction in order to grow; even the "perfect" will not be spared it. We should note here that Wesley insisted that his preachers continue to announce the "good news" of perfection, even as he insisted that the same preachers read Jonathan Edwards' *The Life and Diary of David Brainerd* lest Methodist preachers come to think that their hardship-riddled lives were actually hard.

While Wesley never speaks of growth-spurts, surely the "moment" of "entire" sanctification is such a spurt, admitting as it does of subsequent growth. By extension I wish to suggest that a fruitful elaboration of Wesley's thought concerns not one growth-spurt but any number of them as believers are brought to a crisis. Wesley has spoken of that moment in believers' lives when they become aware as never before of "inbred" sin, of the deeper depredations of their depravity. At this juncture they either seek and await that work of grace which deals with their residual corruption, or they make their peace with their now-evident shoddy

---

13. The affliction can be very subtle, as both Reformers and Roman Catholics knew. See Luther, *Luther's Works*, 14:60 and 42:75 where he insists that the worst form of trial (*Anfechtung*) is to have no trial, since then the believer is without the comfort of knowing that God is at work—albeit "left-handedly"—for the sake of the strengthening of faith. In the same vein Miguel de Molinos (*The Spiritual Guide Which Disentangles the Soul* (1688; 1:63) argues that the worst temptation is be without temptation, for then the believer is tempted to find happiness anywhere but in Christ (3:28).

discipleship—eventually, perhaps, to sink all the way back down into unbelief. For a long time I have thought that under God believers are *repeatedly* exposed, at critical moments in their Christian development, to a startling apprehension of their inbred corruption and/or an undeniable acquaintance with new dimensions and directions of God's will for them. *At this moment* believers are faced with that crisis of which Wesley spoke. *At this moment* we either repent of and repudiate the "monster's face" that has newly loomed before us; *at this moment* we either embrace and abandon ourselves to the will of God for us or we make our peace with a limping discipleship—eventually, perhaps, to find that it doesn't even limp. (Wesley would have said, "inevitably to find....") Either God's will is welcomed without reserve or Christian existence *at any level* shrivels—for to arrogate to ourselves the prerogative of limiting our obedience is to strangle faith. Wesley is helpful in his articulation of such a crisis. But why restrict it to one such crisis? The fact that discipleship is marked by many such crises serves to remind us that faith is always dynamic, never static.

[6] Wesley knew thoroughly the eastern or Greek tradition of Patristics. Therefore he would have appreciated the difference between the Greek *teleios* and the Latin *perfectus*. *Perfectus*, an unnuanced word, has the force of faultless, of not admitting further development. It is a term used of things rather than of persons.

Teleios, on the other hand, is highly nuanced, as its different translations into English indicate; e.g., "Not that I have already obtained this or am already perfect...." (Phil. 3:12), "Let those of us who are mature be thus minded...." (Phil. 3:15) "Perfect" and "mature" translate *teleios* within three verses. *Teleios* is a term more characteristically used of persons, and used specifically of persons in light of their function. It can mean "full-grown" (as opposed to underdeveloped), "mature in mind" (as opposed to someone learning the rudiments of a subject) or "qualified" (as opposed to someone lacking expertise).

Wesley nowhere thoroughly exploits the lexicon with respect to *teleios*. At the same time he frequently says enough to indicate that *perfectus* is not what he has in mind—or could have.[14]

[7] Yet there is a dimension of Wesley's understanding of perfection that appears to have been undervalued in the discussions concerning perfection: mysticism. While the mystical element has been acknowledged[15], mysticism appears not to have been considered as the *essence* of it. Wesley characteristically speaks of both inward and outward holiness, yet always with the understanding that inward holiness (the work of grace upon our "tempers" or dispositions) is the ground of all outward holiness. While many assessments of Wesley's doctrine of perfection probe the theological adequacy and consistency of his argument concerning outward holiness, virtually none seems to consider *gospel-facilitated* and *gospel-normed* mysticism as the essence of inward holiness. Wesley left-handedly indicates his elemental conviction here in *On God's Vineyard* (1787), written ten years after *Plain Account*.[16] This tract states briefly Wesley's persuasion concerning God's raising up Methodism for its unique witness in the church catholic, as well as Methodism's trifling with its birthright. In it Wesley elaborates the essence of Methodism and insists that Methodists are "as tenacious of inward holiness as any mystic, and of outward as any Pharisee"(3:507). The logic of this statement, it seems to me, is the heart of Wesley's doctrine. A subsequent, closer reading of *Plain Account* brought to my attention the nature of

---

14. I appreciate Outler's comment (2:98) that the Eastern tradition understands the *teleios* word-cluster to mean "a never ending aspiration for all of love's fullness (perfecting perfection.)" At the same time this understanding does not relieve Wesley's doctrine of all problems. Wesley urged his people to "*expect* to be made perfect in love in this life" (2:97). Would Wesley have urged his people to *expect* an *aspiration*?

15. E.g., Robert Tuttle, *Mysticism in the Wesleyan Tradition*, 147ff.

16. It should be noted too that in this tract Wesley, now 84 years old and setting down an understanding of Methodism that he had pondered and observed and tested for decades, writes accusingly to Methodist dilettantes, "Were not the fundamental doctrines both of free, full, present justification delivered to you, as well as *sanctification, both gradual and instantaneous*?" (3:516, emphasis added).

the hymns (written by brother Charles) which Wesley brings forward to support or illustrate the points he is endeavouring to make in his *Plain Account*: they support not a notion of sinlessness (especially as this came to be understood in nineteenth-century holiness movements) but a mysticism that is always and everywhere Christ-normed. Before he quotes any hymns in this tract, however, Wesley speaks of our subordinating all to our love for God, adding, "Other sacrifices from us He would not; but the living sacrifice of the heart hath He chosen." The last point points immediately to mystics who preceded Wesley—Pascal or Theresa D'Avila, for instance. The latter spoke like this when a startlingly intense, intimate admittance to God had been vouchsafed to them and their vocabulary, so far from being adequate to it, could only stammer before it. Within a page or two of "Let it [i.e., sacrifice] be continually offered up to God, through Christ, in flames of holy love" (the lattermost expression being common to the mystics) Wesley is quoting hymn-lines whose mystical overtone is undeniable:

> Till all my hallow'd soul be Thine;
> Plunged in the Godhead's deepest sea,
> And lost in Thine immensity. (*PA*, 10)

"All," "plunged," "deepest," "sea," "lost," "immensity": in the space of three lines Wesley co-opts repeatedly the oceanic imagery that the mystics relied on to point to—but never adequately describe, let alone explain—what they knew themselves through an experience of God beyond telling.

Alerted now, I perused the remainder of *Plain Account*, only to find the following:

> A rest where pure enjoyment reigns,
> And Thou art loved alone. (*PA*, 26)

> Let all I am in Thee be lost;
> Let all be lost in God. (*PA*, 27)

> Fulfil, fulfil my large desires,
> Large as infinity,
> Give, give me all my soul requires,
> All, all that is in Thee. (*PA*, 33)

> ...full with everlasting joy;
> Thy beatific face display,
> Thy presence is the perfect day. (*PA*, 39)

(The beatific vision, so very foreign to Protestants, is much-valued by Roman Catholic mystics.)

> Thy soul break out in strong desire,
>   perfect bliss to prove;
> Thy longing heart be all on fire
>   To be dissolved in love. (*PA*, 54)

("Bliss," "longing," "all on fire," "dissolved"; this is how the mystics customarily speak.)

We must note too the paradoxes in mystical testimony as language finally breaks down in apparent self-contradiction before the unspeakable mystery of God:

> And sink me to perfection's height.[17]

[8] Wesley's insistence on the simultaneity of the "inward" and the "outward" prevents the mystical from fleeing the distresses of this world. The mystical is always earthly-concrete, while the earthly is always eschatologically transfigured. The Christian who is "lost" or "dissolved" in God is the same person who campaigns with Wesley for schools, pharmacies, credit unions, and the healing advanced by such as *Primitive Remedies*.[18]

---

17. Quoted in Frank Baker, *Charles Wesley's Verse*, 63.
18. See Wesley, *Primitive Remedies* (Santa Barbara: Woodbridge, 1975).

WESLEY'S UNDERSTANDING OF CHRISTIAN PERFECTION
THE MYSTICAL IN WESLEY'S "PERFECTION"

In his *Journal* entry of 15th June, 1741, Wesley deplored the inadequacies of Luther's *Commentary* on Galatians. Now Wesley said he was "utterly ashamed" of his erstwhile appreciation of the book—not least because Luther "is deeply tinctured with *mysticism* throughout, and hence often fundamentally wrong"(19:200,201).[19] Earlier still (*Journal*, 25th January, 1738) Wesley wrote, "all the other enemies of Christianity are triflers—the mystics are the most dangerous of its enemies. They stab it in the vitals, and its most serious professors are most likely to fall by them. May I praise him who hath snatched me out of this fire likewise, by warning all others that it is set on fire of hell" (18:213).

Note in the foregoing how Wesley's negative conclusion contrasts with his positive beginning: "I grew acquainted with the mystic writers, whose noble descriptions of union with God and internal religion made everything else appear mean, flat and insipid." What was his objection? "But, in truth, they made good works appear so too; yea, and faith itself, and what not? These gave me an entire new view of religion—nothing like any I had before. But, alas! it was nothing like that religion which Christ and his apostles lived and taught"(18:213). Traditional mysticism is a-Christological, and therefore (according to a son of the Magisterial Reformation) not Christian at all.[20]

Despite the foregoing I am convinced that a mystical dimension is to be found in Wesley's groping after adequate theological expression where he and the mystics knew language to be forever inadequate: an acquaintance with God so intimate and intense, exquisite and abysmal that the heart apprehends what the head fails to comprehend—or communicate. (One thinks of the hymn-line of Albert Orsborn, "The mind

---

19. Emphasis Wesley's. In the 1774 edition of his *Journal* Wesley changes "fundamentally" to "dangerously."

20. Thomas Muentzer, the most prominent mystic of the Radical Reformation, consistently undervalued Christology, preferring to have not Jesus Christ but rather mystical experience the foundation of the Christian life. (See Eric Gritsch, *Thomas Muentzer: A Tragedy of Errors*, 61.)

cannot show what the heart longs to know."[21] When the heart moves from longing to know to knowing, the head *still* cannot "show" it.) With respect to this aspect of the economy of faith Wesley consistently exhibited traits of mystical "gold" even as he continued to denounce mystical "dross." We should not lose sight of the fact that eight of the fifty volumes in his *Christian Library* (which library he expected all Methodist Christians to read) were written by Roman Catholic mystics of the Counter Reformation. To be sure Wesley edited these extensively, never hesitating to excise passages that he felt would point vulnerable pilgrims in the wrong direction. Still, in editing them he most certainly recommended them. He published the *Christian Library* between 1749 and 1757, and included in it extracts from Macarius, Fénélon, Pascal, Brother Lawrence, D'Avila, Lopez, Bourignon, and Molina.

Then why did he speak so harshly of mysticism? What was the dross he repudiated?

[1] Mysticism spoke characteristically of union with God where it should have spoken of *comm*union with God. Any suggestion that the creature is absorbed into the deity (the creature losing its essence as creaturely and taking on the essence of the divine) is to be abhorred as unbiblical.[22] (Needless to say, it could always be argued that the mystics didn't mean this either, even though they might be criticized for inaccurate and infelicitous articulation.)

[2] Mysticism undervalued original sin. The mystics were then too close to regarding faith (or at least the capacity for faith or the desire for faith) as a natural human possibility.[23]

---

21. *The Song Book of the Salvation Army* (London: Salvationist Publishing and Supplies, 1953), #478, pp. 333–334.

22. John Calvin accuses Osiander, a Lutheran, of doing just this. (Calvin, *Institutes*, 2.12.6)

23. Compare John Calvin, "There is not in us any commencement of faith or any preparation for it" (*Commentary* John 6:45) and "Away with those who prate about men being prepared for the reception of God's grace by the movement of nature. They might just as well say that the dead walk" (*Commentary*, John 11:25).

[3] Mysticism said much about the "dark night of the soul," the spiritual desolation that Christians undergo as God "withdraws" himself from them. Wesley maintained characteristically that the "dark night" occurred on account of sin: "the most usual cause of inward darkness is *sin* of one kind or another."(2:208)[24] *Sin* beclouds believers' sense of God's presence. (Here Wesley appears one-sided. While sin does as much, Scripture speaks frequently of God's withdrawing himself (as it were), "hiding" himself in order to discipline his people or refine them or strengthen them.)

[4] Mysticism, with its "Spirit-immediacy" (i.e., underemphasis on the Mediator), was always in danger of combining such immediacy with "works-righteousness." Wesley looked askance at what he regarded as the mystics' pitfall, always emphasizing for himself the biblical and Reformation affirmation of "justification by faith."

[5] Mysticism tended to speak too little of the atonement.[25] The mystics, concerned as they were with indescribable intimacy with God, had apparently overlooked the fact that sinners cannot be united with the holy God at all—unless God acts in his unique freedom and grace to make himself and his estranged creation "at one."

Despite the "dross" of the mystics (always corrected by Wesley when he commended their work) Wesley plainly cherished their "gold."

[1] Their all-consuming preoccupation with God. For the mystics God is not a hobby, not an "experiment," not an add-on in life, not the object of speculation. (However abstract their work may appear to others, the mystics testify of God as concrete and of spiritual experience as real as sense-experience). God is their "environment" as surely as water is the environment of fish. For the most part it isn't so much that mystics are aware of living in God as that they cannot understand *not* living in God—unless the "dark night" appears with a torment that is foreign to the spiritually shallow. In view of the mystics' being "lost" in God it is

---

24. See Wesley's letter to Mary Bishop, Sept. 13, 1774: "Darkness...seldom comes on us but by our own fault" (2:223 fn).

25. See Tuttle, *Mysticism in the Wesleyan Tradition*, chapter 5.

not surprising that their writing reflects the passion of God impassioning them. (See Pascal's, "Not the God of the philosophers but of Abraham, Isaac and Jacob.... Fire! Fire! Fire!" Compare this with the Wesleyan hymns, quoted in *Plain Account,* that speak of "flames," etc.)

[2] Their heart-experience. While Wesley resolutely resisted "enthusiasm" (the elevation of experience above Scripture), always wanting Methodism to avoid even the hint of fanaticism, he also opposed "formalism" in equal measure. Formalism was the spiritual inertia of orthodox sterility. Formalism's doctrinal articulation of Truth was unexceptionable at the same time that its evidence of transformation at the hands of the Spirit of Truth was unavailable. The mystics knew that while theological correctness is necessary, it is never sufficient: a doctrine-stocked head does not guarantee a Spirit-infused heart. Academic sophistication is categorically different from spiritual intimacy. Wesley maintained we are to be so close to God, "so nigh as to be one spirit with him. And this is true perfection"(*Notes,* Heb. 7:19).

Here Wesley was surely reflecting the mystical element in the experience of God vouchsafed to many biblical personages. How else can we speak of Elijah's experience of earthquake, wind, fire, and finally the still, small voice?[26] How else of Elisha's "entire" desire of a double portion of Elijah's spirit? Not even Ezekiel's vocabulary can do justice to Ezekiel's Spirit-fired psychedelic drama. What besides "mystical" could be said of Isaiah's prostration in the temple amidst smoking pillars and shouting seraphim and red-hot coals searing his lips (even as other "worshippers" yawned, wondering when the service was going to end)? Isn't it natural for "such an intercourse between God and the soul"(11:53) to end in the orgasmic?

And then there is the apostle Paul. He matter-of-factly tells us he was "caught up to the third heaven...and this man heard things that cannot

---

26. Wesley quotes Ezekiel 36:25 (new heart, new spirit, etc. with Wesley underlining "from *all* your idols I will cleanse you") in the penultimate paragraph of *Christian Perfection* even as he denied perfection to those under the Old Testament "dispensation" (2:121).

be told, which no one may utter." The "third heaven" was an ancient way of speaking of the most intimate, most intense, most vivid presence of God. Three years before he was "caught up to the third heaven" he had been crumbled at the hand of God on his way to Damascus. In addition Paul had had a vision of the man from Macedonia who had pleaded with Paul to go there with the gospel. In addition to the Macedonian episode Paul had fallen into a trance while praying in the Jerusalem temple, and while in the trance had been told to get out of Jerusalem.

Two crucial points must be made here. (i) Paul never makes his mystical encounters the substance of his preaching. He expounds only "the word of the cross." (ii) He never undervalues, denies, or dismisses such encounters. They were immensely important to *him*. Apart from the Damascus road encounter he would still be harassing followers of the Way. Had he regarded his "may not be uttered" engagements with God as insignificant he would have avoided referring to them. Obviously he thought his readers should hear of them.

I am convinced that Wesley's "perfection" has close affinities with the foregoing. The *doctrine* is one thing (and not difficult to criticize, since Wesley often inelegantly and inconsistently attempts to utter "what may not be uttered"); different and distinct is the *experience* of whole-soulled, self-oblivious, horizon-filling, heart-drenching love. An encounter with God that cuts one loose from the clutches (but not the claim) of the earth; the Spirit-filled aspiration to move so deeply into the heart of God as not to think of finding one's way back out; the intimacy and immediacy and intensity of beholding the deepest hues of one's depravity *and* the pardon of God's sin-bleaching love as one is ravished by the flames of a love that scorches and saves in the same instant; to be taken out of oneself (the classical meaning of "ecstasy"—*ek stasis*); to find one's integration as a by-product of a contemplation that eclipses anxieties about integration, frustration, material deprivation, bodily hardship; to be apprehended by the incomprehensible in such wise as to live where doctrine is but the crystallized "exhaust fumes" of that explosive fire which cremates "this body of death"; this is what Wesley is pointing to at the same time that, like Paul, he never substitutes it for "the word of the cross."

[3] Their concern for spiritual discipline. "Methodist" was originally an epithet, but not an undeserved epithet. Spiritual discipline *was* a major concern of Wesley's both before *and after* Aldersgate. Conversion, it must be remembered, redirects one's personality; it doesn't turn one into a disparate personality (surely a sign of psychosis). Wesley repudiated vehemently the Moravian practice of "stillness." Relentless immersion in Scripture, prayer, fasting, frequent attendance at the eucharist, accountability to others through the meetings of "class" and "band," sacrificial service on behalf of the needy; all such rigours were essential to spiritual vigour.

[4] Their self-renunciation. Wesley admired the mystics in this regard. For years he remained perplexed as to why Methodists began with spiritual ardour only to "flatten out" in a spiritual somnolence from which they needed to be awakened (and, sadly, could not be). He could only conclude that the gospel generated a discipleship which, because *not* yet sin-free, repudiated one expression of depravity (vulgarity) only to accommodate another: spiritual indifference born of refinement. As people came to faith, with its attendant sobriety, industry and thrift, their economic fortunes rose. Simultaneously their affluence caused their ardour—and therefore their self-renunciation—to abate. Their swelling savings account meant social superiority—which in turn accustomed them to a life of relative ease. Wesley, nearly frantic now, penned tract after tract.[27] No matter. His newly-affluent people were no longer willing to endure cold, heat, hardship, persecution, deprivation—all of which they had embraced cheerfully when poor. The mystics modelled a self-renunciation for Wesley that he continued to covet for his people.

[5] Their aspiration to holy living. While Wesley was undoubtedly a son of the Reformation (after Aldersgate he always insisted on the primacy of justification by faith), there were aspects of the eastern

---

27. *Sermon on the Mount: VIII* (1748), *The Use of Money* (1760), *The Good Steward* 1768), *The Danger of Riches* (1781), *The More Excellent Way* (1787), *On Riches* (1788), *Causes of the Inefficacy of Christianity* (1789), *On God's Vineyard* (1787), *On the Danger of Increasing Riches* (1790).

church that he preferred to the western (both Roman and Reformed). One such aspect was the east's characteristic understanding of salvation therapeutically rather than juridically.[28] Simply put, the eastern church characteristically emphasizes transformation rather than transaction. While Roman and Reformed traditions underline the work of Christ in terms of transaction (without, of course, denying transformation), Wesley preferred to underline transformation (without, of course, denying transaction).[29] Paramount for Wesley was the *difference* Jesus Christ effects in his people. This motif is found everywhere in Wesley's works. In his *The Duty of Constant Communion* he warns readers against those who claim to know themselves pardoned of the guilt of sin while not yet delivered from the power of sin. It is our deliverance, he insists, that confirms our pardon (3:429).[30]

In addition, Wesley saw around him the wreckage of antinomianism—and never failed to distance himself from the latter. Lawlessness, utter lack of restraint, indifference to God's claim upon our obedience; all of this he anathematized. Holy living was the sign of a holy people, and a conscientiously, intentionally holy people was *the* reason God had raised up the Methodists, he believed. The doctrine of sanctification (including the perfection it implied) was "the grand deposit" that God had entrusted with Methodism.

All of the foregoing is gathered up in the mystics' aspiration to perfection, that singleminded pursuit of self-forgetful *love* of God and humankind. With his Anglican insistence on " that we may *perfectly* love Thee"

---

28. In his *Responsible Grace* Randy Maddox indicates in several places Wesley's affinities with the eastern church.

29. John Calvin, a major spokesperson for the western church, nonetheless foreshadows Wesley in "Yet such is the power of divine light that it attracts us to itself and transforms us in the image of God" (*Commentary,* John 12:40).

30. Here Wesley draws attention to something that is closer to the wider tradition of the church catholic than it is to the narrower tradition of the Reformation churches with their massive emphasis on the forensic dimension of justification and a sanctification that, often put forward as virtually undiscernible now, is affirmed as an eschatological reality.

Wesley, in typical Anglican fashion, highlighted so many strengths of the church catholic: the Patristic note of entire sanctification, the Magisterial Reformation's insistence on the "hinge" of justification[31] as well as its equally strong insistence on the distinction between justification and sanctification[32], the Radical Reformation's urgency concerning detachment from material distractions, the Puritans' esteem of the Law lest sin be reduced to the merely regrettable, the mystics' recognition of the place of extra-material renunciation—with all of this comprehended in "the *fundamental doctrine of the Church*, namely, salvation by faith."(11:82)

To be sure, brothers John and Charles disagreed on what should be denoted by "perfection." John felt Charles "pitched" it so "high" as to render it unattainable. Charles insisted that a perfection that was less than *perfectus* was no perfection at all.[33] John, on the other hand, knew that believers would continue to hunger for deliverance from this or that sin only if they knew there was deliverance from *any* sin. And since it was not the prerogative of Christians to set limits to the incursion and efficacy of grace in this life, then why not deliverance from *all* sin? Charles, disgusted at the overstatements of those whose zeal submerged wisdom, could only bemoan "our darkest ignorance of pride" and decry,

"Believe delusion's ranting sons,
And all the work is done at once."[34]

---

31. Wesley sounds the characteristically Protestant note in his *An Earnest Appeal to Men of Reason and Religion*, "Pardoning love is still at the root of all" (11:70).

32. In *On God's Vineyard* Wesley accused the Council of Trent (1545–1563) of confusing them, even as he argued that in the providence of God Methodism had been *especially* privileged with "a full and clear knowledge of each, and the wide difference between them" (3:506).

33. John indicates he is aware of the difference. "These are now made perfect in a higher sense than any who are still alive. So St. Paul, while on earth, denies that he was made perfect. Phil. 3:12"(*Notes*, Heb. 12:23).

34. John R. Tyson, *Charles Wesley on Sanctification*, p. 251.

John, however, saw that either Methodism risked what Charles deplored or Methodism settled for that fecklessness which had already appeared in those fellowships whose complacency allowed them an offhand accommodation of *simul totus*.

Needless to say critics were not long fastening onto some of the less elegant aspects of John Wesley's exposition of Christian perfection. When his Anglican superiors accused him of importing a novelty into Anglicanism (not understanding how much he hated theological novelty), he asked them, "Why do you fault me? This morning you prayed the Collect for Holy Communion from the Anglican Prayerbook:

> Almighty God, unto whom all hearts are open,
> all desires known, and from whom no secrets are hid;
> Cleanse the thoughts of our hearts by the inspiration
> of Thy Holy Spirit, that we may *perfectly love Thee* and
> worthily magnify Thy holy Name; through Christ our Lord.

When you prayed it, did you mean it?" Do we? Is there "anything more amiable that this? anything more desirable?"

APPENDIX

In his recent book, *Responsible Grace,* Randy Maddox states that Wesley doesn't use "'will' to designate the human faculty of rational self-determination...rather, he equated the will with the affections."[35] In the context of Wesley's hamartiology Maddox speaks of "will—i.e., our affectional nature," and later again, of "Wesley's identification of 'will' and 'affection.'"[36] Since the nature of the will (the precise meaning of "voluntary") appears to be one of the more problematic aspects of Wesley's understanding of perfection, the relation of affect to will should be probed.

---

35. Randy Maddox, *Responsible Grace,* 69.
36. *op. cit.,* 88, 184.

In *The Image of God* (1730) Wesley speaks of the Edenic "endowment" of understanding, and comments, "this comprehensive understanding was the least part of that image of God wherein man was originally made. Far greater and nobler was his second endowment, namely, a will equally perfect. It could not but be perfect while it followed the dictates of such an understanding. His affections were rational, even and regular..." (4:294). Here Wesley appears to uphold the traditional distinctions among will, affect and understanding.

In his subsequent *The Wisdom of Winning Souls* (1731) Wesley stipulates that in seeking the conversion of someone we must first "strengthen his understanding," then move on to "regulating the affections." The head must be enlightened and the heart cleansed. "Otherwise, the disorder of the will again disorders the understanding, and perverseness of affection will cause an equal perverseness of judgment" (4:313). Again it appears that Wesley doesn't equate the will with the affections, even as Wesley does regard them as internally related: the impairment of any one of will, affect and understanding entails the impairment of the others.

Fifty years later, in *The End of Christ's Coming* (1781) Wesley speaks again of humankind's "endowment": "he was endued also with a will, with various affections (which are only the will exerting itself in various ways) that he might love, desire and delight in that which is good; otherwise his understanding had been to no purpose" (2:474). Here Wesley speaks of affection in terms of will (not *vice versa*) yet without equating will and affection.[37] In the same tract Wesley speaks of "liberty," without which "both the will and the understanding would have been useless. Indeed without liberty man had been so far from being a *free agent* that he could have been *no agent* at all" (2:475). Here Wesley mentions "will" in the conventional sense of "the capacity to act."

---

37. Wesley makes much the same point in his discussion of angels where he states, "God has endued them with understanding, will or affections (which are indeed the same thing, as the affections are only the will exerting itself in various ways), and liberty" (3:6).

Months later Wesley penned *On the Fall of Man* (1782). Here he reiterates the fact that humankind was "endued with understanding, with a will, including various affections, and with liberty, a power of using them in a right or wrong manner, of choosing good or evil. Otherwise neither his understanding nor his will would have been to any purpose" (2:409). Once more Wesley speaks of understanding, will and affections without identifying any one in terms of another.

Opposing the notion that God acts irresistibly on humans (as God acted in fashioning the material creation), Wesley writes in *The General Spread of the Gospel* (1783), "He [i.e., the human creature] would no longer be a moral agent any more than the sun or the wind, as he would no longer be endued with liberty, a power of choosing or self-determination"(2:489). In *On the Fall of Man* by "liberty" Wesley had meant the condition of exercising power, he now includes the power of choosing or self-determination. He can even use "liberty" as virtually synonymous with "will"; e.g., " the understanding, the affections, and the liberty are essential to a moral agent"(2:489).

PART II

THE WESLEYAN TRADITION

8

THE METHODIST TRADITION IN CANADA

The Methodist tradition arose chiefly from the activity of John Wesley (1703–1791), born to Samuel Wesley and Susanna Annesley, Dissenters in the Puritan mould who affiliated with the Church of England in their youth. John was nurtured in Anglicanism, was ordained priest and remained a life-long member of it. At Oxford University he, together with several others, formed a group derisively labelled the "Holy Club." It met to encourage study of the classics and the Church Fathers, frequent attendance at Holy Communion, and assistance to the poor and imprisoned.

Still groping spiritually after ordination, in 1736 Wesley moved to Georgia hoping that his work among English colonists and aboriginals would imbue him with spiritual vitality. Upon his return to England in the wake of an unsatisfying ministry in the new world he came to the assurance of saving faith and of sins forgiven on May 24, 1738. Thereafter his ministry, formerly a not uncommon eighteenth-century Anglican blend of mysticism and moralism, was grounded in the Reformation

---

* This chapter was commissioned by the *Encyclopedia of Religions in Canada* (New York: Thomas Nelson and Sons [forthcoming]).

understanding of justification by grace through faith on account of Jesus Christ.

John recognized that "Scripture, from beginning to end, is one grand promise"; namely, salvation known and enjoyed as a present reality, as contrasted with the current Anglican understanding of blessedness in the life-to-come. With his theological emphasis on soteriology, John insisted that God had "raised up Methodism to spread scriptural holiness throughout the land." Whereas his pre-1738 pronouncements (see his sermon, "The Circumcision of the Heart," 1733) had declared that people became holy by means of humility, he now insisted—and never recanted—that holiness was a divine gift, owned in faith, and humanly exercised with unrelenting rigour. While classical Protestantism had stressed justification (pardon, remission of sins, free acceptance), Wesley retained this yet stressed deliverance: God could do something with sin beyond forgiving it; namely, release people not merely from its guilt but especially from its grip or power. In this vein he endorsed "Christian perfection," maintaining that no limit could be set to the scope of God's deliverance in this life. Herein he merged the Puritan emphasis on godliness that he found in his predecessors with the similar emphasis on sanctity found in the church catholic. Strenuously disagreeing with Calvinism's notions of predestination and limited atonement, he maintained that Christ had died for all: all needed to be saved, could be saved, could know they were saved, and could be saved to the uttermost.

Since, Wesley insisted, "the New Testament knows nothing of solitary religion," Methodism characteristically developed the communal dimension of its corporate life. Converts were expected to join in public worship weekly and to receive Holy Communion as often as possible. In addition they were formed into "societies," "classes," "bands," and "select societies" in order to expose themselves to stringent examination from peers and thereby promote self-honesty, mutual correction, encouragement, edification, and service. The "societal" emphasis was marked too by a concern for every aspect of human well-being. To try to mitigate suffering Wesley wrote a textbook of primitive medicine, begged money to establish London's first free pharmacy, developed schools for the disadvantaged children of coalminers, built houses for widows, gathered funds for start-up loans to Methodist entrepreneurs whom the chartered banks would not consider.

In all these endeavours John's brother Charles (1707–1788) supported John, matching him in outdoor "field" preaching. Charles' greatest contribution to Methodism, however, remained his hymn-writing (9,000 poems and hymns), as Scripture-saturated hymns rooted themselves in minds and hearts as often as Methodist people hummed the tunes amidst their daily work.

Following Wesley's death, Methodism ceased to be "leaven" in the Church of England and became a separate denomination. One of its missioners, Laurence Coughlan, arrived in Newfoundland in 1766 and began working among Protestant English and Irish settlers. Five years later William Black, born in England but raised in Nova Scotia, commenced evangelizing in the Maritimes, his work falling under the supervision of British Wesleyans in 1800. In 1855 this body formed the Wesleyan Methodist Conference of Eastern British America.

Under the leadership of William Losee, meanwhile, the Methodist Episcopal Church (U.S.A.), established on Christmas Day in 1784, began work in 1791 among British immigrants to Upper Canada. By 1828 the Methodist Episcopal work in Canada had formally severed ties with the U.S.A. In 1833 most of it joined with the British Wesleyans to form the Wesleyan Methodist Church in Canada, adding to itself the Methodist people of Lower Canada in 1854. That part of it which absented itself from the union re-formed into the Methodist Episcopal Church of Canada (1834), eventually growing into the second largest Methodist body in Canada.

In turn the Wesleyan Methodist Church in Canada and the Wesleyan Methodist Conference of Eastern British America united in 1874, annexing as well the Methodist New Connexion Church in Canada (itself an amalgam of several small groups), thereby forming the Methodist Church of Canada.

In 1884 this body joined with the Methodist Episcopal Church in Canada, together with the Bible Christian Church of Canada and the

Primitive Methodist Church in Canada, bringing to birth the Methodist Church (Canada, Newfoundland and Bermuda.) This lattermost union made the Methodist Church the largest Protestant denomination in Canada. It now included all Canadian Methodists with the exception of several very small groups: the British Methodist Episcopal Church (a development of the African Methodist Episcopal Church, serving chiefly people of colour), two German-speaking bodies (the Evangelical Association and the United Brethren in Christ), and the Free Methodist Church (a body that had begun in New York State in 1860 and extended itself into Canada.)

In 1925 the Methodist Church united with seventy percent of the Presbyterian Church in Canada and ninety-six percent of the Congregational Union of Canada to form The United Church of Canada.

Canadian Methodism distinguished itself on several fronts.

Methodists were committed to missions among aboriginals. The "first nations" had been exploited since the days of the fur trade, the exploitation manifesting itself in alcohol-abetted destitution. Eager to avoid paternalism, the Methodists sought to put mission leadership in the hands of aboriginals themselves. Peter Jones, Chief of the Mississaugas, was ordained the first aboriginal itinerant. Egerton Ryerson, soon to be the best-known Methodist minister, represented Canada in the Society for the Protection of Aboriginal Inhabitants of the British Dominions.

Missions overseas paralleled those in Canada. In 1873 the Wesleyans were the first of the Canadian Methodist "family" to begin working in Japan, concentrating on evangelism, medical assistance, post-elementary education and theological training for Japanese ministers. By 1884 Canadian Methodists had established a theological college in Azabu, supported by the Women's Missionary Society's efforts in training Japanese women for church work. Canadian Methodist missions commenced in China in 1891 amidst circumstances that were uncommonly dangerous.

In the meantime the social position of Methodists was changing in Canada. Earlier the Church of Scotland and the Church of England had formed social elites inaccessible to Methodists, the latter being poor and frequently despised. Zealous in evangelism and ardent in their pursuit of godliness, however, their sobriety, industry and thrift fuelled their social ascendancy. Some Methodist families became wealthy: the Gooderhams from grain and railways, the Masseys from farm implements, and the Flavelles from meatpacking. By mid-nineteenth century they were able to challenge the Anglican monopoly on education and political power.

From this position Methodism was able to make its unparalleled contribution to the public good, a system of high-quality public education. Insisting that education subserved not only the evangelical cause in particular but also the human good in general and the social good more widely still, Methodism's educational architect, Egerton Ryerson, undid the Anglican Church's exclusive control over education. Ryerson implemented the system operative in Canada today: high quality education available to all, without a religious or financial means test.

In addition the Methodists built Victoria College, offering instruction in arts and sciences, later expanding it under principal Samuel Nelles to a full-fledged university by adding faculties of law, medicine and theology, eventually moving the institution from Cobourg to Toronto in order to federate it with the University of Toronto.

Aware of John Wesley's legacy, Canadian Methodists dedicated themselves to the alleviation of human distress on any front, their vision here being no less than social transformation. They exerted themselves on behalf of convicts and ex-convicts, prostitutes and impoverished immigrants, all the while campaigning for better housing, improved public health, unemployment insurance, pensions, compensation for injured workers, the eight-hour work day, humane working conditions and homemaking skills. Salem Bland and James Woodsworth were the most visible exponents of the Social Gospel movement in Methodism, the latter eventually leaving the ministry in order to co-found the Cooperative Commonwealth Federation. The prosecution of social justice, it was thought, would largely eliminate the sources of social disharmony. At the same time leaders such as Samuel Chown continued to uphold the necessity of personal regeneration.

Concern for education and social transformation naturally gave rise to a commitment to publishing. Books, magazines and pamphlets were produced in ever-greater numbers; even by 1884 the circulation of Methodist-backed publications stood at 160,000, excluding the materials produced for overseas missions. Under William Briggs and Lorne Pierce, Methodists became instrumental in promoting a Canadian literary tradition, producing vast quantities of Canadian fiction, poetry, history and textbooks for schools.

Since 1925 smaller denominations such as the Wesleyan Church, the Free Methodist Church, the Standard Church (now merged with the Wesleyan Church), the Church of the Nazarene (extensions of American bodies), and The Salvation Army have endeavoured to maintain the spiritual tradition of Wesley. These smaller denominations, however, now operate in a nation whose ethos has changed to such an extent as to be unrecognizable to the Methodists whose contribution to public life in Canada was unparalleled in the nineteenth century.

In the wake of The United Church of Canada's adoption of a theological liberalism that diverges from the Methodist tradition in many respects, the challenge facing the smaller Methodist denominations is daunting. They will be helped to meet it, however, by such *foci* as the Chair of Wesley Studies at Tyndale University College & Seminary. Established in 1993, the Chair is dedicated to exploring, preserving and expanding the theology, tradition and ethos of the spirit and spunk of a progenitor who fathered, birthed and nourished a movement that continues to infuse and inform Canadian institutions and expectations.

9

THE ARMINIAN ASPECT OF WESLEY'S THEOLOGY

Susannah Annesley, mother of John Wesley, on at least one occasion vehemently came to the defence of her son when he was in the throes of the intra-Methodist dispute concerning predestination. Determined to clear John of the theological slander heaped upon him, Susannah declared "it is a travesty of truth to say that Wesley made salvation dependent on man's (sic) free will. Mr Whitefield was trying to insinuate that Mr Wesley is an Arminian, which he is not."[1]

Yet Wesley unashamedly called the magazine he expected his people to read and absorb, *Arminian Magazine.* Did he and his mother disagree profoundly on the crucial matter of whether the gospel was free for all without qualification or free only for the 'elect,' only for part of a sinful humankind when all humankind deserved condemnation?

Precisely when Susannah was struggling in England to clear her son's name of an evil reputation it did not deserve, Jonathan Edwards was

---

* This chapter was commissioned by InterVarsity Press and appeared in *Biographical Dictionary of Evangelicals* (Downer's Grove: InterVarsity Press, 2002), pp. 18-20.

1. Quoted in Herbert McGonigle, *Sufficient Saving Grace* (Carlisle, U.K.: Paternoster Press), p.128.

using 'Arminian' as a theological swear-word in the New World. Edwards distanced himself from anything resembling 'Arminianism' in that the word had become theological shorthand for a heresy three times over. The heresies pertained to Christology, soteriology and epistemology (or how it is we know what we know).

One hundred and fifty years after the death of Arminius the people who used his name as a label embraced the Christological heresy of Arianism. Arius, the formidable opponent of Athanasius at the Council of Nicaea (325), had stated that the Son (incarnate) was more than human but less than God. Athanasius had replied, as the apostles before him had insisted, that Jesus Christ is simultaneously fully divine and fully human. Those possessed of orthodox faith recognized immediately that anyone who is less than God is not divine at all, while anyone who is more than human is similarly not human at all. Athanasius had rightly seen that someone who is not divine cannot save (since no creature can save fellow-creatures), while someone who is not creaturely cannot be God's agent in bringing forth a new creation. Arius' Christology was heretical and useless in equal measure.

Similarly the label "Arminian" referred to a soteriology (the logic of salvation) that was a compend of divine and human effort. This compend was known as 'semi-pelagianism,' named after a British monk (Pelagius) who had maintained that depraved people could will themselves out of their sinnership and will their reconciliation with God. Semi-pelagianism was the notion that God came part-way to fallen humans while they in turn moved part-way to him, with the result that the chasm between them occasioned through sin had been bridged and reconciliation achieved. In this arrangement humans contributed (fifty percent at least) to their salvation.

Finally "Arminian" referred to an epistemological error wherein humans were said to be able to know God naturalistically. In other words, the Fall had not impaired humankind's capacity to know God. Humankind could gain a knowledge of the Creator in the same way it gains a knowledge of the creation. Forgotten here was the truth that the Fall had 'darkened' human understanding concerning knowledge of God (and of the human) to the point of 'futility.' (See Romans 1 and Ephesians 4.) Overlooked completely was the apostolic conviction that only as we are bound to the Son in grace-given faith do we know the Father.

Wesley repudiated without hesitation and without qualification every aspect of the three-fold heresy outlined above. For this reason his mother denied him to be "Arminian."

The theology Wesley would espouse for the rest of his life was in place before he had read a word of Arminius. Then why did he insist tirelessly that he and his people were Arminians?

For Wesley "Arminian" was shorthand for an affirmation of the universality of the atonement and the universality of the save-ability of every last human. Wesley found abhorrent the Calvinistic notion of double predestination; namely, that on account of a divine, eternal decree (i.e., a decree enacted prior to the creation of humankind) some people were destined to salvation and others to condemnation. The former could never forfeit their salvation; the latter had no opportunity whatever of coming to love the Saviour. Wesley found especially abhorrent the fact that since the decrees of election and reprobation preceded the decree of creation, the reprobate had been appointed to condemnation not on account of their sin but before they were born and therefore before they could have sinned.

Related to the "horrible decree" (Calvin's expression) was the notion that Christ had died not for all of humankind but only for the elect. Wesley's understanding of the gospel and its inherent impulse to evangelism required that he be able to approach anyone at all and say "Jesus Christ has died for you"—without a secret, under-his-breath 'perhaps' or 'let's hope he has.'

None of the above means that Wesley had a shallow understanding of the Fall. With the apostles he agreed that sinners are not sick but dead, "dead in trespasses and sins" before God (Ephesians 2).

With the Reformers he maintained that "Total Depravity" (the utter inability to save oneself) described the human predicament. Contrary to the accusation many predestinarians levelled at him, Wesley never maintained that the faith by which we are bound to the Saviour is our contribution to our salvation, while he always maintained that such faith was—and had to be—our commitment, even as this commitment was God's gift, albeit a gift that the Holy Spirit enabled us to exercise.

In describing himself and his people as "Arminians" Wesley maintained that Christ had died for all; the Holy Spirit now lapped and nudged every last human being; the gospel was to be commended to all, and all could exercise Spirit-wrought faith in the crucified as the gospel was declared and embraced. There was no one whom the arms of the crucified did not enfold; and there was no one whom God had pre-appointed to eternal loss.

For Wesley's theological opponents 'Arminian' entailed a three-fold heresy that Wesley recognized and rejected; for Wesley, however, 'Arminian' was a glorious affirmation that no human being was God-forsaken now, beyond the reclamation of the gospel.

WHO WAS JACOB ARMINIUS?

Arminius, Dutch Remonstrant Reformer, was born Jacob Harmenszoon c.1559 in Oudewater near Utrecht. His middle-class family was devastated when his father, a maker of kitchen utensils, died during Arminius' infancy and his mother, together with all his siblings, were slain during his adolescence in the Spanish massacre of Oudewater in 1575. Thereafter family friends raised him. Like most classically trained humanist scholars of his era, he eventually Latinized his name, recalling the "Arminius" who had been a first-century Germanic leader noted for his resistance to the Romans.

In 1574 he began his studies at Leiden, a university whose mood had retained for decades much of the pre-Magisterial Reformation ferment of the North Netherlands. Studies were pursued as well at Geneva, Basel, and Geneva again, culminating, after years of leadership in city, church and university, in a doctorate from Leiden in 1603.

In Leiden, where Arminius studied initially, the atmosphere included a biblically-informed piety, a sacramentarianism that viewed medieval sacraments as largely superstitious, and a humanist perspective that identified Roman Catholic corruption of the church. It would be anachronistic to speak of this movement as (proto-)Lutheran or Zwinglian, as these latter descriptions entail a doctrinal specificity that was not operative in what had flowed from the fourteenth and fifteenth centuries. The city and the university of Leiden, at the time of Arminius' sojourn, accommodated the older reform as well as the precise Calvinism that Reformed refugees had brought with them. The ensuing conflict was less concerned with predestination (albeit never far from the surface) than with the relation of Calvinist consistory (an ecclesiastical court in Reformed churchmanship) and the city (reflecting the less doctrinally exact, humanist-informed piety indigenous to the Low Countries). The consistory, for instance, in the spirit of Calvinist rigour, opposed observing Christian festivals (e.g., Christmas and Easter) that happened not to fall on Sundays.

Financed by Amsterdam merchants, Arminius began studying under Beza at Geneva on New Year's Day, 1582. Beza, Calvin's 62-year old successor, was venerated in Reformed constituencies everywhere. By rearranging Calvin's emphases Beza largely retained the major tenets of Calvin's theology while significantly altering its spirit. While Calvin, for instance, had spoken of the grandeur of God and the majesty of God but not of the "sovereignty" of God, Beza thrust into the centre of his thought a sovereignty that was to appear to Remonstrants indistinguishable from the arbitrary assertion of naked power. And where Calvin had focussed on the believer's life or participation in Christ, with predestination merely the means whereby sin-deadened people come to be "in Christ," Beza made predestination a controlling principle. Calvin's emphasis on the living person of "Christ clothed with his gospel" gave way to assorted decrees and a preoccupation with their respective priority.

Having been graduated from Geneva, Arminius studied next at Basel, and then at Geneva once more. A trip to Italy in 1587 found him accused of compromising himself with Roman Catholic potentates and also of having "lost his [Calvinist] faith" through exposure to Jesuits.

Upon returning to Amsterdam he was ordained pastor to the "Old Church," the focal point of church life in the city. In 1590 he married

Lijsbet Reael, an aristocrat who thereafter ensured that he orbited among the most influential merchants and leaders of the city. Like all the Magisterial Reformers before him, Arminius would remain a pastor for virtually all of his working life, spending fifteen years in the Amsterdam pulpit and six in the Leiden. (Worth pondering is his conviction that exercising the pastoral office, rather than theological wrangling, facilitates the holiness of the minister.) From 1603 until his death in 1609 he was professor of theology in Leiden, where he was also elected Rector (president) of the university even as a theological minority opposed him. In Leiden he gathered up the fruit of his writing in behalf of earlier controversies and in 1608 published his most mature work, *Declaration of Sentiments*.

While the notions pertaining to the name "Arminius" are commonly thought to suggest exclusive rejection of all things Calvin, his appreciation of Calvin's Commentaries is noteworthy. They occupy, he said, second place only to Scripture: "I recommend that the Commentaries of Calvin be read.... For I affirm that in the interpretation of the Scriptures Calvin is incomparable, and that his Commentaries are more to be valued than anything that is handed to us in the writings of the Fathers—so much so that I concede to him a certain spirit of prophecy in which he stands distinguished above others, above most, indeed, above all."[2]

His preaching through Romans became the occasion of a theological controversy that he was never to escape. His first opponents were humanists who denied original sin. Succinctly he replied to them, "I believe that our salvation rests on Christ alone and that we obtain faith for the forgiveness of sins and the renewing of life only through the grace of the Holy Spirit."[3] Opposition arose next from the Calvinists who differed from him on his insistence that Romans 7 describes the pre-Christian. Immediately he was accused of Pelagianism, Socinianism (unitarianism) and non-compliance with the Belgic Confession and the

---

2. Quoted in Carl Bangs, *Arminianism: A Study in the Dutch Reformation* (Grand Rapids: Zondervan, 1985), p. 287.

3. See *op. cit.*, pp. 337–340.

Heidelberg Catechism. Not trusting the Calvinist clergy of the church courts, he defended himself on charges of doctrinal deviation only in the presence of civic officials whom he recognized as his assessors. They acquitted him.

Differing from Gomarus, his principal opponent in his latter days as professor in Leiden, he continued to claim that the "wretched man" of Romans 7 is not the apostle speaking autobiographically but is rather the unbeliever. He added in support:

— this viewpoint has been defended through the church's history and has never been deemed heretical;

— no heresy, including Pelagianism, can be derived from it;

— the viewpoint of modern theologians (e.g., Beza) that Romans 7 speaks of the Christian is a viewpoint that none of the Church Fathers upheld—including Augustine, the Father dearest to the Calvinists;

— to say that Romans 7 describes the Christian is to slight the grace of God (grace appears impotent in the face of sin) and to foster wanton behaviour (even the regenerate cannot help doing the evil they do not want to do).

— the pre-regenerate person can possess an awareness of sin.

In his detailed exposition of Romans 9, another major area of protracted controversy, Arminius articulated a doctrine of grace that recognizes the irreducible humanness of the beneficiaries of grace and that unfailingly honours then as human agents, certainly not synergistic contributors to their salvation and therefore co-authors of it, yet just as certainly God's covenant-partners made in God's image whose co-operation recalls the Patristic subtleties around the Fathers' repudiation of co-redemption and yet their affirmation of *gratia operans/co-operans*. Arminius protested any sugestion that even sinful humans are entities like sticks and stones to be manipulated mechanically. Fallen humans, admittedly "dead in trespasses and sins," are nonetheless fallen humans, and as graced by God, response-*able* and therefore response-*ible*. This notion underlies Arminius' distinction between the act of believing as belonging to grace and the ability to believe as belonging to nature.

Concerning Romans 9 Arminius insisted

— the question that his opponents said predestination answered, namely, "Why do some individuals believe and others do not when all alike are dead *coram Deo* [before God]?" is neither asked nor answered in the chapter;

— the chapter does not discuss individuals but rather classes of people: those who affirm righteousness by faith in the Righteous One and those who seek to merit God's recognition;

— to speak of the predestination of individuals before they have been created, and therefore to speak of the reprobation of individuals before they could have sinned, is to render God monstrous;

— to postulate both a hidden and a revealed will of God is to falsify the New Testament's declaration that in Jesus Christ (whom everyone admits to be God's revealed will) "the whole fullness of deity dwells bodily" (Col. 2:9);

— God's command and God's promise are co-extensive. It is not the case that God commands all to repent and believe but visits only some with the mercy that quickens both repentance and faith. God does not predestine who will or will not believe; rather God predestines to salvation in Christ all who believe in Christ;

— the position of Beza and his supporters can only mean that God is deemed to be the author of sin. (Cardinal Bellarmine agreed with Arminius, adding that the high Calvinist position rendered God the only sinner.) This notion undercuts human culpability and renders God's judgment pointless.

Arminius' chief writing during his pastorate in Amsterdam, *Examination of Perkins' Pamphlet,* has often been judged his single best contribution to theological discussion. Perkins (1558–1602), the major spokesperson for English high Calvinism, maintained as a strong supralapsarian that creation and fall are (merely) the means whereby the decree of election or reprobation is implemented. Arminius' arguments here are those found throughout his works. However, their exposition is more detailed and more nuanced in the *Examination* than anywhere else. Most pointedly Arminius insists that grace is the love of God meeting humankind as sinful; grace is not a synonym for "decree" or "will" or "sovereignty";

i.e., grace is God's love addressing humans in their depravity rather than "affecting" them as creatures without reference to their sin.

While Perkins maintained that Christ died only for the elect, the parameters of the atonement being identical with the parameters of faith, Arminius countered that Christ had died (and thereby gained salvation) for all, but only some are saved; i.e., the cross is sufficient for all but effectual only in believers. Arminius' distinction here reflected his convictions concerning the bondage of the will. He insisted that the will of fallen humans was "bound" in that of itself it can will only its depravity. He insisted too, however, that the fallen will is never merely "of itself"; grace attends all fallen creatures, with the result that the graced will is enabled to affirm or endorse the grace that has elevated it beyond mere (fallen) nature. The graced will is "free" in that it is the non-coerced act of a genuine human agent. In other words, the graced will does not contribute to its salvation yet necessarily concurs in it, or else it is not a human creature that is saved.

Consonant with his understanding of the free will, Arminius eschewed the notion of the Christian life as the "state" of grace (and therefore static), preferring to understand it as dynamic: graced concurrence acknowledges and appropriates greater grace in an upward spiral that also finds the believer advancing in godliness through greater immersion in grace. Whereas Perkins had said this position to be Pelagian, Arminius maintained that Pelagianism predicated the will's response to grace entirely to nature or partially to nature (in the case of semi-Pelagianism), whereas the will's response to grace is grace-wrought without being grace-wrenched. A concomitant of his position is that believers can "make shipwreck" of faith. Yet they need not fear doing so, paradoxically, in that the gift of grace (and therefore of faith) includes a gift of filial fear that renders believers non-presumptuous and non-cavalier but ever spiritually vigilant and therein "kept" by the power of God.

While those who esteem Arminius frequently do so on account of his views concerning predestination, he must not be thought to be a one-issue thinker. Unlike the first and second generation Magisterial Reformers, Arminius is a scholastic evincing immense affinities with the scholastic "family" whether Roman Catholic and predestinarian (Bañez and Baius), Roman Catholic and non-predestinarian (Suarez and Molina), Protestant and predestinarian (Junius and Gomarus) or Protestant and non-predestinarian (his successors, Episcopius and Limborch). While the non-predestinarian, biblical humanism of the older North Netherlands is found in Arminius, it does not typify him. Rather he is indebted to late medieval and Renaissance Aristotelianism.

Like all scholastics Arminius has a metaphysical concern foreign to the earlier Reformers, and unlike the latter a debt to Thomas Aquinas. In fact Aquinas is the most frequently quoted thinker in Arminius' works, and the only scholastic whom he names as an ingredient. Certainly not a Jesuit, Arminius nonetheless preferred the Jesuit reading of Aquinas to the Dominican reading with its Augustinian cast of Thomas.

None of this is to suggest that Arminius is crypto-Roman Catholic. Still, he stands squarely in a tradition indebted to Thomistic metaphysics and Aristotelian logic (despite an appreciation for the bifurcationist logic of Ramus). Protestants typically are unaware that these features characterize the theologies of the seventeenth century.

Whereas the Reformed schools differed markedly on the issue of supra- or infralapsarianism, Arminius differed from both with respect to his understanding of God's will and foreknowledge. Here he owed much to Molina's *scientia media:* God foreknows future contingencies without thereby determining them. Molina furnished him with a matrix that included God's foreknowledge, the efficacy of grace, and a freedom of the will that is genuine rather than seeming. In short, Arminius adopted the Jesuit-Thomistic tradition of *scientia media* that denied divine determination yet preserved the infinitude of the divine intellect and the scope of human freedom.

Arminius' life unfolded amidst relentless conflict. Denied external tranquility, he was never distracted from the practical, non-speculative understanding of theology he absorbed from his reading of the medieval Duns Scotus, and credibly stated that his sole ambition was "to inquire in the Holy Scriptures for divine truth... for the purpose of winning some souls for Christ."

10

CHARLES WESLEY AND THE METHODIST TRADITION

The output of Charles Wesley (1707–1788), the younger brother of John Wesley, is prodigious: 9000 poems; 27,000 stanzas; 180,000 lines. Charles wrote three times as much as William Wordsworth, one of England's most prolific poets. While Charles didn't write poetry every day, his output averages out to ten lines of poetry every day for fifty years.

Was he sane? In Henry Rack's recent biography of John Wesley, Charles is described as "seeming[ly] almost a manic-depressive personality."[1] Had Charles suffered from bi-polar affective disorder (i.e., alternated between psychotic states of floridness and near-immobility) he would never have been able to accomplish what he did as itinerant evangelist and spokesperson for the Methodist movement. On the other hand, mood swings that are non-psychotic yet more extreme than those of most people are labelled today as "cyclothymic." While psychiatric speculation can never be confirmed, from Charles' correspondence and journals it

---

1. Henry Rack; *Reasonable Enthusiast* (Nashville: Abingdon, 1992), p.252.

appears incontrovertible that he suffered more than most in this regard. Poets routinely do. Today he would strike us as eccentric to say the least. He wore his winter clothing throughout the year, even in the hottest summer weather. Whenever poetic inspiration fell on him he became preoccupied to the point of semi-derangement. Seemingly unaware of where he was or what was in front of him, he would walk into a table or chair or desk, stumbling, lurching, crashing, not helped at all by his extreme short-sightedness. He would stride into a room, oblivious of the fact that a conversation had been underway before he invaded, and begin firing questions at those present, these people now startled at the apparent rudeness and effrontery of the man whose lack of social perception allowed him to continue interrogating people who couldn't reply and who weren't answerable to him in any case. Not waiting for their response, he would pour out aloud the poetry that was taking shape in his head, then turn on his heel and walk out. If he happened to be on horseback when lines fell into place in his head, he would ride to the home of an acquaintance, hammer on the door and cry, "Pen and ink! Pen and ink!" The poetry safely written down, he excused himself and went on his way.

Charles could write poetry for any occasion. When his wife was about to enter upon the rigours of childbirth, for instance (made even more rigorous in the eighteenth century on account of the primitive state of obstetrics), he wrote a poem for her which she could use as a prayer:

> Who so near the birth hast brought,
> (Since I on Thee rely)
> Tell me, Saviour, wilt thou not
> Thy farther help supply?
> Whisper to my list'ning soul,
> Wilt thou not my strength renew,
> Nature's fears and pangs control,
> And bring thy handmaid through?

At the funeral of George Whitefield, the Anglican evangelist who was a much more dramatic preacher than either John or Charles Wesley,

Charles praised his departed friend in a poem 536 lines long. While his poetry concerned chiefly the themes of the gospel message, he also tried, as imaginatively as he could, to empathize with all sorts of people in their manifold stresses and strains and griefs. For this reason he has left us poetry about wives and widows, coalminers and criminals, high school students and highwaymen, saints and soldiers, particularly soldiers who were loyal to the crown of England during the American War of Independence.

Charles was born in 1707, the eighteenth of nineteen children, eleven of whom survived the ravages of childhood disease. He gained his eccentricity from both his mother and his father. When his mother, Susannah Annesley, was only 12 years old she defied her father, a learned Puritan minister, and informed the family that she was becoming an Anglican. The Anglican Church, the state-church, had persecuted Puritan Dissenters for decades, frequently making martyrs out of men who wanted only to preach the gospel according to their conscience. The 13-year-old voiced no reason for her decision; she was content to tell her hurt and horrified parents that she was convinced of the soundness of her position and had inscribed it in her diary. (Years later her diary disappeared in the house-fire that nearly carried her off with her husband and children. Therefore no one knows to this day what reasons she had advanced.) Susannah was unyielding. When she married, several years later, her father wasn't allowed to officiate, since no non-Anglican minister could preside at a service of the state-church. Her father was crushed at his being excluded.

The father of Charles, Samuel Wesley, was eccentric too. Fancying himself a poet, he published a book of entirely forgettable verse. The title of his book of poems was simply *Maggots*. The single illustration adorning the book was a drawing of Samuel himself with a large maggot sitting on his forehead. The poems are unusual: "The Grunting of a Hog"; "A Box like an Egg"; and, perhaps the most unusual, "The Tame Snake in a Box of Bran".

Samuel and Susannah married, eventually having nineteen children. John was the fifteenth, Charles the eighteenth. (Kezia was the last of that generation.)

Both boys possessed awesome academic talent. When he was still a teenager Charles competed in what was known as a "Challenge," a scholarly joust wherein one fellow tried to stymie another on any of a hundred subtle questions concerning Greek grammar. The competition began early in the morning and continued until nine at night, three or four nights a week, for eight weeks. Much was at stake, since the winner would be named a "King's Scholar" and guaranteed entrance to Oxford or Cambridge University. Charles triumphed and moved on to Oxford.

Following his ordination to the Anglican priesthood Charles ministered in Georgia for six months where he proved himself to be a most obnoxious clergyman: prickly, opinionated, self-righteous, condescending, prying. Upon his return to England he rejoined his sister Kezia, the youngest of the nineteen Wesley children. Kezia's adolescent frivolity had infuriated Charles earlier, for Kezia used snuff, the eighteenth-century equivalent of marijuana. Her frivolity behind her now in her new-found maturity, Kezia told Charles she believed that God could and did work a work of grace in the human heart. Believers, she said, were granted new standing before God, a new nature, new outlook, new motivation, new affections. Then on 21st May, 1738, Kezia's conviction and experience of the truth became his. Charles wrote in his journal, "by degrees [the Spirit of God] chased away the darkness of my unbelief. I found myself convinced.... I saw that by faith I stood."[2] Whereupon he wrote a hymn that Christians continue to find a ready vehicle of their own experience of grace:

> And can it be that I should gain
> An interest in the Saviour's blood?
> Died he for me, who caused his pain?

---

2. Charles Wesley, Journal, May 21st, 1738; quoted in Arnold A Dallimore, *A Heart Set Free: The Life of Charles Wesley* (Westchester: Crossway Books, 1988), p. 61.

> For me, who him to death pursued?
> Amazing love! how can it be
> That thou, my God, should'st die for me?

Three days later John came to the same awareness. Methodism was born. In the meantime their friend George Whitefield (unlike the Wesleys, George Whitefield had not been born to the privileged clergy class but rather was the child of an English barmaid); Whitefield, an Anglican priest like the Wesleys, had been expelled from Anglican pulpits. Like John the Baptist, Whitefield never left any doubt as to where he stood. "I am persuaded," he wrote, "that the generality of preachers talk of an unknown and an unfelt Christ. The reason why congregations have been so dead is because they have had dead men preaching to them. How can dead men beget living children?"[3] Soon Whitefield was joined by the Wesleys in outdoor preaching, where they addressed crowds of up to 25,000.

In 1740 Charles visited Wales for the first time. On the whole the Welsh people loved him. In Cardiff, however, he had his first taste of violence (although by no means his last). An aristocrat who heard him was incensed at being told that moral rectitude was no substitute for clinging in faith to the sin-bearing Christ. Angrily he demanded that Charles recant. Charles refused and replied to him, "You cannot endure sound doctrine...you are a rebel against God, and must bow your stiff neck to him before you can be forgiven."[4] Whereupon the angry man assaulted Charles with his cane. A mêlée developed, in the course of which a Mrs. Phipps was struck as well. Her name will never be forgotten only because of her proximity to the assault on Charles—as Pilate is immortalized on account of his proximity to the crucifixion.

Not only was Charles a forceful evangelist, he was a diligent pastor. Like any good pastor, he spent much time at deathbeds. His journal

---

3. Harry S. Stout, *The Divine Dramatist* (Grand Rapids: Eerdmans, 1991), p. 131.
4. The quotations in the following paragraphs are found in Dallimore, *A Heart Set Free*.

entry of 4th March, 1741, reads, "I saw my dear friend again, in great bodily weakness but strong in the Lord.... I spoke with her physician who said, 'She has no dread upon her spirits...I never met such people as yours.'" In the same year he buried a young woman, Rachel Peacock, and subsequently wrote, "At the sight of her coffin my soul was moved within me and struggled as a bird to break the cage. Some relief I found in tears, but still was so overpowered that unless God had abated the vehemence of my desires, I could have had no utterance. The whole congregation partook with me of the blessedness of mourning."

When Charles was 39 years old he married Sarah Gwynne, daughter of Marmaduke Gwynne, a Welsh magistrate. Sarah, known to everyone as "Sally," was 20. Before she married him she told him he had to take better care of himself physically. To this end she urged him to stop getting up every morning at four and to sleep in until six; to stop sleeping on boards and begin sleeping in a bed; and lastly, if she was going to marry him he would have to take off his clothes when he slept. Extraordinarily beautiful, Sarah sat for several portrait painters. She had been married for only two years when smallpox overtook her. She lingered near death for days. Her 18-month-old son, "Jacky," succumbed. Sarah regained her health even as her face, hideously disfigured now, was more than many people could bear to look at. When someone who hadn't seen her since her illness blurted to Charles that his wife's appearance was repulsive, Charles commented, "I find her beautiful." Theirs was a marriage of storybook romance. Ultimately eight children were born to them, five of whom died in infancy or early childhood. Two sons, Samuel and Charles II, would distinguish themselves as musical performers and composers. (Samuel Sebastian Wesley, the best-known of the musical Wesleys, has tunes in every denomination's hymnal. In addition he wrote twenty oratorios.)

Yet not everyone among the Wesley brothers and sisters had a marriage like theirs. Mehetabel or "Hetty," the favourite sister of both John and Charles, was intelligent, vivacious, wonderfully gifted as a poet and sensitive to a degree that only her two dear brothers appeared to grasp.[5] When Hetty was 25 years old a suitor called on her several times. Her father, Samuel, disapproved of the suitor and told him not to come back. Samuel reinforced his decree by sending Hetty to a wealthy family where she worked as an unpaid drudge. She had been wounded by her father's heavy-handedness, was desperately lonely, and lacked utterly the intellectual company she craved. She wrote John vowing that she would never return home. She was home in less than a year, five months pregnant. Her father, heavy-handed still and enraged now as well, forced her to marry Mr. William Wright, a coarse, insensitive fellow as unlike Hetty as any man could be, and habitually drunk as well. Her baby died before it was a year old. A second infant died, and then a third. Hetty was crushed. Her grief found expression in her poem, "To an Infant Expiring the Second Day of its Birth":

> Tender softness, infant mild,
> Perfect, purest, brightest child!
> Transient lustre, beauteous clay,
> Smiling wonder of a day!
> Ere the last convulsive start
> Rend thy unresisting heart,
> Ere the long-enduring swoon
> Weigh thy precious eyelids down,
> Oh, regard a mother's moan!
> Anguish deeper than thy own!
> Fairest eyes, whose dawning light
> Late with rapture blessed my sight,
> Ere your orbs extinguished be,
> Bend their trembling beams on me.

---

5. The eldest brother, Samuel Wesley, never sided with the eighteenth century Awakening. He was ordained to the Anglican ministry, became headmaster of a boys' school, and established a poetry journal. John and Charles appear to have had little to do with him.

> Drooping sweetness, verdant flow'r,
> Blooming, with'ring in an hour,
> Ere thy gentle breast sustains
> Latest, fiercest, vital pains,
> Hear a suppliant! Let me be
> Partner in thy destiny![6]

John was irate at his father's callousness and preached a sermon, "Showing Charity to Repentant Sinners." The sermon excoriated father Samuel and was meant to acquaint him with his cruelty. The older man remained unaffected, however, his heart hardened against his daughter forever.

When Hetty fell mortally ill while still a young woman, Charles attended her. "I prayed by my sister," he wrote, "a gracious, trembling soul; a bruised reed which the Lord will not break." The day Hetty died John was absent in London. Charles conducted the funeral service for his favourite sister, preaching on Isaiah 60:19, "The Lord shall be thine everlasting light, and the days of thy mourning shall be ended.' That night he wrote in his journal, "I followed her to a quiet grave, and I wept with them that wept."

While Charles had no dispute with his sisters, he had several with John. They disagreed sharply over the matter of lay-preachers. As Methodism gathered more and more people it found itself without sufficient preachers. While John and Charles were Anglican priests and intended being nothing else, relatively few Anglican clergy sided with the Methodists, knowing that to do so would render them suspect to Anglican officialdom. As a result, the Methodist movement had to use more and more lay-preachers. These lay-preachers were zealous, sincere men whose dedication entailed enormous personal sacrifice but who lacked formal academic training. Oxford-educated himself, John had insisted that they study five hours each day. His mandate here was unrealistic in view of

---

6. M. Wright, "To an Infant Expiring the Second Day of its Birth"; quoted in R. Lonsdale, ed. *The New Oxford Book of Eighteenth Century Verse* (Oxford University Press, 1984), pp. 165–6.

their lack of academic formation and even lack of time. Admittedly, their theological under-exposure tended to foster doctrinal imprecision, this in turn occasionally giving rise to preaching that Charles found to be full of sound and fury yet signifying little. Concerning one such lay-preacher, Michael Fenwick, Charles wrote,

> Such a preacher I have never heard, and hope I never shall again. It was beyond description. I cannot say he preached false doctrine, or true, or any doctrine at all, but pure, unmixed nonsense. Not one sentence did he utter that could do the least good to any one soul.[7]

John, however, insisted that Methodism couldn't survive without lay-preachers and sharply rebuked Charles for his fussiness. (In this regard John was vindicated conclusively. Methodism wouldn't have survived its first flowering without lay preachers whose sacrifice was nothing less than exemplary. While the British Crown guaranteed Anglican clergy an annual income of thirty pounds, lay preachers—John was careful never to call them "clergy" or "ministers" and thereby violate not only canon law but even the law of the land—were paid only fifteen pounds per year.) Charles was forced to tolerate the preachers whose utterance frequently grated on him.

The doctrine of Christian perfection, however, remained the area of sharpest contention between the brothers. John insisted, in conformity with the tradition of the church catholic, that there was no limit to the scope of God's delivering his people from sin's guilt *and* grip *in this life*. To deny that God could "break every fetter" *now* was to condemn the habituated to life-long bondage, offering them only the faint comfort of release *in articulo mortis* [in the instant of death]. While always reading the word "perfection" as "single-minded"—the meaning it had in the King James Version of the Bible, John never thought it to mean "flawless" or "faultless." Charles riposted that eighteenth-century people invariably heard "perfection" as "faultless." Charles found "perfec-

---

7. Quoted in Dallimore, *op.cit.*, p.189.

tion" unhelpful; worse, disastrous, spawning as it did (he maintained) unrealistic self-estimation and insufferable spiritual pride, only to be followed by unforeseen vulnerability and embarrassing collapse. John thought Charles held out too little for people struggling with sin's addiction; Charles thought John held out too much. Charles reiterated that if by "perfection" John meant something less than what others generally understood, he should stop using the term. John insisted that the term was scriptural.[8] Mordant pen in hand, Charles scripted some of his sharpest exchanges with his brother:

> If perfect I myself profess,
> My own profession I disprove:
> The purest saint that lives below
> Doth his own sanctity disclaim,
> The wisest owns, I nothing know,
> The holiest cries, I nothing am.[9]

Sharper still, perhaps is his

> Longer than all should forward press,
> Should see the summit with his eyes,
> Impatient for his own success
> BE PERFECT NOW, the preacher cries!
> He ruins by his headlong haste,
> The wheat is choak'd with tares oer'run,
> And Satan lays the lunacy and waste.[10]

By 1756 Charles no longer had the stamina for an itinerant ministry on horseback. He was 49 years old, had spent years being rain-soaked, frozen, poorly-fed and assaulted by angry mobs. He gave up the travelling ministry and established residence in Bristol, preaching there and in London regularly.

---

8. For a detailed discussion of this point see chapter 7 above.
9. Tyson, *Charles Wesley: A Reader*, p. 389.
10. Ibid., p. 387.

By 1780 Charles was 73. Confusion had overtaken him. Poetry no longer leapt to his mind. When he preached now he paused at length between phrases, trying to recall what he wanted to say. In frustration he would thump his chest with both hands while mumbling incoherently. Then, tired, he would lean on the pulpit with both elbows. If he wanted more time he had the congregation sing a hymn; and if more time still, another hymn.

He lived another eight years.[11] John was in Newcastle when he learned of the death of his brother. Next Sunday John was conducting worship, entirely composed, when the congregation happened to sing one of Charles's earliest hymns. When the congregation came to the words

> My company before is gone
> And I am left alone with Thee

John unravelled. He staggered back into the pulpit chair, weeping profusely. The congregation waited for him, and he recovered enough to finish the service.

Sarah, Charles's widow, moved to London and lived there with her daughter and son. She died in 1822 at the age of 96.

THE ART OF CHARLES WESLEY[12]

To be sure, Charles Wesley was a genius, yet "genius" wasn't the only ingredient in his poetic mastery. His classical education and his unrelenting assiduity were equally important.

Charles left home for high school when he was eleven years old. On Monday mornings the lower form boys wrote an English prose précis of the sermon they had heard the day before; the middle form boys wrote a Latin prose précis; the upper form boys, a Latin verse précis. (Is there

---

11. When Charles was ready to dismount his animal appears to have been ready to have him do so: Charles had ridden the same mare for fifteen years.

12. For what follows I am largely indebted to Frank Baker, *Charles Wesley's Verse* (London: Epworth Press, 1964).

a high school student in Canada today who could write a Latin verse précis of last Sunday's sermon?)

After high school Charles moved on to Oxford University where he studied Latin and Greek for nine years, with concentration in Latin poetry. By age 30 he had written hundreds of poems, even though he had not yet penned any of the hymns that would issue from his spiritual awakening. When the awakening did occur, immersing him in a new world, it was so huge an event that Charles likened it to the creation of the cosmos. Certainly he had read aright the Greek text of 2 Corinthians 5:17: the man or woman renewed in Christ lives in a new *creation.* He compared the brooding of the Spirit over him to the brooding of the Spirit over the primeval chaos when the Spirit first brought the world into being:

> Long o'er my formless soul
> The dreary waves did roll;
> Void I lay and sunk in night.
> Thou, the overshadowing Dove,
> Call'dst the chaos into light,
> Badst me be, and live, and love.

All poets read other poets and are thereby informed by the poets they read. Charles was no exception. He read chiefly Shakespeare, Milton, Herbert, Dryden, Pope, Prior and Young. (Prior's poem, "Solomon," is 100 pages long, and Charles expected his daughter, Sally, to memorize all of it.) Yet none of the poets he read had anything like the influence on him of Scripture. Subsequently his hymn-poems became conduits whereby the Methodist people were steeped in Scripture as they hummed tunes in the course of their daily affairs. Generally Charles embedded one Scripture text at least in each hymn line:[13]

| With glorious clouds encompassed round | Ex. 24:16, 17; Ps. 97:2; Ez. 10:4 |

---

13. Quoted in *WJW,* Vol. 7, pp. 730, 731

Whom angels dimly see,	Isaiah 6:2
Will the Unsearchable be found,	Job 11:7; 23:3,8,9; 1 Tim. 6:16
Or God appear to me?	Isa. 59:2; Hab.1:13; 1 Cor.15:8

Come, then, and to my soul reveal	Dan. 2:22
The heights and depths of grace,	Eph. 3:18
The wounds which all my sorrows heal	Isa. 53:4-5; 1 Pet. 2:24
That dear disfigured face.	Isa. 52:14; 53:2

While Charles's themes came from Scripture, his poetic vocabulary was entirely his own, a fine blend of English words from Latin roots and English words from Anglo-Saxon roots. His basic vocabulary was Anglo-Saxon. Anglo-Saxon words are largely monosyllabic; e.g., *hit, wind, swept, thrust.* They are more vigorous than Latin words and have greater impact. English words derived from Latin, on the other hand, tend to be polysyllabic. They suggest not action but contemplation. They are capable of greater precision of thought.

> Those aramanthine bowers
> Inalienably made ours.

(*Aramanthine* means "never-fading.") Charles was especially fond of Latinisms ending in -able, -ible, -ably and -ibly. Note his Christmas hymn on the incarnation:

> Our God contracted to a span,
> Incomprehensibly made man.

In this vein we should note his hymn, "O Thou who camest from above":

> There let it for thy glory burn
> With inextinguishable blaze.

(It might be noted in passing that William Tyndale, the master of early-modern Saxon vocabulary, never used Latinate polysyllabic words, always preferring the force of monosyllables; e.g., "My sin is more than I can bear.") If today we find Wesley's vocabulary difficult to understand in places because strange to us, we should know that his vocabulary is the most modern of all eighteenth-century poets.

By dint of his nine-year immersion in classical poetry Charles absorbed thoroughly the poetic conventions used so very tellingly by the classical poets.

(i) Some of the rhetorical devices CW used.

Anaphora: repeating the same word at the beginning of consecutive phrases or sentences. E.g. (with respect to God's grace),

> Enough for all, enough for each,
> Enough for evermore.

Anadiplosis: beginning a stanza with the theme (re-stated, but not reproduced word-for-word) of the last line of the preceding stanza. E.g., in "Jesus, lover of my soul,"

> stanza 3, last line: "Thou art full of truth and grace."
> stanza 4, first line: "Plenteous grace with thee is found."

And again, e.g., in "And can it be that I should gain"

> stanza 1, last line: "That thou, my God, should'st die for me!"
> stanza 2, first line: "'Tis mystery all: th'immortal dies."

Epanadiplosis: beginning and ending a line ("book-ending" the line) with the same word:

> E.g., "Come, desire of nations, come."

Epizeuxis: repeating a word or phrase within a line.

> E.g., "Who for me, for me hast died."

(The foregoing four devices are forms of repetition used to lend emphasis, continuity or cohesion.)

Aposiopesis: the speaker comes to a complete halt in mid-stanza.

> E.g., "What shall I say?"

Oxymoron: inherent self-contradiction.
>E.g., "I want a calmly-fervent zeal."

Parison: an even balance in the expressions or words of a sentence.
>E.g., "The good die young;
>>The bad live long."

(Wesley used many more rhetorical devices as well.)

(ii) Some examples of CW's vocabulary.

(He liked to retain or recover literal meanings.)
>expressed: shaped by a strong blow (as from a die)
>illustrate: illuminate
>secure: free from care
>tremendous: terrifying
>virtue: manliness or power (Latin: *vis*, power; *vir*, man)
>pompous: dignified (but not ostentatious)

(iii) Some of the figures of speech CW used.

Metaphor: an implied comparison between two things.
>E.g., "He laid his glory by,
>>He wrapped him in our clay."

Synecdoche: one aspect of a person represents the whole of the person.
>E.g., "The mournful, broken hearts rejoice."

Antonomasia: a proper name is used as a general epithet.
>E.g., "Come, all ye Magdalens in lust."

Hypotyposis: lively description.
>E.g., "See! He lifts his hands!
>>See! He shews the prints of love!"

Hyperbole: exaggerated language used to express the inexpressible.
E.g.,
>I rode on the sky
>(Freely justified I!)
>Nor envied Elijah his seat;
>My soul mounted higher

> In a chariot of fire,
> And the moon it was under my feet.

(Here CW was speaking of his experience of that grace which had pardoned him. ("Freely justified I!")

(iv) Metre (/ = *accented syllable;* ' = *unaccented syllable.*)

iambic	' /
trochaic	/ '
anapestic	' ' /
dactylic	/ ' '
spondaic	/ /

CW wrote chiefly in iambic metre. Isaac Watts did too. E.g.,

> And then shall we for ever live
> At this poor dying rate?
> Our love so faint, so cold to Thee,
> And thine to us so great!" (Watts)

(Watts wrote 1000 poems, of which only twenty-two were in trochaic and five in anapestic.)

While Charles Wesley preferred iambic, he also wrote significantly in trochaic and anapestic, sometimes combining them: iambic-anapestic (e.g., "Nor envied Elijah his seat") or iambic-trochaic (e.g., "Jesus! the name that charms our fears"—trochaic-iambic). He rarely wrote in dactylic (unlike Longfellow's *Evangeline:* "This is the forest primeval," or even "Hickory dickory dock.") While most poets can work well in one metre only, CW could write superbly in any.

(v) Stanza Form

Charles Wesley wrote many fine hymns in 4-line stanzas, the 1st and 3rd lines having 8 feet (syllables), and the 2nd and 4th lines 6. E.g.,

> Jesus, united by thy grace,
> And each to each endeared,
> With confidence we seek thy face
> And know our prayer is heard.

He preferred 6 lines with 8 feet (8.8.8.8.8.8). E.g.,

> Then let us sit beneath the cross,
> And gladly catch the healing stream,
> All things for him account but loss,
> And give up all our hearts to him;
> Of nothing think or speak beside,
> 'My Lord, my Love is crucified.'

(Note the rhyme scheme here: ABABCC)
His next favourite stanza form was 8.8.6.8.8.6. ("romance metre") E.g.,

> If pure, essential love thou art,
> Thy nature into every heart,
> Thy loving self inspire;
> Bid all our simple souls be one,
> United in a bond unknown,
> Baptized with heavenly fire. (AABCCB)

(vi) Endings

Lines that end in an unaccented syllable are said to possess feminine rhyme: ("Love divine, all loves excelling"); lines ending in an accented syllable, masculine ("O what shall I do my Saviour to praise?"). Masculine rhymes were thought to be "stronger," imparting greater emphasis. CW wrote 300 hymns in feminine rhymes, 8700 in masculine.

While the native genius and the formal training of Charles Wesley were important ingredients in his hymn writing, they weren't the most important. What counted above all was his life in God, in particular his experience of the Crucified. Repeatedly in his *Journal* Charles summarized his ministerial endeavour and its Spirit-authored fruit, "She received the atonement." His hymns sing pre-eminently about the cross.

MERCY IMMENSE AND FREE

Despite his 9000 published poems, the depth and wonder and force of his immersion in God is finally inexpressible. His matchless words, "Depth of mercy, can there be / Mercy still reserved for me?" point us to the heart of One before whom all of us (Charles too) are ultimately wordless.

11

EGERTON RYERSON AND PUBLIC EDUCATION IN CANADA

Egerton Ryerson was born March 24, 1803, in Vittoria (near Port Dover, Ontario), one of nine children of Joseph Ryerson and Mehetabel Stickney. His parents were descendants of Dutch Protestants who had wearied of the suffocation born of Europe's class confinement and craved the opportunities the New World afforded. His oldest New World ancestor, Martin Reyerzoon, had landed in New Amsterdam before the British conquest rendered the settlement New York (1664). In the wake of the British victory the family name was Anglicized to "Ryerson." Joseph Ryerson, Egerton's father, forsook Dutch Calvinism and embraced the Church of England.

In 1815, at the close of the War of 1812, Ryerson's three older brothers, George, William and John, underwent that precisely demarcated shift "from darkness to light" by which Methodism had come to be identified. Soon the twelve year-old Egerton was listening with similar intensity to Methodist preachers. One such, a former blacksmith, unashamed to be known now as "The Old Hammer," became the means whereby the youngster's heart was heated white-hot and forged forever.

Ryerson continued farming and studying until he was eighteen, when he thought he should identify publicly with the movement through which he had been spiritually awakened. His father, upon hearing that Egerton had joined the Methodists, responded swiftly and surely: "Leave them or leave home." Ryerson left home, supporting himself as a student-teacher in the local grammar school.

Rescinding the expulsion, Ryerson's father pleaded with his son to return. Egerton's prompt return indicated that he was now as unembittered and unresentful and as he had earlier been courageous—character traits that would mark him throughout the struggle and strife soon to surround him for the rest of his life. Labouring on his father's farm for one year, he left home for good, this time with Joseph's blessing.

In August 1824 he began studying Latin and Greek with assistance from a near-by schoolmaster. Then in the midst of protracted, serious illness he found himself "addressed" once again in a manner no less turbulent than his spiritual awakening. This time he acknowledged not a summons to discipleship but a vocation to the ministry. One month later he was astride a horse, itinerating throughout the Niagara Peninsula as a Methodist Probationer. Although his formal education was restricted to a few months of instruction in the classics, he immersed himself in Locke's *Essay Concerning Human Understanding* (Locke was the principal English philosopher of the Enlightenment), Paley's *Moral and Political Philosophy* and Blackstone's *Commentaries*. (Ironically, the man who was to design and inaugurate public education in Ontario and whose work would be copied throughout the Canadian nation was almost entirely self-taught, and would continue to school himself for the rest of his life.)

Ryerson preached his first sermon in Beamsville, Ontario. (This village has become dear to many United Church clergy and their families on account of its Albright Gardens and Manor, the final earthly residence for ministers who retire without the means to house themselves.) Before long he was minister of the Yonge Street Circuit. The circuit gathered up the people in the triangle whose outermost points were Pickering, Weston and the south shore of Lake Simcoe. It took him a month to visit all the preaching points within it. On a typical Sunday the 22-year-old Ryerson found himself riding thirty miles, preaching three times, and addressing two classes.

Then there occurred the momentous event that brought him unprecedented opportunity, altered forever his public image and fixed his name in Canadian history. In 1825 Bishop Mountain of Quebec died. Toronto's Bishop John Strachan preached on the occasion of Mountain's death, turning the sermon into both a panegyric lauding the rise and riches of the Church of England in Canada and a poniard aimed at the heart of all who declined the denomination, but with especial denunciation reserved for Methodists.

For years Strachan had been the power broker of the Family Compact, the "Compact" consisting of a handful of rich families who exercised a monopoly on business, finance and education. It aimed at petrifying the social stratification that allowed the privileged to exploit the New World's version of Britain's class structure, the worst in Europe. Earlier Strachan had candidated for the ministry of the Church of Scotland. Rejected by the Presbyterians, he had turned to the Anglican Church and then had turned on all who didn't belong to it. Rising to episcopal pre-eminence, he sought to punish any who didn't support the Compact's constellation of power, piety, prestige and privilege.

Strachan denigrated the Methodist people, faulting them for a putative American origin and accusing them of American leanings. The Methodist clergy, however, he more than denigrated: he ridiculed them, his scurrility stooping to sneer at them as irremediably ignorant in view of their having inflated themselves into preachers when their intellectual mediocrity should have chained them to plough and shop. Following up his sermon with concrete designs to suppress Methodists, Strachan asked the government for exclusive Anglican access to the Clergy Reserves (the Clergy Reserves being land and the income it generated reserved for the sole use of the church), in addition to a large grant, thereby assuring a Britain made nervous by the nation to the south that Upper Canadian Anglicanism was loyal to the crown. In addition, of course, the inequity of withholding from Methodists the right to solemnize marriages as well as to hold title to church buildings, parsonages and cemeteries; this was to be perpetuated.

Methodists were outraged at Strachan's vilification of their clergy and his accusation of political treachery and his enforced injustice. They looked around for someone to champion them. Ryerson, only 25 years old, penned Methodism's reply. The pseudonymously written "Review of a Sermon, Preached by the Honourable and Reverend John Strachan" appeared in William Lyon Mackenzie's paper, *The Colonial Advocate*. Ryerson voiced Methodism's disgust at the Anglican Church's political prostitution. Stressing again that he had no complaint with Anglican doctrine or liturgy, Ryerson noted that Strachan appeared unaroused on matters pertaining to the gospel yet implacably vehement and venomous when finances were at stake. Replying to Strachan's assertion that a Christian nation without an established Church was inherently self-contradictory, Ryerson reminded readers that the gospel had thrived in the hands of the apostles even though the latter had been without state support. As for the "ignorance" of the Methodist clergy, Ryerson listed the books mandated for Methodist candidates for ordination, and recalled John Wesley's insistence that all Methodist preachers study five hours per day. Concerning the imputation of American origin, Ryerson noted that the Wesleyan Methodists had never known an American root, while by 1825 there were scarcely any in the Methodist Episcopal Church (a denomination that had originated in the United States) who were American-born. He reminded his accusers that his parents had been United Empire Loyalists who had left the Republic out of loyalty to the British Crown. He argued conclusively that Strachan's sly slander concerning "U.E.L.s" (they were not to be trusted since they might have absorbed unknowingly the worst of republicanism with its rejection of tradition and its elevation of the masses and its affinity for a government that Strachan's echelon regarded as little more than mob rule); this innuendo was groundless. Methodists weren't American sympathizers infested with republicanism.

Furthermore, why should the state favour the Church of England when only thirty-one of 235 clergy in Upper Canada were Anglican? George Ryerson, brother to Ryerson, weighed in with his written comment that non-preferential treatment shouldn't be accorded the "temple of spiritual tyranny." Father Joseph, now aware of his sons' role in the dispute, cried, "We are all ruined." Egerton himself relished none of this, finding that controversy, however necessary, issued in "leanness of soul." Notwithstanding his fear of spiritual enervation, Ryerson's gospel-engendered polemics bore incontestable fruit: within four years legislation appeared that permitted Nonconformist denominations to own land and their ministers to marry and baptize. The dissolving of the Clergy Reserves took another twenty-five years, when the land was sold off with revenues returning to the government, most of which were redistributed for education.

Ryerson's concern to counter the Family Compact's ascendancy, however, never acidulated his spirit or eclipsed all other aspects and implicates of the gospel. After the Methodist Conference of 1826 in Hamilton, he began living among the aboriginal people on the Credit River. Introduced to Peter Jones at a camp meeting of Mississaugas and Mohawks, Ryerson found a spirit-mate in the young native Methodist preacher who had evangelized his people and whose father (Augustus), like Ryerson's, had been a United Empire Loyalist and whose mother (Tuhbenahbenahneequay), was an Ojibwa. Able now to elicit the help of the aboriginals who trusted him, and recognized precocious besides (within months he could preach to the people in their language), Ryerson's linguistic ability saw him commissioned to produce a grammar and lexicon of the Mississauga dialect. Immediately he set himself to raising money to build a school and chapel for the natives. Knowing that the Credit River people could furnish few funds for the project, Ryerson returned to his former circuit and old friends, unashamed, like Wesley before him, to beg from door-to-door for an undertaking whose worth neither he nor they ever doubted. The structure was completed in six weeks. Drawing on his agricultural expertise he convinced the natives that fenced land and cultivated fields produced vastly more than either bartering hand-made goods or hunting and gathering in the wild. Their chief, understanding the restless nature of the Methodist itinerancy, dubbed him "A Bird-on-the-Wing."

The Anglican hierarchy recognized the young minister's talent and offered to finance a fine formal education if he consented to honour his vocation within the Church of England. Characteristically neither envying nor toadying, he graciously declined the offer, convinced that only crass opportunism would see him leave the people among whom he had come to know God for the sake of self-advancement. He insisted he believed the "Articles of Religion" of the Methodists; he agreed with their constitution; and he never doubted that they were "church" as depicted in Scripture. Never hostile to the Church of England, he would nevertheless remain immovably opposed to its efforts to get itself "established" (thereby making it an aspect of the state), its attempts at preserving its endowments, and its prerogatives that demeaned those less privileged. (When he came to marry, for instance, he and Hannah Aikman had to travel twenty miles to find a Presbyterian clergyman to preside, Presbyterians from the Church of Scotland being allowed some of the privileges denied all Methodists.)

By now the Methodists knew that they had to have their own journal if they were to forestall fragmentation. The Methodist Conference of 1829 minuted the founding of a weekly paper, the *Christian Guardian*. (All papers in Upper Canada at this time were weeklies.) Ryerson was elected its first editor. Initially distributing 500 copies, in three years it swelled to 3,000. In no time it was the most widely read paper and the most influential of any in the province. The *Guardian* gathered up Methodist theological concerns, religious issues in everyday life, discussions of the sort of government the people currently had or ought to have, educational reform (always a priority with Ryerson), as well as practical advice in household economics. The paper eclipsed the official *Upper Canada Gazette*.

Methodism's successful venture into journalism expanded into book publishing. The *Guardian*'s first editor opened a bookstore, selling chiefly books imported from Britain and the U.S.A. The seed was small yet the yield, as in the parable, unforeseeably huge as the Methodist Book Concern metamorphosed into the largest printing and publishing enterprise in Canada. Its sales of imported books underwrote the publishing and distribution of indigenous writers, among whom were Charles G.D. Roberts and Catherine Parr Traill. Renamed "The Ryerson Press" in 1919 in honour of its founder, it continued to support the work of Canadian writers, including that of two famous poets, Earle Birney and Louis Dudek. Surviving until 1970, it did much to shape the Canadian identity in the twentieth century through the novelists, poets, biographers and historians whose works it made available across the land.

Ryerson's contribution to the Canadian people through literature developed into a related contribution through a major academic institution, Victoria College. Bishop Strachan had long campaigned for a charter for "King's College" (later to become the University of Toronto), replete with Anglican privileges. All its professors, for instance, would have to endorse the Thirty-Nine Articles (Anglicanism's normative doctrinal statement), while veto power over the institution's council would rest with the Bishop of Lower Canada (Quebec). The Methodists countered with their own college, situating it in Cobourg, Ontario, at that time the hub of Methodist strength in the province. (Non-Anglican "dissenters" of Calvinist persuasion supported Ryerson in his efforts to end Anglican hegemony in higher education.) In 1836 the Methodists erected Upper Canada Academy, expanding it into Victoria College (1841) and Victoria University (1865, when faculties of law and medicine were added). Named Victoria's first principal, Ryerson announced a curriculum as broad as it was deep. In addition to classics (a mainstay at any university at this time), he added a science department offering courses in chemistry, mineralogy and geography, as well as new departments of philosophy, rhetoric and modern languages (French and German). Always eschewing one-sidedness anywhere in life, he insisted that each student pursue a balanced programme of the arts and the sciences.

Indisputably, however, Ryerson became a household name, with churches and streets named after him in scores of cities and towns, on account of his colossal achievement concerning public education. Dismayed to see one-half of school-aged children with no formal education and the remaining half averaging only a year's, and horrified at the poor training and brutal disposition of what passed for "teacher" in too many villages, Ryerson's people had mirrored the prophet's word, "precept upon precept...here a little, there a little" (Isaiah 28: 13) as they had pried open the grip of the Family Compact. Ryerson himself was handed unparalleled opportunity the day he was appointed Chief Superintendent of Common Schools for Canada West in 1844. (A "common" school was the social opposite of the elitist private schools.) He was only 41. Two years later he was promoted to Chief Superintendent of Education, an office he occupied for the next thirty years, leaving it only to retire. Ryerson persuaded the provincial government to assume responsibility for education. Soon common schools, aided by government grants, appeared wherever twenty students could be gathered. The arrangement was a quantitative leap over the log cabin schoolhouses whose instructors were frequently minimally literate themselves.

Thinking ill of a British school system that perpetuated the worst class divisiveness in Europe, Ryerson visited Continental common schools in Holland, Italy and France, "bookending" his trip with visits to Germany where he could observe the education system that Philip Melanchthon had implemented 300 years earlier.

Melanchthon (1487-1560) had been the first systematic theologian of the Magisterial Reformation. While Luther had penned theological tracts to respond to exigencies in church and society, Melanchthon had "bottled" Luther's rich "geysering," scripting his *Loci Communes* ("Commonplaces") into a theological textbook that had seen eighteen Latin editions in a few years, as well as numerous German printings.

Yet Melanchthon had wanted to be relieved of his teaching responsibilities in theology in order to concentrate on the humanities. Superbly trained as a humanist (he was recognized the best Greek scholar in Europe following the death of Desiderius Erasmus), he was enormously gifted as linguist and philologist, yet equally at home in philosophy. He had always maintained there to be no substitute for schooling in the humanities and the sciences. (Physics, said Melanchthon, illustrated the harmony of the creation.)

As early as 1524 (he was then only 27 years old) Melanchthon had begun developing public schools throughout Germany; he had reorganized the universities; he had fashioned the pedagogical methods in which hundreds of teachers were trained; and he had written school textbooks, subsequently used by countless pupils.

Germany's system of public education seared itself upon Ryerson as holding greater promise for Canada than that of any other European nation. Upon his return to Canada he wooed the provincial government into marrying education and tax revenues, thereby providing free education for all. Of course the rich objected, arguing that they shouldn't have to support the schooling of their social inferiors. Ryerson triumphed. His free education was soon compulsory as well. In it all he elevated teaching from a miserable job to a calling akin to that of the ordained ministry.

George Brown, editor of Toronto's *Globe* newspaper, ranted that Ryerson had imported "Prussian" education into Ontario. Ryerson, cultured where Brown was crude, quietly immersed himself in French literature, having taught himself the language so well that he and the pope had conversed in it during his visit to Italy. (Ryerson was prescient in his awareness that all public figures in Canada would have to be conversant in French. In addition he was aware that everywhere in Europe—and therefore why not in Canada—French was the language of culture. No educated person boasted of being unilingual, and no one who aspired to the world of letters was inept in French. Earlier, while principal of Victoria College, he had taught himself Hebrew.)

Ryerson always knew that the life of the mind was a good in itself. The life of the mind was its own justification. Furthermore, it was his conviction that people are commanded to love God with their minds. While it wasn't sin to be ignorant, it was sin to be more ignorant than they had to be. And it was sheer wickedness for a society to relegate the relatively disadvantaged to lifelong ignorance.

While Ryerson knew that the life of the mind was an end in itself, he also knew that the life of the mind was useful; it had utilitarian significance. People with greater education in fact could do more of greater social usefulness than those who had been unable to gain adequate education. Ryerson knew, then, that the public good was always served by better quality public education.

He knew something else; namely, education didn't merely equip people to know more; it expanded the universe in which they lived. Education equipped them to live in a different world, a richer world, a world of greater complexity and greater wonder. Deprived of adequate schooling, people would be confined to a much smaller world outside and a commensurately smaller world inside.

Ryerson knew too that public education was essential to social democracy. Political democracy was relatively easy to achieve: each citizen was given the right to vote. Social democracy, however, occurred when all citizens had equal access to opportunities within a society. Ryerson knew that apart from a vibrant public education, social gains couldn't be retained. The cruel class stratification, with its "invisible ceilings" that precluded socio-economic mobility and frustrated people in private and public "prisons," would reappear as surely as Strachan and his supporters wanted it to reappear. Like any nineteenth-century thinker apprised of the French Revolution, Ryerson knew that if public education didn't thrive and with it the release of resentment engendered by the limitations of the place on the social spectrum where one had been born, then different clusters in the society, now frozen into immobility, would turn inward for support and then turn outward in hostility. His educational vision entailed vastly more than schooling: it entailed a vision for a nation, its people and its future.

Ryerson struggled to give birth to, refine, and expand public education with his second last breath. His last breath, of course, was reserved for what was incomparably dear to him and his educational mentor, Philip Melanchthon. "Next to the gospel," the multi-talented German reformer had exclaimed, "there is nothing more glorious than humanistic learning, that wonderful gift of God."

A RECOGNITION

Streetsville Methodist Church (now Streetsville United Church, Mississauga, Ontario), where the author ministered for twenty-one years, was constructed in 1876. Egerton Ryerson delivered the sermon at the dedication of the building. At the conclusion of the service the congregation, consisting of the financially unremarkable people who typified the Methodists of nineteenth-century Ontario villages, had subscribed enough in cash and pledges to pay for the new edifice. In one evening Ryerson had 'preached the church out of debt.' When the author was called to the Streetsville congregation in 1978 the story was still told and Ryerson's name still redolent.

12

NEW CONNEXION METHODISM AND WILLIAM BOOTH

I: FROM JOHN WESLEY TO THE METHODIST NEW CONNEXION

Wesley himself had anticipated a connectional crisis in Methodism. In 1766, twenty-five years before his death, he became aware of a demand for

> a free conference; that is, a meeting of the preachers, wherein all things shall be determined by most votes . . . . It is possible, after my death, something of this kind may take place. But not while I live. To me the preachers have engaged themselves to submit, and to 'serve me as sons in the gospel' . . . . To me the people in general will submit. But they will not yet submit to any other.[1]

---

* This chapter was commissioned by the Canadian Methodist Historical Society and appeared in the *Papers of the CHMS* (Toronto: CHMS, 1993), pp. 91–108.

1. *Minutes* of Wesleyan Conference, 1812 ed., (1766), p. 60. For much of the information in this part of the paper I am indebted to Davies, George and Rupp (eds.), *A History of the Methodist Church in Great Britain* (London: Epworth Press, 1965), Vol. 1.

Wesley may have been prepared to have his death dispel his autocracy and forestall any one else's; but only his death would do it. He had no intention whatever of sharing his authority with others within the Methodist precincts. As discerning as he was totalitarian, however, he unerringly forecast a rent in the seamless garment of the movement. In fact he foresaw three groups forming. (i) Up to one-quarter of the Methodists (he meant Methodist preachers) would attempt to "procure preferment in the Church"[2]—that is, the Church of England, the established church. Presumably these would be those who had grown weary of being looked upon as second-class citizens, marred by "enthusiasm" and social inferiority. This group was farthest removed from the New Connexion. (ii) Other preachers would become congregationalists and secure pastorates in this milieu. While Wesley did not specify who would constitute this second group, most likely they were those ministers who, having taken Wesley at his word—"There is but a hair's breadth between me and Calvin"—and who, aware too of the modified Puritanism which remained in Wesley, decided to move closer to a Christian body which was self-consciously informed by Calvin and Calvin's Puritan heirs. (iii) The third group, the largest, would remain steadfast at the centre of the Methodist ambit, and would continue to preach Methodist doctrine and uphold Methodist discipline.

Wesley, concerned as to what kind of leadership might replace his autocracy, appointed the One Hundred Preachers as heirs to his authority. This arrangement was facilitated by means of the Deed of Declaration of 1784. To be sure, the company of One Hundred were to exercise a benign and benevolent dictatorship:

> I beseech you, by the mercies of God, that you never . . . assume superiority over your brethren; but let all things go on . . . exactly in the same manner as when I was with you . . . do all things with a

---

2. Davies, George and Rupp, 276.

single eye, as I have done from the beginning, without prejudice or partiality.³

Government was to be exclusively in the hands of preachers, men, currently Wesley's assistants, whom he felt he could trust to maintain the ethos he had imparted.

Those Methodists who did not want an institutional rupture with the Church of England were aware that such matters as the administration of sacraments had to be settled in conformity with Anglican tradition. Wesley, it must be remembered, insisted to the last that he was an Anglican priest. Quickly it was asked if only those preachers whom Wesley himself had ordained were permitted, and this would scarcely have satisfied the Anglican hierarchy, since Wesley was not a bishop, or if all itinerant preachers were allowed. By 1795 it was agreed that anyone authorized by the Methodist Conference could, while each society was to determine who would administer the sacraments. This decision, along with the decision to allow Methodist services of worship during the hours of Anglican worship, effected a *de facto* separation from the established church.

A comparably vexatious matter pertained to the role of the laity in church government about which Wesley had written

> As long as I live the people shall have no share in choosing either stewards or leaders among the Methodists. We have not and never had any such custom. We are not republicans, and never intend to be. It would be better for those who are so minded to go quietly away.⁴

At least fifty people, immediately upon Wesley's death in 1791, so far from going quietly away, decided to make a noise. They proposed startling changes for church government, among which were: class

---

3. *Minutes*, 1791, p. 234. Wesley reiterated his point in 1788. See *The Letters of John Wesley*, ed. by John Telford (London: Epworth, 1931), Vol. VII, p. 266.
4. *Letters*, VII, 196.

members were to choose their own leaders, society members were to choose society stewards, preachers could admit a member to or expel a member from a society only with the consent of a majority of that society, and itinerant preachers could be assigned their duties only by stewards at the quarterly meeting.

In the meantime the company of One Hundred Preachers, the collective successor to Wesley himself, had circulated a letter reminding the Methodists that the One Hundred were the sole rulers of the movement. In no time disputes over lay jurisdiction abounded. For instance, in 1792 a Methodist preacher, having administered the Lord's Supper, found that church trustees (lay persons who in this particular case wanted Methodism to identify with the established church) barred him from preaching in other chapels on the circuit. Did lay persons have the right to circumscribe the ministry of someone who had been ordained by Conference? If so, then lay control was operative.

The controversy appeared to come to a head quickly with Alexander Kilham, a preacher whom Wesley had accepted in 1785. Kilham, not unlike many Methodist preachers, identified himself not with the Anglican supporters among the Methodists but with those who favoured affiliation with Dissenters. A Dissenter replete with the courage of his convictions, Kilham announced that collaboration with the Church of England was evidence of the world's infestation of the Christian's mind and heart. In the face of his Anglican-leaning fellows, Kilham circulated a letter arguing that many Methodists did not receive Holy Communion inasmuch as they could not receive it conscientiously from ungodly clergy in the midst of ungodly communicants. Kilham insisted that all Methodists were *de facto* Dissenters. And since Methodist preachers were every bit as qualified as other Dissenting ministers, why not have them administer the sacraments instead of referring their people to an Anglican priest? In a second pamphlet Kilham replied to those who had rebutted him tartly.

At the following Conference, dominated, of course, by preachers, Kilham was strongly censured and his pamphlet condemned. Despite

Kilham's praise of John Wesley, he was accused of defamation. Nonetheless, a motion to expel him was defeated.

In a third pamphlet Kilham argued that every circuit or district should be represented at Conference by a delegate of its own choice—the incipient democratization of church government. A fourth pamphlet followed, signed "Martin Luther." Clearly Kilham was telling whoever would listen that he regarded the administrative structures of Methodism as little better than papal tyranny. The fifth pamphlet Kilham delivered to Conference in person. It argued that Scripture was normative even in administrative matters. Here the Calvinist influence is unmistakable, transmitted through Puritans and Dissenters, and exemplified for Kilham by the Scots Presbyterians whom he came to cherish when he was Methodist minister in Aberdeen and in whose denomination he saw lay representation in the church courts.

Kilham's *magnum opus* was not long coming: *The Progress of Liberty Among the People Called Methodists*.[5] It was a plea for freedom of conscience. In it he wrote, "is it not amazingly strange that any sect or party should refuse to give to their brethren what the laws of our country so cheerfully allow?[6] This document detailed matters which he claimed were supported by Scripture; for instance, members should determine their own class leaders, the circuit meeting should approve any preacher proposed for the itinerary, circuits should appoint lay delegates to district meetings, district meetings should appoint lay delegates to the Conference of Preachers where these lay delegates, along with preachers, would have jurisdiction over both spiritual and temporal affairs.

Opposition was swift and sure and severe: London preachers urged Newcastle District to put Kilham on trial. The district in turn deferred trying him until Conference met. Kilham went to ecclesiastical trial in Wesley's Chapel, London, in 1796. When he requested a copy of the charges, his request was denied. Conference expelled him in July, 1796,

---

5. Kilham, *The Progress of Liberty Amongst the People Called Methodists* (Alnwick: 1795).

6. Kilham, 18–19.

having tried him without formally charging him. Subsequently he asked if he might be allowed to preach as a layman. A few Methodist ministers were assigned to meet with him for the purpose of assessing his suitability. The meeting occurred. He was asked to recant and to refrain from further criticism of any sort. He refused, and his excommunication was sealed. A biographer later wrote of him, "it is impossible not to conclude that the sentence of expulsion was unmerited, and that he was not treated with either charity or justice by the Conference."[7] Everything that Kilham had suffered to see implemented Conference then turned down.

In August, 1797, three other preachers, William Thom, Stephen Eversfield, and Alexander Cummin, left the Conference and met with Kilham to form "The New Itinerary," renamed eventually "The Methodist New Connexion" [MNC]. In this latter body, administrative responsibilities were shared jointly by clergy and laypersons. Five percent of the Methodists joined. Their representative statement at the second Conference of the MNC merits perusal.

> It was not from an affectation of singularity that determined us to proceed in supporting the rights and liberties of the people . . . .
> It was a conviction arising from Scripture that all the members of Christ's body are one; and that the various officers of it should act by the general approbation and appointment of the people.[8]

Kilham laboured indefatigably on behalf of the MNC, and died in 1798 at the age of 36. He had spent himself to overturn Methodism's exclusion of lay jurisdiction, concerning which a highly-placed Methodist official had written, "We have the most perfect aristocracy existing perhaps on God's earth. The people have no power; we have the whole in the fullest sense which can be conceived."[9]

---

7. Alexander Kilham Townsend, *The First Methodist Reformer* (London: 1889), 72.
8. *Minutes of the Methodist New Connexion*, 1798 10.
9. Coke, *Cardinal Examination of the London Methodist Bill*, in Edwards, *After Wesley* (London: Epworth Press, 1935), 50–51.

The MNC grew very slowly. After ten years it had only thirty-five ministers, eighty-four chapels, and 7,202 members. Since mainstream Methodism was firmly ensconced in the more densely populated areas of Britain, the MNC attempted to move into sparser regions. Indeed, so sparsely populated were they that it was difficult to generate a congregation. The MNC ministers were paid a pittance, while the physical demands on them were overwhelming. Not surprisingly, then, almost fifty percent of MNC ministers who were admitted in the first seventeen years of the denomination resigned after an average service of only six years. Moreover, it came to light that trust deeds did not permit chapels to be transferred from the Wesleyan body to the MNC. Litigation ensued frequently, as unpleasant as it could only be. Members were often politically suspect, thought to be possessed of convictions similar to those of revolutionaries in France and anarchists in Britain. After fifty years it had 19,289 members (including 3,201 in Canada). The name of one of its members, however, was destined to be heard around the world.

II: FROM THE METHODIST NEW CONNEXION TO WILLIAM BOOTH

William Booth (1829–1912) was first a minister among the Wesleyan Reformers.[10] His people cherished him and pressed him to remain in their communion. Catherine Mumford, later his wife, urged him to join the MNC inasmuch as this off-shoot was better organized, in her opinion, (Booth himself regarded the Wesleyan Reformers as organizationally chaotic) was more widely distributed, and hence afforded a wider sphere of service, albeit chiefly in the urban areas of heavily-industrialized north England.[11] Ironically, of course, so far from providing a larger sphere of service Booth was soon to find the MNC so cramped as to be a strait-jacket.

---

10. For much of the following I am indebted to Begbie, *Life of William Booth*, Vols. I and II. (London: MacMillan, 1923) and Collier, *The General Next To God* (London: Collins, 1965).

11. *Encyclopedia of World Methodism* (Nashville: Abingdon, 1974), II, 156–7.

MERCY IMMENSE AND FREE

From the inception of his theological training, Booth's heart ached for the wretched of soot-corroded England whom he saw, as Wesley had seen before him, when most church leaders saw no one at all. In his diary he wrote that he felt "much sympathy for the poor, neglected inhabitants of Wapping [an area of east London] and its neighbourhood as I walked down the filthy streets and beheld the wickedness and idleness of its people."[12]

Booth's ability was as great as his compassion. While MNC ministers were generally granted permission to marry only after four years' probation, Booth's exceptional gifts won him permission to marry Catherine after only one year. The reputation of the spellbinder-preacher spread throughout England like wild-fire. Invitations to preach deluged him. The MNC knew by now that Booth was a star in its firmament. Nevertheless, the denomination remained ambivalent about him. On the one hand he had given the MNC household familiarity; on the other hand several denominational authorities disapproved of his methods. By now the MNC, along with the parent Methodist body, had been granted the social respectability so long denied, while with respectability came spiritual vacuity. Early in his ministry MNC authorities had rebuked Booth for welcoming so-called riff-raff to worship. He had been told that they could attend worship if they entered and left by the rear door of the chapel, and, once inside, remained behind the pulpit platform where they could not be seen. Booth was a dramatic preacher, intense to the point of being uncomprehending when he found other preachers dawdling over a second cup of tea while millions lived in temporal squalor and faced eternal ruin. Yet millions venerated him. When he left the island of Guernsey in 1854 following a preaching mission, countless people lined the pier to bid him adieu. His popularity did nothing to endear him to denominational hierarchs who regarded his theology and his presentation as deficient in taste.

---

12. Quoted in Begbie, *op. cit.*, I, 181.

NEW CONNEXION METHODISM AND WILLIAM BOOTH

Booth himself was aware that dross could be alloyed with precious metal. When he beheld the distress of the people who streamed to the communion rail, weeping and crying out, he wrote to Catherine, "Amidst all this I could not help but reason, Is it right? Is this the best way?"[13] Yet he remained convinced that it was a way, a way through which he witnessed the transformation of those who had languished in a spiritual wasteland and the deliverance of those who had been enslaved in a manner which social historians have described hauntingly.

At the same time Booth knew that popularity as such did not betoken spiritual depth. God alone could render fruitful the work of even the most gifted servant; of himself, the preacher could generate nothing. "My present popularity almost frightens me," he wrote Catherine; "I am alarmed as to the maintaining of it. I mean the carrying out of the work of God. Yesterday morning was a perfect failure. But God can, and I firmly believe God will, work."[14] Booth knew too that popularity is the most dangerous threat to any preacher. What would be gained if the world gathered at his feet if he, meanwhile, had forfeited himself before God? To Catherine he wrote once more, "My soul pants for something deeper, realler, more hallowed in my soul's experience. *If I fail it will be here.*"[15] Discerning in his awareness that other ministers were devoid of zeal for the gospel, Booth was prescient in recognizing that his own zeal would immerse him in trouble with fellow clergy. On his 26th birthday he wrote Catherine, "I cannot but be surprised at the want of any aspiring emotion so apparent in many of our ministers; they are nothing and seem content. I deplore this, yet if I was like them I should be very much happier."[16]

Institutional wisdom outweighed clergy resentment and antipathy sufficiently to let the Annual Conference of the MNC free Booth of circuit fetters in London and appoint him to wide-ranging evangelistic

---

13. Ibid., I, 194.
14. Ibid., 197.
15. Ibid., 197 (emphasis added).
16. Ibid., 201.

MERCY IMMENSE AND FREE

work. It was felt that Booth might even lend a tonic to those circuits whose anaemia had heretofore been incurable.

This is not to say that Booth's ego swelled in proportion to the crowds who hung on him. On the contrary he had moments when he was riddled with self-doubt. At such times he doubted the sincerity of many who had newly made profession of faith; he doubted his vocation; he wondered if anything lasting would come of his work. Telling Catherine of a woman who had claimed to be the beneficiary of the Saviour's mercy only to be found, a day or two later, stumbling further into the darkness, he wrote, "I find so few who seem to me to live Christianity. *Who is there?*"[17] At the nadir of his self-doubt he considered abandoning his evangelistic work in order to seek a position in commerce, however slender, that would feed him, his wife and their family adequately. He concluded that he lacked the friends and influence needed to land him a "secretaryship" or similar position.

Booth's occasional self-doubt, however, was nothing compared to the hostility of the MNC. Institutional nastiness now varied directly with the crowds who turned out at his services and the penitents who responded to the gospel-invitation he articulated. Everything about him was denounced. The towns and cities where he had announced the bad news of God's judgment and the good news of God's mercy and patience hungered to have him return. The denomination did not shut him down at first, not wishing to incur adverse publicity, but neither did it allow him to proceed unopposed.

Many clergy-colleagues bitterly resented Booth's notoriety. They had no idea what his ministry was costing him and his family: long periods away from home, energy-depletions which left him exhausted, next-to-no money, no fixed address as the family moved frequently in and out of shabby lodgings, and a wife whose health, never robust, was now chronically sub-standard even as she struggled to speak in public while sustaining numerous pregnancies.

---

17. Ibid., 201 (emphasis Booth's).

NEW CONNEXION METHODISM AND WILLIAM BOOTH

Booth was careful to submit to denominational oversight inasmuch as he reported duly to superiors whenever they wanted to query him on matters pertaining to his ministry. Nevertheless, in 1857 denominational authorities decided to curtail him. At the Annual Conference he was told that his days as itinerant evangelist were over; he was being reassigned to circuit work. To his parents-in-law he wrote,

> For some time I have been aware that a party was forming against me. Now it has developed itself and its purpose. It has attacked and defeated my friends, and my evangelistic mission is to come to an immediate conclusion. On Saturday, after a debate of five hours, in which I am informed the bitterest spirit was manifested against me, it was decided by 44 to 40 that I be appointed to a circuit. The chief opponents to my continuance in my present course are *ministers*. . . . I care not so much for myself . . . . My concern is for the Connexion—my deep regret is for the spirit this makes manifest, and the base ingratitude it displays.[18]

A perceptive and sympathetic layman, not infected with the clergy's *rabies theologorum*, wrote to Booth,

> I believe that as far as the preachers have power, they will close the New Connexion pulpits against you. Human nature is the same in every Conference, whether Episcopalian, Wesleyan, New Connexion, Primitive [i.e., Primitive Methodist] or Quaker. And the only way for men such as you to escape the mental rack and handcuffs is to take out a licence to hawk Salvation from the great Magistrate above, and absolutely refuse to have any other master.[19]

The Booths were appointed to Brighouse, a grimy, industrial town, and were accommodated in the worst part of it. Catherine quickly added up the spiritual emptiness of their superintendent, "a sombre, funereal kind of being, utterly incapable of cooperating with Mr. Booth in his ardent

---

18. Ibid., I, 244 (emphasis Booth's).
19. Ibid., I, 244.

views and plans for the salvation of the people."[20] William, saddened and disappointed at the treatment accorded him by denominational authorities who seemed unable to grasp what impelled him, fervently wished to be "independent of all conclaves, councils, synods and conferences."[21]

This is not to say that Booth had no supporters among the ministers. A few brave men courted denominational sanctions in standing by someone institutionally regarded as an ineradicable irritant. Indeed, following his ordination in 1858 (Booth had been the focus of undisguised denominational outrage before he was even ordained) he wrote of the event,

> I was surprised to find so large a number of revival friends at the Conference. John Ridgeway, William Mills, William Cooke, Turnock and many others are anxious on the question of my reappointment to evangelistic work. Birmingham, Truro, Halifax (my own circuit), Chester, Hawarden, and Macclesficid have presented memorials praying Conference to reinstate me in my former position. The discussion had not come on when the business closed last night.[22]

Booth and others had known that the controversy surrounding him would be a major item on the Conference agenda. The reader can only be struck by the administrative conjuring; the most controversial item in the denomination managed not to get to the floor.

A compromise was suggested at the Conference meeting of 1861. Booth insisted that his vocation could not endure it. The president of Conference, Henry Lofts, decided to settle Booth's future in a private meeting to which only delegates were admitted. He ordered that the chapel gallery be closed immediately. Catherine, seated there, saw at once what Crofts was going to do. Leaping to her feet she cried, "Never!" "Close the doors!" the enraged president of Conference fumed.[23] William

---

20. Ibid., I, 245.
21. Ibid., I, 194.
22. Ibid., I, 248.
23. Collier, 35.

bowed to the president chairing the meeting and walked to the narthex, where he met Catherine at the foot of the gallery stairs. They embraced each other and together departed from the denomination which had frustrated and harassed them for years.

Almost at once he was invited to conduct a short series of meetings in Cornwall. The "short" series continued for eighteen months, during which both William and Catherine preached night after night to the fishermen and townspeople who had rowed and walked miles to attend. The Methodist New Connexion failed to understand that it needed Booth desperately, while he had no need of it at all.

Denominational authorities were glad to see him go. The ferment his ministry fostered inconvenienced bureaucrats. Little wonder that one of Booth's several biographers wrote of the institutional hounding of someone the world will never forget, "Officialdom exists in a system; officialdom has its own dignity to consider; officialdom is mediocrity in purple."[24]

In his letter of resignation Booth was content to leave his exoneration in the hands of God.

> Looking at the past, God is my witness how earnestly and disinterestedly I have endeavoured to serve the Connexion, and knowing that the future will most convincingly and emphatically either vindicate or condemn my present action, I am content to await its verdict.[25]

No one pretends that the future condemned his action.

III: RETENTION AND REPUDIATION

Most significantly Booth retained what he believed to be the substance of Wesley's theology. In 1885 a Methodist writer, Hugh Price Hughes, interviewed Booth for an article in *The Methodist Times*. "Have you any

---

24. Begbie, I, 230.
25. Ibid., I, 253.

special advice for us Methodists?," Hughes asked the now-famous Booth. The latter's reply was swift and simple: "Follow John Wesley, glorious John Wesley."[26] Wesley, it must be remembered, looked upon the doctrine of sanctification as "the grand depositum which God has lodged with the people called Methodists."[27] The doctrine, and, Wesley would have reminded us, the reality of which the doctrine spoke, was characteristically substantive of the Methodist movement, the principle of cohesion of all that it believed and did. William Booth and his followers continued to emphasize sanctification, or renewal by God's Spirit through faith. While Wesley and Booth did not disagree with the sixteenth-century Reformers' understanding of total depravity ("Allow this," said Wesley of total depravity, "and you are so far a Christian; deny it, and you are but a heathen still"[28]) as well as the transaction wrought in the atonement, they both considered the Reformed tradition to have undervalued transformation; they were convinced that God could do something with sin beyond forgiving it.

This is not to say that everything in Booth's understanding of sanctification and holiness can be found explicitly in Wesley. In fact for years many have felt that The Salvation Army's understanding of sanctification lies closer to that of John Fletcher, a Methodist thinker whom Wesley knew and loved, than precisely to that of Wesley himself. Nevertheless, the spirit of Wesley's doctrine is the spirit of Booth's. Nowhere, as far anyone knows, has Booth spoken a critical word about Wesley.

Again, this does not mean that Booth shared Wesley's theological sophistication. Wesley was steeped in Patristics; Booth would not have known Athanasius from Ambrose. Wesley was Oxford University trained and multi-lingual; Booth left school early in order to apprentice to a pawnbroker. Wesley was schooled in the Reformers and drank deeply of the Puritan wisdom lodged in his grandfather and his wife's grandfather

---

26. Hughes, "An Interview with William Booth on The Salvation Army," *The Methodist Times*, 5 February 1885, 81–82.
27. Wesley, *Letters*, VII, 15 September 1790.
28. Wesley, *Sermons* (Burwash, ed.), "On Original Sin."

as well; Booth merely insisted that the doctrine of double predestination was an abomination. Nevertheless the ethos of Wesleyanism, particularly the vision of such thoroughgoing transformation as to set no limits to the efficacy of God's grace, Booth believed himself to have retained in his work and witness. One might say that while Booth possessed relatively little of that theological erudition which saturated Wesley, he profited much from the explicit theology which Wesley breathed into his followers.

Another Wesleyan aspect which Booth retained had to do with the unchurched. When the MNC forbade Booth to be an itinerant evangelist and instead appointed him to circuit work, he did not find himself preaching to an empty church. Wherever he preached the sanctuary overflowed—often more than a thousand attempted to hear him. The problem for him was not that no one came to church; the problem was that those who came were the Sunday congregation. Repeatedly he asked himself one question: "Why am I here with this crowded chapel of people who want to hear the message? Why am I not outside bringing the message of God to those who don't want to hear it?[29] Before Booth, Wesley had taken up outdoor preaching when he was startled at its effectiveness with George Whitefield. Since Whitefield, a spirit-quenching superiority had settled upon the MNC; it felt that such an endeavour decidedly lacked that taste preferred by those with social aspirations. For this reason Booth also rented buildings to which came hordes of people who would never have attended a conventional place of worship.

When Wesley had commended the gospel at mineheads, in factories and in the marketplace to those who would otherwise never have heard it, it was a miracle that he could communicate with people who were light-years removed from him in terms of formal education; it was surely a greater miracle that he wanted to. (An equal miracle, albeit remote from Booth's passion, was found in George Whitefield; the son of an English barmaid communicated effectively with England's social elites.)

---

29. Collier, 33.

Like Wesley, Booth was extraordinarily gifted at speaking compellingly to those whom the church customarily slighted.

Another retention has to do with hymnody. Virtually everyone in Wesley's family was gifted poetically, his younger brother, Charles, outshining them all. Charles, it must be remembered, wrote three times as much poetry as William Wordsworth. Booth was similarly gifted, as were several others in his family, especially his son, Herbert. Booth's hymns are idiosyncratically marked by images of vastness.

> O boundless salvation, deep ocean of love,
> O fullness of mercy Christ brought from above.
> The whole world redeeming, so rich and so free,
> Now flowing for all men, come roll over me.[30]

Perhaps the best evidence of Booth's retention of Wesley is found in The Salvation Army's hymnbook: the genius of Charles Wesley has been preserved.

Booth's repudiations of the Methodist New Connexion abound. He repudiated entirely the MNC's characteristic sharing of church government with lay people. While no Christian leader to his time had used lay people as effectively as Booth, he refused to share authority with them. Modelling his organization on the military and naval mindset of the British empire in the Victorian era, Booth insisted that the distinction between clergy ("officers") and lay people remain ironfast. In this regard he repudiated the MNC but retained the autocracy of Wesley himself. Booth had become exasperated with the ponderous, cumbersome stodginess of lay committees and subcommittees which debate and defer only to delay or defeat the deployment of the one thing which the Spirit is urging for needy people. When asked why The Salvation Army had so few committees Booth replied laconically, "If there had been committee meetings in the days of Moses the children of Israel would never have got across the Red Sea." (It is only fair to add that Booth's totalitarianism

---

30. *The Song Book of the Salvation Army* (London: Salvationist Publishing and Supplies, 1953), #167.

was the source of major grief and disruption relatively quickly; several of his relatives departed, unable to endure a dictatorship with whose edicts they disagreed.) In Booth's defense it should be stated that upon leaving the MNC and forming The Christian Mission he was saddled with a committee of thirty-four which met only once a year. In view of the rapidity with which Booth added up what had to be done and the speed with which he himself wanted to move in doing it, and in view of the formative decisions which have to be made quickly in the birth of a new movement, the committee of thirty-four was hopelessly inefficient. George Scott Railton, an early and ardent supporter of Booth, himself fed up with procedural labyrinths, turned to Booth and said, "*You* tell us what to do and we shall do it."[31] While Wesley was alive he and he alone ruled Methodism; when Elijah's mantle fell on Booth (Booth thought), Booth liked the fit. Here Booth repudiated everything Kilham and his colleagues had suffered to effect in the New Connexion.

Booth, it must be remembered, insisted initially that he did not want to found a sect. He wanted only to form an evangelistic agency for those for whom (namely, all of us) the hands of the clock registered two minutes to twelve. All authority is given to military officers in combat inasmuch as any other arrangement will only guarantee the destruction of those in danger. For Booth waging war was more than a metaphor; waging war was literal truth.

Another aspect of nineteenth-century Methodism which Booth repudiated was its non-deployment of women preachers.[32] In the course of Sunday worship during their sojourn in Brighouse, Catherine arose from her seat and walked slowly down the aisle towards her husband. He

---

31. Ibid., 55.
32. While Wesley had ordained no women, he had permitted women to preach. Upon his death, however, women preachers were silenced. The principal issue at the Methodist Conference of 1803 was, "Should women be permitted to preach among the Methodists?"" For amplification of this point see Victor Shepherd, "Women Preachers in Early Day Methodism," *Fellowship Magazine* (Barrie: United Church Renewal Fellowship, Sept. 2001), 10–11.

assumed that his wife was ill and needed assistance. Instead she ascended the pulpit stairs, stood beside her husband, and announced that she had come forward to make public confession of sin. "I have been disobeying God," she blurted as she unfolded her resistance to her vocation to preach.[33] Booth, aware that this was a vocation, and aware too that it was anathema in the churches of his era, yet also knew that vocations must be confirmed and sealed. He informed the congregation that Catherine would preach that evening. In no time she enthralled crowds, and in no time MNC authorities disapproved. Catherine was adamant:

> I have searched the Word of God through and through. I have tried to deal honestly with every passage on the subject . . . I solemnly assert that the more I think and read on the subject, the more satisfied I become of the true and scriptural character of my views . . . what endears the Christian religion to my heart is what it has done, and is destined to do, for my own sex.[34]

She preached until she died at age sixty-one. The daughter of a clergyman and better educated than her husband, schooled in philosophy, literature and history, she was transparently possessed of compassion for addicted men and women, many of whom were illiterate. Not content to address these people, she fearlessly walked indescribable streets where desperate human beings lived in near-savagery. Subsequently she wrote,

> I remember in one case finding a poor woman lying on a heap of rags. She had just given birth to twins, and there was nobody of any sort to wait upon her . . . . By her side was a crust of bread and a small lump of lard . . . . The babies I washed in a broken pie-dish, the nearest approach to a tub that I could find. And the gratitude of those large eyes, that gazed upon me from that wan and shrunken face, can never fade from my memory.[35]

---

33. Ibid., 34.
34. Begbie, I, 208 (emphasis Catherine Booth's).
35. Ibid., 1, 249.

NEW CONNEXION METHODISM AND WILLIAM BOOTH

For years William Booth quipped, "Some of my best men are women." Among his officers he never hesitated to promote women over men. (This tradition continues. A recent leader of The Salvation Army was a woman, Eva Burrows.)

A third area where Booth distanced himself from his precursors concerns the sacraments. He never forbade his people to partake of the sacraments, and in fact continued to administer them himself for several years after leaving the MNC. In his preoccupation with evangelism, however, he noticed increasingly that people put their confidence in the sacrament itself, rather in that reality (namely Jesus Christ) to which the sacrament pointed and which can be received only in faith. Convinced that we are born in sin, are not heirs of the kingdom of heaven, and urgently need a new standing before God (forgiveness) and a new nature as well (regeneration), Booth regarded any notion of sacramental efficacy as superstitious (because untrue) and dangerous (because deceptive). The water of baptism does not cleanse anyone of original sin; the rite of baptism does not alter the child before God. Since baptism, for Booth, was symbolic, his people could submit to it if they felt that doing so strengthened their faith; they could also, Quaker-like, decline it. Ever on the lookout for religious formalism devoid of spiritual reality, Booth suspected any churchly activity which diminished one's awareness of the need of conversion. There is but one genuine baptism, he insisted, the baptism of the Holy Spirit. There is but one genuine communion, faith-communion with Jesus Christ. Here, of course, Booth repudiated Wesley utterly. As an Anglican priest, Wesley not only had insisted that Methodists be faithful in their attendance at Holy Communion; Wesley had even said that the Lord's Supper was a converting sacrament, as well as a confirming one.

The sixteenth-century Reformers had said that the sacraments were God-ordained primarily to strengthen weak faith. Booth maintained that they could strengthen weak faith for those who thought they could; increasingly, however, he came to feel that more often than not the sacraments, or at least the public's quasimagical view of the sacraments, obscured the need for faith, and to this extent could be spiritually deleterious. Oddly enough, when in 1882 The Salvation Army still administered the sacraments, a magazine article noted that for the first time in the history of the church, Holy Communion had been administered by women.[36] At an Exeter Hall meeting in 1889, Booth said characteristically, "Neither water, sacraments, church services nor Salvation Army methods will save you without a living, inward change of heart and a living, active faith and communion with God."[37]

In any discussion of Booth's repudiations it is natural to look for formal theological disagreement since so many denominational splits are rooted in doctrinal differences. It is all the more surprising, then, to realize that with one exception (the role of the laity in church government) Booth never distanced himself doctrinally from the MNC. The cleavage lay, rather, in ethos. While Booth and the MNC used the same vocabulary and subscribed to the same doctrine, he felt the denomination now upheld the 'salvation' of the newly-respectable, whereas he saw all of humankind facing the same judge, meriting the same condemnation, standing together on the brink of eternal loss. His passion for evangelism was commensurate with his conviction of human peril. In addition, while MNC authorities opted to do nothing for those deemed not to be "our sort of people," Booth's heart was broken by the material bleakness, degradation and dehumanization which was largely the part of the masses whose lives were governed by the "Satanic mills" of urban putrefaction. His denomination never owned his zeal, his compassion, his urgency, his preoccupation. This is not to say that it was wrong and Booth right. Neither is it to say the converse. It is, however, to recognize afresh that wisdom always awaits justification at the hands of her children.

---

36. "Noncomformist and Independent," 9 February 1882 in Kew, *Closer Communion* (London: Salvationist Publishing and Supplies, 1980), p. 42.

37. Kew, 50.

13

THOMAS C. ODEN

Exemplar of the Methodist Ethos

Thomas C. Oden, a lifelong Methodist, was a noted professor and writer prior to his 'self-outing' as an evangelical three decades ago. Since then his name has become fragrant in behalf of several important concerns.

One such is the leadership he has afforded his own denomination, The United Methodist Church (U.S.A.). Here he has proved himself an articulate spokesperson of theological recovery and a credible leader of spiritual renewal.

Another is the encouragement he has provided for beleaguered pastors, denominational officials, and near-voiceless lay people in mainline denominations. The latter have been declining since the mid-1960s. While it would be an unrealistically roseate reading of the situation to suggest that the decline has been halted, members of these denominations are reluctant to abandon them if only because such members

---

* This chapter was commisioned by and appeared in *Biographical Dictionary of Evangelicals* (Downer's Grove: InterVarsity Press, 2002), pp. 484-487.

recognize that their institution is rooted more deeply than most of the newer denominations in the tradition of the universal church. The deeper root means that sorely-needed water and nutrients can be accessed. Such water and nutrients may yet irrigate and invigorate parched, anaemic areas of the wider church whose future is otherwise bleak.

Oden is not naïve. He is aware that theological and spiritual and pastoral negligence have put North American mainline denominations at risk. But neither is he pessimistic. Aware at all times of church history, he is no less aware that the ship under the cross has taken on water perilously many times over, only to be stabilized and re-directed by the Lord of the church who has pledged himself irrevocably to his people.

In the earlier part of his career Oden, by his own admission, uncritically borrowed from the mind-set of modernity, incorporating it unwisely into the theology he was writing at the time. While not aspiring now to be a theological romantic who no less uncritically adulates the pre-modern, Oden has nevertheless come to appreciate the wisdom of the early church, especially that of the Church Fathers. Aware that keel and ballast in a sailboat allow it to sail across or against the wind (without keel and ballast a sailboat can only be driven before the wind, welcome or not), and aware too that keel and ballast allow the same boat to right itself after being knocked over in sudden squalls, Oden has come to see that the Church Fathers, together with the recognized giants of the Christian tradition, provide the church with a stability and recoverability without which it will either meander or sink. In other words, the great weight of the tradition is the instrument the Lord of the church uses to see his people home at last.

In respect of his appreciation of the Church Fathers Oden has undertaken the editorship of the *Ancient Christian Commentary on Scripture*. He knows that we are not the first generation of Christians; that our foreparents have much to teach us; that the challenges facing the church today are not new (e.g., multiculturalism and religious diversity); that there are many family-groups among Christ's people that any one family has overlooked if not dismissed. In this regard Oden has probed the contribution of the Eastern Church as well as the Western, the Fathers as well as the apostles, and the medievalists. Not surprisingly his *Ancient Christian Commentary on Scripture* has drawn on Greek, Latin, Coptic and Syriac sources.

In all of this Oden resembles his theological progenitor, John Wesley. Wesley was a student at Oxford University at the close of an era of fertile Patristic scholarship there. Wesley absorbed the Fathers, had a thorough command of their theology and referred to them normatively throughout the three-dozen volumes he penned. He maintained that the best way of avoiding theological seduction was to school oneself in Scripture and the Fathers. He was thoroughly apprised of the Eastern contribution. (While not disdaining the Western Fathers, he remained suspicious of the West's most visible representative, Augustine, on account of the latter's espousal of predestination.)

Oden resembles Wesley no less in his concern for the spiritual wellbeing of the people of God. Just as Wesley wrote and spoke so as to be understood by those without his educational privilege, Oden has concerned himself with pastoral theology and practice in a way that keeps pace with his academic research.

In much the way that Elijah's mantle fell upon Elisha, Wesley's cloak has come to adorn Oden. He remains a faithful steward of Wesley's legacy, a diligent explorer of long-buried riches now being unearthed, and, not least, a Methodist thinker with the heart of a Methodist evangelist.

A BIOGRAPHICAL SKETCH

Thomas Clark Oden was born on October 21, 1931, in Altus, Oklahoma. His father was a lawyer and his mother a music teacher. In 1949 he enrolled in the University of Oklahoma and graduated with a B.Litt. in 1953. He began studying theology formally at Perkins School of Theology (Southern Methodist University), graduating with his B.D. in 1956. Ordained by the Oklahoma Conference of the United Methodist Church (deacon, 1954; elder, 1956), he served in varied parish ministries. Beginning in 1956 he studied at Yale University, and was awarded his

M.A. in 1958 and his Ph.D. in 1960. Hans Frei and H.Richard Niebuhr supervised his work. His doctoral dissertation, revised for publication, was published as *Radical Obedience: The Ethics of Rudolf Bultmann*. One year of postdoctoral study followed at Heidelberg.

In 1958 he began his professional teaching career as an instructor at Perkins School of Theology. From 1960 to 1970 he was associate professor and then professor at Phillips University. In 1971 he became the Henry Anson Buttz Professor of theology at Drew University, where he taught until his retirement.

Oden has also been a guest lecturer or visiting professor at Moscow State University, Oxford, Edinburgh, Duke, Emory, Princeton and Claremont. In addition he has been consultant to the Ethics and Public Policy Center of Washington, D.C., the White House Dialogue on Urban Initiatives (1985), and Public Information Office Briefings (1984–1986.)

Oden has published approximately forty books and eighty articles.

Following his *Agenda for Theology* (1978) republished as *After Modernity, What?* (1990) with four additional chapters and an introduction by J. I. Packer, Oden described himself as an "out-of-the-closet evangelical." He has continued to distance himself from the ethos of the institutions, images and "isms" that earlier he wore as a badge. His *Requiem: A Lament in Three Movements* (1995) is anguished autobiography concerning the lethal stranglehold that totalitarian "liberals" have on denominational bureaucracies, church conferences, and seminary education. A former left-wing radical, he now affirms the genuine radix of the Scripture-normed authority of the post-apostolic writers. His "new" radicalism, inspired and measured by the gospel, nevertheless finds him still espousing out-of-step causes, such as the utter unreformability of the seminaries unless the practice of tenure is overhauled.

Recently Oden has become a contributing editor of *Christianity Today*. His position there magnifies his influence enormously, as this magazine is the most widely-read evangelical journal in North America.

Never backing away from rendering the judgments that he deems gospel-fidelity to enjoin, Oden has made the rare move of publicly faulting another denomination in another country. The United Church of Canada

(Canada's largest Protestant denomination, formed in 1925 of Methodists, Presbyterians and Congregationalists), Oden has pronounced devoid of ecumenical identity, "and is no longer thought properly to be called an ecumenical communion"; i.e., is no longer the church in that it has abandoned consensual teaching on creation, sin, covenant sexual fidelity and the blessings of marriage.

By his own admission every turn that Oden took on his way to the theological position with which he is now identified was a left turn. The "turn" that "righted" him, however, was not a right turn or series of compensatory right turns but rather a turn back into the Fathers. Startled at the shallowness and virulence of 1960s radicalism, he looked for theological resources and discovered that Patristic thinkers exhibited a profundity and pertinence that few modern authors could rival.

Oden describes himself as an "orthodox, ecumenical evangelical," where orthodoxy "is nothing more or less than the ancient consensual tradition of exegesis." His work aims at articulating, in the spirit of Vincent of Lérins, the faith of the universal church.

Its focus is the consensus of the first five centuries, since "antiquity is a criterion of authentic memory in any historical testimony." His preoccupation with antiquity means he refuses to renounce his "zeal for unoriginality....the apostles were testy with revisionists."

Its mood is evangelical, reflecting throughout the gospel's particularity and inherent militancy. This mood contrasts sharply with a theological modernity whose treachery has rendered evangelism impossible and orthodoxy unrecognizable. An evangelical invitation suffuses his work as he urges readers to decide for Christ, warning them tenderly yet solemnly about the peril of procrastination: "One who neglects an opportunity at hand may not have another."

Its centre is the rediscovery of ancient ecumenical theology and the recovery of classical Christianity in his evolving Wesleyan tradition.

Its target audience is the working pastor, since Christian teaching is healthy only where living tradition is embodied by an actual community. (See, for instance, his *Pastoral Theology: Essentials of Ministry*).

Its orientation is that for which he commends Arminius and those after Arminius; viz., "the gradual Protestant retrieval of the ancient ecumenical consensus on grace and freedom." In this regard Oden consistently disavows the predestinarianism of the later Augustine (even as Augustine remains one of the ecumenical giants) that emerged so very strongly in the Magisterial Reformers. Oden regards this deterministic misunderstanding of election as a departure and declension from the received faith. Characteristically the church has upheld the inviolability of the humanness of God's covenant partners. At the same time Oden discerns and denounces the error of Pelagianism, together with the more subtle seductiveness of semi-Pelagianism. His work incorporates everywhere a nuanced discussion of *gratia operans/gratia co-operans* that, while strange to Protestants who are unacquainted with Patristic thought, is crucial in any approach to him.

Its most recent expression is the project he is masterminding, *Ancient Christian Commentary on Scripture*, whose purpose is the recovery of classical Christian exegesis. A major strength of this project, he maintains, is the reviving of texts so very old that they contain no trace of European imperialism (and therefore no inherent revulsion, for instance, for Asian and African Christians). These texts will therein prove singularly significant as they are brought to bear on the cultural formation of both West and East. In addition ancient exegesis will expose readers to the intimate connection between prayer and study, to the relation of theology to vibrant Christian community, and to worship as the context in which Scripture is read. Oden hopes that Protestants especially will peruse the *Ancient Commentary*. Their doing so will remedy the theological one-sidedness that arises on account of Protestantism's neglect of pre-Reformation texts, and also reduce Pietism's extreme vulnerability to modern consciousness. They can expect to be startled, for instance, by Nazianzen's theological power and Jerome's transparency to the Spirit's energy.

Repeatedly Oden indicates why he has written polemically and prolifically. While theology as the inquiry into God is inherently the most engaging of all subjects, theologians have turned it "into a yawning bore," boring just because it is so very destructive: heresy is treasonous, and when protracted, tedious. Aware, however, of the presumption that laps at anyone claiming to be a corrective, the stated motive for his three-volume *Systematic Theology* (1987, 1989, 1992) was an invitation for readers to test his own fallibility.

Everywhere Oden sees his work as setting a limit to the license of "guild" (i.e., academically appointed) theologians and exegetes whose perfidy has summoned him to be "someone to teach you the elementary truths of God's word all over again." (Heb. 5:12) For this reason his work as a whole and his systematic theology in particular repristinate the elemental, doctrinal "building blocks" of the faith; specifically, theological matters that are articulated in the creed and that appear in the standard *regulae fidei*. (Precise studies of more detailed matters such as anthropology, liturgy and ethics will be developed in subsequent works.)

Throughout his writings Oden looks first to the four great Patristic thinkers of the east and west: Athanasius, Basil, Gregory Nazianzen, John Chrysostom, together with Ambrose, Augustine, Jerome, Gregory the Great. These exegetes consistently clarify the mind of the believing church; "we are more indebted to these eight exegetes than any since the apostles." While Oden cites other thinkers frequently (especially Thomas Aquinas, Luther and Calvin) they are invoked where they amplify the aforementioned consensus, not where their work is idiosyncratic. Other thinkers deemed non-consensual (e.g., Menno Simons) are scarcely mentioned at all.

Oden's single largest work is his *Systematic Theology* (1500 pages, 15,000 references to classical writings.) Its purpose is "to set forth an ordered view of the faith of the Christian community upon which there has generally been substantial agreement between the traditions of East and West, including Catholic, Protestant and Orthodox." Unlike virtually all systematic theologians, however, Oden insists that the exposition of the traditional theological topics in his work serves primarily as an introduction to the annotations; i.e., the annotations embedded in the text are more important than the text itself. True to Scripture, to his native Wesleyanism, and to the Fathers, he regards God's holiness as the linchpin of the entire theological enterprise.

Oden's theological "journey" brought him to this point after earlier starts that if not false were hesitant at least.

He names five theological instructors who shaped his thought: Albert Outler, Rudolf Bultmann, H.Richard Niebuhr, Karl Barth and Will Herberg. Despite the apparent neo-orthodoxy of three of these men, Oden subsequently criticized neo-orthodoxy for its non-interest in worship, sacrament, pastoral care, the concrete tasks of ministry, and the holiness of the church. His "best" teacher was Outler, who introduced him to Augustine and Wesley. Although his Ph.D. dissertation was a comparative study of Bultmann and Barth, he soon repudiated the favoured Bultmannism that had first brought him to theological prominence and concentrated on Barth. In the 1960s Oden was concerned chiefly with the relation of theology to psychotherapy. Attentive now to the necessity, nature and integrity of human agency, he came to regard the Eastern church fathers as a corrective to Barth's one-sidedness.

Upon Oden's appointment to Drew University his friend and colleague, Will Herberg, persuaded him to ground his thinking in classical sources. Ironically, says Oden, a conservative Jew was his chief mentor in classical Christianity. With the arbitrariness and weakness of his earlier liberalism now exposed, and repulsed by his former support of the abortion platform, he abandoned situation ethics and with it the entire liberal worldview. Rejecting too his earlier notion that novelty is the task of theology, he jettisoned "creativity," now convinced, thanks to J.H. Newman, that his responsibility was to listen to the deposit of truth already sufficiently given. Intrigued by the decisions of the ancient Ecumenical Councils, he plunged into Patristics. Quickly he identified himself in terms of "paleo-orthodoxy," an expression coined to indicate the distance now between him and neo-orthodoxy. By his own admission modern psychology had taught him to trust his experience, whereas ancient writers now taught him to trust that Scripture and tradition would transmute his experience.

THOMAS C. ODEN

Oden has endeavoured to honour his theological parents by means of two books related to Wesley. *Doctrinal Standards in the Wesleyan Tradition* (1988) assesses the nature, place and function of normative doctrine in the United Methodist Church specifically and in the churches of the Wesleyan family generally. It aims at healing the doctrinal amnesia that has largely afflicted mainline North American Methodists.

John Wesley's Scriptural Christianity (1994) expounds Wesley's theology on all major points, beginning in the time-honoured way with God's attributes and concluding with eschatology. It is a contemporary exposition and interpretation of Wesley's thought, aiming always at fidelity to Wesley's text. Its subordinate purpose is to convey Wesley to other branches of the Christian family in view of the fact that non-Wesleyans are much less acquainted with Wesley's thought than are non-Magisterial thinkers, for instance, with that of the sixteenth-century Reformers.

Finding Wesley rooted in the Patristic, Anglican, holy living and Puritan traditions, he sees Wesleyanism as a bridge between Protestants and Catholics, even as it has profound affinities with the Eastern Church tradition. He deems Wesleyanism's characteristic resistance to co-optation at the hands of party or fad to be one of its major strengths.

Two areas that seem problematic for evangelicals are his seemingly uncritical espousal of the Fathers and an "ecumenical" view of baptism that some may find indistinguishable from sacramental regeneration.

Concerning the first matter Oden affirms repeatedly his agreement with the Fathers that in the "theandric" (sic) One the humanity suffers but never the deity. Specifically he denies that the Father suffers in the Son's crucifixion. Nowhere does Oden acknowledge that the risen, exalted Lord continues to suffer. In the same vein the neo-Platonism of the Fathers is unchecked. Oden cites with apparent approval the Patristic neo-Platonism concerning sexual matters, such as Nazianzen's pronouncement that Christ's birth "didn't have its origin in weakness... for sensual pleasure did not precede the birth." A similarly neo-Platonic argument is advanced as to why there will be no marrying in heaven. Circumcision is understood to consecrate "that organ...which...is most likely to be corrupted by idolatry and sin." (His commentary on the

Pastoral Epistles, relieved of uncritical support of the Fathers, upholds a more Hebraic understanding of sexuality.)

Concerning the second matter Oden, to be sure, insists "it is not baptism of itself that saves," yet he appears to undo this assertion throughout his discussion of baptism, as in his remark, "The Holy Spirit through baptism offers, calls forth, and elicits regeneration in a spiritually blessed water in which the whole triune God is by grace effectively present," and "The Spirit remains in those who have received the grace of baptism, who remain indelibly known to God." He appears impelled to speak this way inasmuch as the Fathers do.

Oden predicts that a sign of hope in twenty-first century Christian thought will be its preoccupation with the rediscovery of boundaries in theology: "I would love to find a seminary where a discussion is taking place about whether a line can be drawn between faith and unfaith."

A diligent student and teacher of Kierkegaard for decades, Oden's mature work can be summarized in an item cited in his *Parables of Kierkegaard* (1978.) Faith disrupts, says the Dane, and where public disruption isn't observable, faith hasn't occurred. If as "believers" we nevertheless protest that we have faith, we are theologians; if we know how to describe faith, we are poets; if we weep in describing faith, actors. But only as we witness for the truth and against untruth are we actually possessed of faith.

14

NEITHER MIST NOR MUD

In the summer of 1976 I was visiting professor at Memorial University of Newfoundland. A nearly-retired clergyman who had been in Newfoundland all his life commented on Newfoundland churchmanship of yesteryear: "The Presbyterians had scholarship, while we Methodists had religion." The disjunction he spoke of is non-biblical, since, for one, God is to be worshipped with the mind, and for another, to worship one-knows-not-what is simply to worship an idol. I shall not comment on turn-of-the-century Methodism in Newfoundland. But I can tell you what Wesley's reaction would have been if such a disjunction had been attributed to him: he would have considered himself falsified, even maligned.

There is no doubt concerning the theological dilution of the largest Methodist body which formed the larger part of The United Church of Canada in 1925; i.e., no doubt concerning the doctrinal flaccidity of this branch of the Wesleyan family. As I have sought to find out why and how the largest segment of the Wesleyan family in Canada could unravel

---

* An address delivered at the installation of the Rev. Dr. Victor A. Shepherd in the Donald N. and Kathleen G. Bastian Chair of Wesley Studies, Tyndale University College & Seminary.

theologically so very badly I have heard countless references to Wesley's sermon, "Catholic Spirit."[1] It is often suggested to me that Methodism is characteristically theologically indifferent, even suggested that Wesley himself was—as "Catholic Spirit" is referred to (but not quoted unless quoted out of context) again and again.

The truth is Wesley knew that doctrine has to do with the truth of God; that doctrine is essential to the soundness of anyone's faith and essential to the soundness of the church. Then what of his sermon, "Catholic Spirit"? Did he lapse momentarily in this one sermon and unwittingly sow the seeds of the very distortion which has haunted at least the larger North American bodies which bear his name?

In fact Wesley never jettisoned—nor thought could be jettisoned— what he held to be the core, the essentials, of the Christian faith. At the same time, to be sure, he deplored what he deemed to be unnecessary quarrelling among Christians. For instance, while he remained enormously indebted to Puritan thinkers of the preceding century, he thought Puritan disputants themselves unnecessarily contentious. Wesley stood opposed in equal measure to dogmatism with respect to non-essentials and indifference with respect to essentials. Then does his "Catholic Spirit" atypically support the cavalierness to the substance of the faith which the sponsors of the chair I am to occupy rightly resist as surely as other denominations with a Wesleyan root have not resisted?

The text for "Catholic Spirit" is 2 Kings 10:15 (KJV). "And when he [Jehu] was departed thence, he lighted on Jehonadab the son of Rechab coming to meet him. And he saluted him and said, 'Is thine heart right, as my heart is with thy heart? And Jehonadab answered, It is. [Jehu said], If it be, give me thine hand." We know that Wesley preached on this text on November 23, 1740; September 8, 1749; and November 3, 1749. Likely he preached on it on other occasions as well. The sermon was first published in 1750, then republished in 1755 and 1770. Evidently

---

1. For all references to Wesley's sermon "Catholic Spirit" in the remainder of this chapter see *Works of John Wesley, Bicentennial Edition* (Nashville: Abingdon Press, 1987) pp.79–96.

Wesley deemed its subject-matter important. The latter two editions were graced by the addition of Charles's forty-two line hymn, "Catholic Love," one stanza of which is

> Weary of all this wordy strife,
> These notions, forms, and modes and names,
> To Thee, the Way, the Truth, the Life,
> Whose love my simple heart inflames,
> Divinely taught, at last I fly,
> With thee and thine to live and die.

Then did Charles support the notion that any attempt at doctrinal precision is but "wordy strife"? In order to answer this question we must probe the sermon itself.

Wesley's first point is that "love is due to all mankind"—including, he is careful to add, those who curse us and hate us. Yet there is a "peculiar love" which we owe fellow-believers. All Christians know this and approve it; and just as surely all Christians fail here. Wesley adduces "two grand general hindrances"; Christians "can't all think alike, and in consequence of this...they can't all walk alike". He admits that differences in opinions or modes of worship may prevent "entire external union"; but "need it prevent union in affection?....May we not be of one heart, though we are not of one opinion?"

As he ponders the text Wesley notes that it "naturally divides itself into two parts": Jehu's question to Jehonadab, and Jehu's welcome to Jehonadab following the latter's positive reply. Wesley immediately notes that Jehu's question concerns Jehonadab's heart, not Jehonadab's opinion. And to be sure Jehonadab had opinions unusual in Israel, impressing as he did upon his children and grandchildren the Rechabite vow which eschewed wine, and forswearing the security of farms and homes for the landlessness and tents of nomads. Jehu, for his part, so far from being offended or contemptuous, was content to "think and let think"—and a good thing too, says Wesley, since as we "see in part" (1 Cor. 13:12) we shall not all see things alike. Then he adds a comment which all Wesleyans (indeed all Christians) must note carefully. Our not all seeing things alike is a consequence of "the present weakness and shortness of human understanding," to be redressed only in the eschaton. Our not all seeing things alike with respect to opinion is not the consequence of that darkened, foolish mind which is a predicate of human depravity. Culpable ignorance of God, on the other hand—always to be distinguished from differences of opinion—is the product of the darkened mind of the depraved, as Wesley acknowledges throughout his works.

Concerning opinion Wesley mentions modes of worship. Some Christians are convinced of the virtues of the Anglican Prayer Book while others are convinced of the virtues of the Free Church tradition. We "think and let think." However, he adds immediately, a churchless Christian is a contradiction in terms. One is a Christian only as one worships with fellow-Christians in a particular congregation. Plainly the mode of worship is of the order of opinion, while corporate worship is of the order of essential.

Jehu's question, "Is thine heart right...?" has to do not with opinions but with essentials. What are they, or at least some of them?

The first, according to Wesley, is, "Is thy heart right with God? Dost thou believe his being, and his perfections? His eternity, immensity, wisdom, power; his justice, mercy and truth?....Hast thou a divine evidence, a supernatural conviction, of the things of God?" Obviously our belief in God's attributes and activity does not concern opinions but essentials; and just as obviously Wesley is careful to balance the objective and the subjective, head and heart. Judiciously he avoids identifying Christian experience ("Hast thou ...a supernatural conviction...?") with mere doctrinal assent; and just as judiciously he avoids identifying Christian experience with normless subjectivism.

The next aspect in Wesley's delineation of what it means to have one's heart right is, "Dost thou believe in the Lord Jesus Christ, 'God over all...'?" The doctrine of the incarnation is bedrock-essential. Nothing less than the most elemental apostolic confession, "Jesus is Lord," will do. There is no suggestion in Wesley of a crypto-Arianism or crypto-unitarianism. And then once again there is that careful balance, typical of Wesley, between objective truth and the believing subject's appropriation of the person of him whose truth it is: "Dost thou know 'Jesus Christ and him crucified'?....Is he 'formed in thy heart by faith'?" Then Wesley adds what he, a son of the Reformation, will always insist on; namely, justification by faith. "Having absolutely disclaimed all thy own works, thy own righteousness, hast thou 'submitted thyself unto the righteousness of God', 'which is by faith in Christ Jesus'?" And lest those rendered righteous (i.e., rightly related to God) by faith think that anything but lifelong struggle and discipline await them Wesley comments, "And art thou through him [Jesus Christ] fighting the good fight of faith, and laying hold of eternal life?" Justification by faith is non-negotiable, as is vigorous, rigorous discipleship.

Next Wesley discusses matters which force his readers to search their hearts, as he sounds like a spiritual director, having inherited the seventeenth century Puritan tradition of spiritual direction. Puritanism abounded in those who were especially adept at helping others discern the movement of grace within them and helping them discern and deal with impediments to this movement. Here Wesley is brief and blunt: "Dost thou seek all thy happiness in him [God] alone?....Has the love of God cast the love of the world out of thy soul?" And then he zeroes in: we must love God for no other reason than God is who God is. We are not to love God instrumentally (that is, because we need something from God); neither are we to love God primarily to avoid the perils of judgment. "Art thou more afraid of displeasing God than either of death or of hell?"—otherwise, Wesley knows, our fear is still an excrescence of that self-preoccupation from which we need to be delivered.

Lastly he asks, "Do you 'love your enemies'?"

The foregoing has nothing to do with opinion, everything to do with essentials. Therefore, says Wesley, he will extend his hand to anyone whose heart is right in the sense of what has been outlined above.

It remains for him to tell us what it means to give one's hand to another. It does not mean that the two shaking hands will hold the same opinion. Nevertheless, it will mean that they genuinely love each other. Lest such "love" be nothing more than sentimental rhetoric Wesley pleads, "Love me with a very tender affection...as a friend that is closer than a brother." In case we still fail to understand him Wesley amplifies this: "Love me with a love...that is patient if I am ignorant and out of the way, bearing and not increasing my burden...." And if you, a believer, find me, a believer too, sinning, says Wesley, love me so as to recognize that I sinned "in sudden stress of temptation."

To give one's hand to another, Wesley informs us briefly, is always to pray for one another and to encourage one another in love and good works.

Then what does Wesley say a catholic spirit is not?

It is not "speculative latitudinarianism." Christians are not indifferent to opinion. The baptist is as sincere, convinced, in fact, in espousing believer's baptism as the paedobaptist is in espousing the understanding associated with this practice. Since a catholic spirit is not even indifference to opinion, how unthinkable that it could ever be indifference to the essentials of the faith. "A man of truly catholic spirit...is fixed as the sun in his judgment concerning the main branches of Christian doctrine." Those who boast of possessing a catholic spirit "only because you are of a muddy understanding; because your mind is all in a mist"; *those* people, Wesley insists, don't even know what spirit they are of. To sit loose to the substance of the faith is simply to display a mind of mist and mud. These self-deluded people think they "are got into the very spirit of Christ" when in fact they are "nearer the spirit of anti-Christ." Wesley's assertion here must be allowed its full weight: theological indifference reflects the spirit of anti-Christ.

In the second place a catholic spirit is not "practical latitudinarianism." Here Wesley repeats his earlier insistence concerning public worship and "the manner of performing it," as well as his insistence that all Christians must be intimately bound to a congregation which is so dear to us that each of us "regards it as his own household."

Wesley's last admonition to us in his sermon, "Catholic Spirit," is for us to remember that the true catholic spirit is manifested in the daily exercise of catholic love, until that day when faith gives way to sight and we behold that love which God is. Until such time, Wesley advises, "keep an even pace, rooted in the faith once delivered to the saints [for him there could never be any other root] and grounded in love, in true, catholic love, till thou art swallowed up in love for ever and ever."

If any doubt remains as to Wesley's doctrinal orthodoxy and the spiritual rigour required by, because first facilitated by, the One whose truth doctrine apprehends, such doubt is dispelled by one reading of Wesley's sermons. Not all one hundred and fifty need be perused; consulting the first four will suffice. They are "Salvation By Faith," "The Almost Christian," "Awake, Thou That Sleepest," and "Scriptural Christianity."

The first, "Salvation By Faith" (1738), Wesley delivered at Oxford University following his Aldersgate awakening, when he flew his evangelical colours. Here he declared himself one with the sixteenth-century Reformers.

The second sermon, "The Almost Christian" (1741), isn't so much about those who are about to enter the kingdom (or about not to enter it) as it is about the disparity between nominal Christianity and genuine faith in a living Lord. This was not a new theme in British Christendom, the Puritan divines before Wesley having expounded it many times. Still, here Wesley publicly declared himself one with the seventeenth-century Puritans. When Wesley was about to preach this sermon (also at Oxford) he was told that Oxford's theological hostility would find his address without credibility. "I know that," he had replied; "however, I am to deliver my own soul, whether they will hear or whether they will forbear."

The third sermon, "Awake, Thou That Sleepest" (1742), was actually written by Charles and endorsed without qualification by John; it too is a throbbing evangelical statement.

The fourth, "Scriptural Christianity" (1744), Wesley delivered on August 24, the anniversary of two dreadful persecutions visited on people of gospel-conviction: the St.Bartholomew's Day massacre in Paris (1572) and the Great Ejection in England (1662) in which both Wesley's grandfathers suffered cruelly. By this time Wesley knew the price to be paid for adhering to that faith attested by apostles, church Fathers and

Reformers. In his journal he wrote on August 24, 1744, "I preached, I suppose, for the last time at St.Mary's [Oxford]. Be it so. I am now clear of the blood of these men. I have fully delivered my own soul."[2]

And yet it is still heard in some areas of the contemporary church that Wesley had a shallow view of human depravity, that his view of Total Depravity was less "total" than that of the Reformers. This is not true. In his sermon, "Salvation By Faith," Wesley insists that humankind's "heart is altogether corrupt and abominable," that salvation is always and everywhere "an unspeakable gift." "Of yourselves," he continues in the same article, "cometh neither your faith nor your salvation.... that ye believe is one instance of grace; that believing, ye are saved, another." Two hundred plus years earlier John Calvin had spoken of faith as an "empty vessel,"[3] meaning that our faith does not contribute to the substance of our salvation, and therefore we cannot boast that we have, however slightly, saved ourselves. In the same vein Wesley writes, "faith is...a full reliance on the blood of Christ, a trust in the merits of his life, death and resurrection, a recumbency upon him as our atonement and our life...." Then he adds, "in consequence hereof a closing with him and cleaving to him as our 'wisdom, righteousness, sanctification and redemption....'" His citing 1 Corinthians 1:30 here is surely telling, since this text was Calvin's favourite. Wesley did not have a diminished understanding of human helplessness before God; he was not less profound than his Reformation predecessors. In a pithy aphorism reflecting the style of Puritan thinkers dearer to him than even most Methodists grasp, he comments tersely, "none can trust the merits of Christ till he has utterly renounced his own."

Wesley had no truck with a gospel-less Pelagianism or a Christ-less Arianism or a Trinity-less unitarianism; neither did he have any truck with that for which he is blamed often, a degenerate Arminianism. His theology was as soundly apostolic as his spirit was truly catholic.

---

2. *WJW*, Vol. 20, p. 36.

3. Calvin, *Institutes of the Christian Religion* (Philadelphia: The Westminster Press, 1960), 3.2.7.

I was privileged to be the first inductee of the Donald N. and Kathleen G. Bastian Chair of Wesley Studies, Tyndale Seminary. For as long as I occupied the Chair I aspired to hold up before students and faculty, and through them before the wider church, John Wesley himself, in order that they and I, learning together from him, might ever reflect the same passion for the apostolic confession of Jesus Christ, the same zeal for holiness and the same catholic spirit that renders our faith ever that faith which works through love (Galatians 5:6).

PART III

SERMONS

15

SUSANNAH ANNESLEY

Mother of the Wesleys and a "Mother In Israel"

Following the service at which Samuel Annesley baptized his newest daughter he wrote to a friend informing the man of what he had done, adding that his children now numbered "two dozen or a quarter of a hundred, I am not sure which." The latter estimate was correct: Susannah was the most recent—and also the last—of twenty-five children. (Samuel had had one child by his first wife, twenty-four by his second.)

Yet the hardship in Susannah's home during her infancy did not come chiefly from the cash-shortages inevitable in a minister's home with a bevy of children; hardship came rather from the harassment visited on her father and his friends on account of their convictions. In 1662 the British government passed the Act of Uniformity, outlawing any clergyman whose conscience would not allow him to endorse every last aspect of the Church of England. Clergy who objected theologically were deemed untrustworthy politically (i.e., a supposed theological test was used to accuse people of treason). What followed—"The Great Ejection"—hounded ministers out of their pulpits and impoverished their families. Puritan clergy (also known as "Non-conformists" or "Dissenters") hid themselves in haystacks and barns, culverts and "safe houses,"

MERCY IMMENSE AND FREE

preaching clandestinely to the brave people who gathered together secretively. Then in 1672 King Charles II promulgated the Declaration of Indulgence. Now Dissenters could worship in public without being charged with a criminal offence. One year later, however, the Declaration of Indulgence was revoked. To be sure, Dissenters were never set upon again as fiercely as they had been at the time of The Great Ejection; nevertheless, incessant persecution made life difficult for them. In 1682 authorities raided Samuel Annesley's house and seized his goods to pay for fines which had been levied just because he conducted services of worship without reference to the Anglican liturgy. The fines levied against the Puritan clergy were huge. One London minister was fined 840 pounds, when a minister's yearly stipend was commonly thirty pounds.

In view of the savage treatment Annesley received for not conforming to the state church (Anglican), he was dumbfounded when his 12-year-old Susannah told him she was determined to join the state church. Samuel himself had contributed as much as he could spare to the Common Fund, a fund set up to assist Non-Conformist clergy like himself, whose families were in desperate straits. He could not understand why his 12-year-old daughter would make this move. Her reasons for the move were certainly clear to her, for years later she wrote them down and filed them with her papers in the parsonage where she was living as a married woman. No one will ever know what her reasons were, however, as all her papers were destroyed in the famous fire of 1709, the conflagration which nearly consumed her six-year-old son, John. Her father could only remain wounded and perplexed in equal measure.

In an era when the education of girls was largely neglected Susannah's intellectual formation was uncharacteristically rich. She immersed herself in the weighty tomes on her father's library shelves: Reformation and Puritan writings, to be sure, but also the works of Anglican divines, Renaissance humanists, and the classics from the ancient world. Early in life she was exposed to the substance, argumentation and vocabulary of learned people as two dozen Puritan ministers gathered every Monday in her home to discuss the finest points in theology and philosophy. Not surprisingly, her theological knowledge excelled that of many of the clergy of her day, and she learned to use the English language with remarkable precision.

When Susannah was 13 and a guest at her sister's wedding she met a 19-year-old fellow who was instantly attracted to her. Samuel Wesley (it's difficult to keep the "Samuels" straight in this story since Susannah's father, brother, husband, eldest son, and grandson were all given this name) waited six years to marry her in 1688. (By now she was 19, he 26) Susannah's father, a dissenting minister, was forbidden by law to take part in the service.

Almost immediately Susannah's husband (Samuel) displayed the financial recklessness (or at least the financial incompetence) which was to haunt him, her and the children for decades. Samuel could not manage on the clergy stipend of thirty pounds; whereupon he signed on as chaplain of a British warship where he was paid fifty pounds per year. He failed to last even one year, however, appalled as he was at shipboard living conditions. Meanwhile Susannah was living in a boardinghouse in London. Soon her unemployed husband joined her. And soon she was pregnant. Her husband, an assistant minister now in London, divided his time between his ministerial duties and his vainly-conceived literary career. The senior minister, displeased at the lack of attention paid to pastoral matters, fired him. Samuel's literary career was vainly conceived in that he fancied himself a gifted poet and biblical commentator when in fact he was neither. He spent most of his time apparently "lost in inner space"; his poetry—two books of which were titled *Maggots* and *The Tame Snake in a Box of Bran*—was entirely forgettable. He spent twenty-five years and much money preparing a useless commentary, in Latin, on the book of Job. His family in penury now, and his wife continually pregnant, he wrote the Archbishop of York asking for financial assistance, explaining his situation as "one child at least per annum, and my wife sick for half that time."

One suppertime, as prayers were read from the Anglican prayerbook, Samuel noticed that Susannah had not said "Amen" to the prayers for the king. He asked her why she hadn't. "Because he is no king," she replied, "he is but a prince." William of Orange was the ruler at that time. Descended from Dutch royalty, and the husband of the daughter of one of England's kings, he was nonetheless not part of that British royal family appointed to rule Britain, in Susannah's opinion. Her defiance of her husband enraged him, especially as he was counting on his reputation as a supporter of the current king to gain him a better position in the church. "If there are going to be two kings in this family," Samuel fumed, "then there are going to be two beds." He stormed away from his rural parish and headed to London, vowing he would rather do anything than live with someone who was "the declared enemy of his country." He said he would return if Susannah apologized. She countered that she would apologize if it could be shown her where she was wrong. But to apologize when she felt herself to be right; this would be manifest insincerity and therefore sin. Susannah wrote to the archbishop maintaining (i) that she was maritally deprived (by now she had had fourteen children, six surviving), (ii) her husband's absenting himself from her on the grounds of a political disagreement was an infringement of his marriage vow. The archbishop agreed with the latter point. Five months later Samuel was home again. The night he and Susannah were reconciled John Wesley was conceived. Twenty-two years later Susannah wrote John, "'Tis an unhappiness almost peculiar to our family that your father and I seldom think alike."

We can never overestimate the courage and the resilience and the determination which Susannah exemplified every day. By the time she was 36 years old Susannah's husband was in jail for debt. (In other words, the family was penniless.) Unending financial difficulties and more than a dozen pregnancies had worn her down. And then in June, 1705, her 3-week-old baby died. "She composed herself as well as she could," her husband wrote of Susannah at this time, "and that day got it buried." To help release her husband from debtor's prison Susannah sent him her wedding rings. Declining to sell them, however, he sent them back to her. While her husband was in prison she was left with all the domestic responsibilities of her large household.

Yet hardship never deflected her from the one concern which above all rendered her a "mother in Israel," her concern with the intellectual and spiritual formation of her children. As soon as each child reached the age of 6 she instructed the child six hours per day in her home-school. "It is almost incredible," she wrote at this time, "what a child may be taught in a quarter of a year by vigorous application, if it have but a tolerable capacity and good health. Kezzy excepted ["Kezzy" was her daughter Kezia] all could read better in that time than most of women can do as long as they live." Susannah, living in an era when the education of girls was largely overlooked, was most careful that her daughters receive adequate schooling. With her own daughters in mind she wrote that "no girl be taught to work until she can read very well... for the putting of children to learn sewing before they can read perfectly is the very reason why so few women can read fit to be heard, and never well enough to be understood."

Nevertheless Susannah always insisted that the ultimate end of education was not literacy as such but rather spiritual formation. She steeped her children thoroughly in the truth that our joy is to be found in discerning and doing the will of God; the child must grasp early in life that indulgent selfism never spells happiness but rather misery. Her husband, a man of little patience and a hair-trigger temper, was amazed to hear Susannah repeat the same point twenty times to her child. Surprised at her husband's amazement she replied, "If I had satisfied myself by mentioning it only nineteen times I should have lost all my labour. It was the twentieth time that crowned it."

Yes, she taught her children reading, writing, and "casting" (arithmetic); but she also schooled them in Scripture, church history, devotional literature, and that Puritan wisdom which ran so deep in her. Yet she was careful not to render the daily lives of her children bleak or joyless. Thomas à Kempis, a medieval writer whose devotional material was popular even in the eighteenth century, Susannah regarded as a weak spiritual guide since he regarded all amusements as sinful. Her educational program always had time for recreation and fun, including a game of cards.

As her children grew older she set aside an hour or two each week for the spiritual assistance of each child in addition to the time spent schooling them in academic subjects. "On Monday I talk with Molly; on Tuesday with Hetty; Wednesday with Nancy; Thursday with Jacky..." (as she always called him). Years later, when John was a student at Oxford University and undergoing much inner turbulence he wrote his mother and asked her to pray for him just as she had done years ago. "If you can spare me only that little part of Thursday evening which you formerly bestowed upon me in another manner...," he asked of her. Susannah's influence upon John in the sphere of education, especially concerning the bond between education and faith, education and ministry, proved to be immense. When he was 86-years-old John instructed his preachers as to what they should urge upon the children in Methodist circles. He specified five things his preachers must do: the fifth, "Preach expressly upon education... 'But I have no gift for it?' Gift or no gift, you are to do it; else you are not called to be a Methodist preacher."

The 86-year-old man who said this very nearly didn't get past six. In 1709 the family's home had caught fire. The parents had managed to get out with as many children as they could corral on the way through the smoke—only to have found, once outside, that John was still inside. He had appeared at a second storey window. Several neighbours had pyramided themselves in order to reach him and lift him off seconds before the building had collapsed and fallen in. Thereafter John had always spoken of himself as "a brand plucked from the burning," citing Amos 4:11. Susannah had resolved to be especially solicitous of John, whom she had regarded ever after as providentially spared. Her diary records her prayer: "I do intend to be more particularly careful of the soul of this child that Thou hast so mercifully provided for, than ever I have been."

Susannah's husband, insensitive as always, remained disdainful of her educational zeal. Priding himself on his university training (she had never gone to university) he told her she ought not to trespass in the field of scholarship. She bit her tongue but wrote in her diary that people who style themselves learned have inflated opinions of themselves. With her husband's inflated self-importance in mind, together with his undisguised attempts at social climbing, she wrote, "Let those that desire a reputation in the world seek ways to obtain it."

SUSANNAH ANNESLEY

The order and regularity, simplicity and seriousness which filled the home lent her household a monastic quality. It was the same monastic quality which would have been found earlier in any conscientious Puritan household. The weightiest Puritan vocabulary is found in her writings, and found in her writings inasmuch as the weightiest Puritan vocabulary described her home and her heart; words such as *method, discipline, duty, reason, conscience, experience* and *holiness*. It is through her that the glorious riches of Puritanism were preserved and passed on to the Methodist movement. To be sure, her best-known sons, John and Charles, provided a unique setting, a distinct ethos or spirit for all of this, as Methodist congregations exuded a different spirit from the more sombre Puritan congregations of fifty or 100 years earlier. Nonetheless, Susannah preserved and passed on to her sons, and through them to others, the richest Puritan distinctives which she had inherited herself. What were these distinctives? An esteem for both reason and experience, disciplined discipleship, a concern to do the truth and not merely understand it, heartfelt personal appropriation of the gospel, a magnification of the believer's assurance concerning the effectual mercy of God, an intense concern for evangelism, a passion for pastoral care which was genuinely caring, a veneration of the sovereignty of grace, and a simple life-style uncluttered by the world's craze for trinkets and toys and trifles. Financially hardpressed as Susannah always was, she advised her children, "Learn by practice to love God above all things, and you will be out of the power of the world; and then to be without wealth will give no uneasiness." Another Puritan emphasis was her insistence on the necessity of reasoned preaching. Preaching, she maintained, must never be an anti-rational appeal to the emotions. At the same time she knew that while reasoned preaching was necessary, reason alone was not sufficient: only God, by means of his Spirit, could render the preached word transparent to God himself. For this reason she cautioned people against knowing God "only as a philosopher"; she meant that no abstract information about God was a substitute for the living engagement with the person of God.

When over-exuberant converts stated that unless one could specify the precise moment of one's coming to faith then one was not a Christian, she replied, "I do not judge it necessary to know the exact time of our conversion." When she came upon new-born believers who were too concerned with taking their own spiritual temperature, too inward-looking, too much overtaken by a one-sided subjectivism, and above all too prone to chatter about it so as to cheapen it, she wrote, "I find this way of talking…has offended me, and I have often wished [such people] would talk less of themselves and more of God. I often hear loud complaints of sin, etc., but rarely, very rarely, any word of praise and thanksgiving to our dear Lord."

By the summer of 1742 (Susannah was now 73) she had buried her husband, several infants, and her eldest son. Now she knew she was dying. John was made aware that his mother was near death and rode quickly from Bristol to London. "I found my mother on the borders of eternity. But she had no doubt or fear, nor any desire but (as soon as God should call) 'to depart and be with Christ.'" To her children who were able to gather around her bed she said, "As soon as I am released, sing a psalm of praise to God."

It was said of Deborah of old that she was "a mother in Israel" (Judges 5:7). The woman who was mother to John and Charles, and through them mother to Methodist descendants without number, including the congregation of Streetsville Methodist Church; this woman, Susannah Annesley, was herself no less "a mother in Israel."

16

"OUR DOCTRINES"

A Sermon on Wesley Day (May 24)

It would be difficult to imagine anyone more rigid, more defensive, more inflexible—in a word, more "uptight"—than Anglican clergyman John Wesley in Georgia, 1737. When day-old infants were brought to the church for baptism, Wesley insisted on immersing them completely three times over. As horrified mothers objected to this dangerous practice (wasn't it enough that the infant-mortality rate was already 50 percent?) Wesley reacted by refusing to serve Holy Communion to the mothers themselves.

At this point in his life Wesley was a moralist. He thought the mission of the church to be that of improving the moral tone of the society. Like all moralists he was also a legalist; that is, he thought that people were admitted to God's favour on the basis of rule-keeping. Like moralists and legalists in general, he was a snob: superior, disdainful, autocratic, unbending—in a word, obnoxious.

Obnoxious he certainly was; stupid, however, he was not. A graduate of Oxford University, Wesley was proficient in the ancient languages: Latin, Greek, Hebrew. He knew philosophy, history, literature, logic, theology. French appears to have been the only modern language in which he was schooled formally. Still, on the three-month voyage to Georgia he taught himself German so thoroughly that years later he translated dozens of Paul Gerhardt's hymns from German to English. In the New World he came upon some Italian settlers who were without a clergyman. Wesley conducted worship for them, reading the Anglican Prayer Book service to himself while translating it aloud into the Italian he had recently taught himself. In Frederica, a village a few miles from Savannah, Wesley came upon a Jewish community. The Jewish people were from Portugal but spoke Spanish. Whereupon Wesley taught himself Spanish in order to converse with them.

Then disaster overtook him. He was 34 years old and had become infatuated with an 18-year old woman, Sophy Hopkey. She rejected him in favour of another man whom she subsequently married, Mr. Williamson. Hurt, frustrated and angry all at once, Wesley found excuses to withhold Holy Communion from Sophy, thereby suggesting to the public that she was scandal-ridden. Her husband was outraged. He had the politically powerful summon a Grand Jury. The Grand Jury indicted Wesley, and he took the next ship back to England in order to escape a lawsuit.

Why had he gone in the first place? He had gone inasmuch as he was a spiritual groper. He had thought that going to the wilderness in the New World would somehow translate into a fresh start for him in his spiritual quest. Candidly he said he'd gone in hope of saving his own soul.

Having returned to England a disillusioned man, haunted by his failure and tormented by his quest, he floundered for months until one Sunday evening he went to a service in London. He says he went "very unwillingly," no doubt because he felt there was no point to going: his situation was hopeless and he himself helpless. Listen to Wesley now in his own words:

> In the evening I went very unwillingly to a society in Aldersgate Street, where one was reading Luther's preface to the Epistle to the Romans. About a quarter before nine, while he was describing the change which God works in the heart through faith in Christ, I felt my heart strangely warmed. I felt I did trust in Christ, Christ alone for salvation, and an assurance was given me that he had taken away *my* sins, even *mine*, and saved *me* from the law of sin and death.

"OUR DOCTRINES"

It was May 24, 1738, the occasion of the long-awaited turn-around in his life. His moralism and legalism were behind him forever. Immediately his preaching shifted from moral exhortation to gospel-offer. His attitude to people, especially those beneath his social position, shifted from contempt to compassion. His rigorous self-discipline shifted from an achievement by which he sought to gain favour with God to a simple life-style that freed up everything about him and made it available to others. It happened on May 24, 1738, a day that his followers thereafter knew as "Wesley Day."

Years later he and his people (Methodism at this time was still a renewal movement within Anglicanism) began to speak of "Our Doctrines." Their doctrines, however, weren't unique to them. "Our Doctrines" were the doctrines of the church-at-large. There was nothing novel about them. Wesley abhorred theological novelty, insisting that anything novel had to be heretical. "Our doctrines" were Anglican, and Wesley considered them the doctrines of Christians everywhere. At the same time, Wesley insisted that his people own them, and own them with mind and heart, understanding and zeal.

[1] First among "Our Doctrines" is justification by faith. Justification or righteousness means right-relatedness to God. Justification, right-relatedness by faith is always to be contrasted with justification by something else; namely, justification by achievement. The issue is this: is our righted-relationship with God, our standing with God, a gift from God, or is it something we earn and therefore merit? With the help of friends who were spiritual descendants of Luther, Wesley came to see that Scripture clearly affirms our right-relationship to God to be God's gift, a gift that we possess by faith.

To say that sinners are justified is to say that those in the wrong before God are put in the right with God. It's to say that they are pardoned, or forgiven, or acquitted, or freely accepted. All these terms mean the same. To say that this happens through the faith of the believing person is to say that such a person welcomes God's forgiveness, endorses God's acquittal, accepts God's acceptance of oneself. Needless to say, faith must never be construed as a virtue that God recognizes and rewards. Faith must never be construed as an achievement that merits pardon with God.

Faith is simply the bond that binds us to Jesus Christ. Isn't Jesus Christ the Son with whom the Father is well-pleased? Then as we are bound to Christ in faith, and bound so closely to him as to be identified with him, we are now the son or daughter with whom the Father is pleased. Isn't Jesus Christ the only covenant-partner of God who keeps the covenant with his Father? Then as we are bound to Jesus Christ in faith and thereby identified with him, we who are covenant-breakers in ourselves are now deemed covenant-keepers in Christ. Isn't Jesus Christ the one whose cross bore the sin of humankind? Then as we are bound to him in faith and identified with him our sin is borne away.

The apostle Paul gloried in the truth of justification by faith. Yet we mustn't think that Paul invented the doctrine. He had found it everywhere in the earthly ministry of Jesus.

Our Lord told a parable of two men who went to church to pray. One fellow, indisputably a moral giant, tried to use his moral attainment as a bargaining-chip with God. The other fellow could only plead, "God, be merciful to me a sinner." "I tell you," said Jesus, "this man went home justified."

Justification by faith is the beginning of the Christian life; it's the beginning of the Christian life and the stable basis for all else in the Christian life. Justification by faith is first among "Our Doctrines."

[2] Second is the new birth. Whereas justification is a change in the believer's standing before God (from condemnation to acquittal, from rejection to acceptance, from expulsion to welcome), regeneration or new birth is a change within the believer herself. Wesley spoke of justification as a relative change (relative because of a changed relationship) and of new birth as a real change.

Through the prophet Ezekiel God had promised to create a new heart, a new spirit, within his people. Ezekiel contrasts the new "heart of flesh" with the old "heart of stone." The heart of flesh beats, pulsates, throbs. It invigorates someone who is alive. The heart of stone, on the other hand, is the heart of a corpse, a heart taken over by rigor mortis. The difference between the heart of flesh and the heart of stone is the difference between someone who is alive unto God and someone who is inert before God. It's the difference between someone who is responsive to God, engaged with God, and someone who is insensitive, unresponsive, indifferent.

As glorious as justification is (the freely-bestowed forgiveness of God), Wesley knew it wasn't enough. He asked himself a question as simple as it was profound: can people be changed, really changed, changed from the inside out? Everyone knew that behavioural conformity could be fostered. (Moralists and legalists major in this.) But could a change so very profound occur that someone was given new aspiration, new motivation, new obedience, in short a new nature? Wesley knew that either God can make a real change in us or the most the gospel offers is a pronouncement of pardon upon our bondage to sin even as that bondage is unrelieved. As glorious as he knew forgiveness of sin to be, Wesley knew that God could do something with sin beyond forgiving it. He insisted that the gospel not only relieved people of sin's guilt; it also released them from sin's grip. Life could begin again.

People can change; better, people can be changed. God will grant them a new heart. God can do something with sin beyond forgiving it. The person he forgives he also remakes. Either this is true or the gospel isn't good news. It is true. Deliverance can be experienced. The relative change of the remission of sin is always accompanied by the real change of regeneration. Believers have a genuine future.

[3] Third in "Our Doctrines" is the witness of the Spirit (i.e., the witness of the Holy Spirit). The children of God can know themselves to be such. When people come to faith in Jesus Christ and are renewed at his hand they are no longer mere creatures of God but are now children of God. God seals this truth upon them so as to leave them with every assurance that they are his.

Wesley was aware that the spiritually hungry look to our Lord in hope of being fed. Plainly a sense of need has impelled them to look to him. Plainly the more urgent their sense of need, the more anxiously they look. If in looking to Jesus Christ they lack assurance that they have met him and are now fused to him, then their everyday bundle of anxieties remains unrelieved and is in fact swelled by a fearsome religious anxiety. Then it's crucial that those who have passed from death to life know it.

Wesley found the witness of the Spirit writ large in Scripture, largest of all in Romans 8:15 where Paul exclaims, "The Spirit, God himself, constrains us to cry out, 'Abba, Father.' As the Spirit pulls this cry out of us the Spirit himself bears witness to us that we are children of God."

Wesley knew that one thing only relieved anxious people concerning their standing with God: the incursion of that Spirit who floods believing people so as to authenticate their adoption at God's hand, and this indubitably.

The witness of God's Spirit resembles happiness in one respect: if we pursue it, it forever escapes us. Happiness, everyone knows, overtakes people when they aren't looking for it but are getting on with what they have to do. In the same way God's Spirit assures us of our standing with him ("No condemnation now I dread" wrote Charles) as we are preoccupied with what God has given us to do.

[4] Fourth among "Our Doctrines" is the declaration of the law to believers. Believers have to be guided on the road of discipleship.

Over and over throughout the history of the church, wherever the glorious truth of justification by faith has been declared, some people have drawn the wrong conclusion. They say "If we are set right with God by our faith in the provision he has made for us in his Son, then it makes no difference what we do thereafter." The apostle Paul had to contend with the same misunderstanding during his ministry. When he announced the good news of the gospel (we are justified by grace through faith, not on account of our conformity to law), some hearers assumed that the law of God had been overturned. "By no means," the apostle expostulated. "On the contrary, faith upholds the law." The law of God is necessary if believers are to live out, live rightly, the new life they have received in Christ.

"OUR DOCTRINES"

Once again, Wesley didn't invent anything here. Apart from Scripture's insistence on the law of God as a guide to believers Wesley took it most immediately from the Puritans who had preceded him. The Puritans took it from Calvin, who found it ultimately in Melanchthon, the fellow who "packaged" Luther's theology. Melanchthon called it "the third use of the law."

The first use, Luther had said, was to order the society, to prevent social breakdown, even social chaos. The second use was to convict people of their sinnership as they came to see that they violated the law of God and were therefore guilty before God. The third use of the law was to guide believers along the road of discipleship.

Think, for instance, of the prohibition concerning theft. The first use of the law forestalls a social chaos wherein nobody can survive. The second use convicts people of their deep-down sinnership and points them to the gospel for relief. After all, the prohibition against theft includes envy, greed, covetousness—sins of which everyone is guilty. The third use guides believers along the road of discipleship as believers now know they must repudiate any envy, greed, covetousness that laps at them even as they must put everything they own at the disposal of their neighbour.

Did I say that the third use of the law is to help believers along the road of discipleship? I did. But isn't Jesus Christ our companion on the road? He is. Then the law of God, for believers, is simply the claim of Jesus Christ upon our obedience. Our Lord himself insists that we obey *him*, obey him *in person*. Then the third use of the law is simply our Lord's relentless insistence that we obey him and thereby walk in that newness of life which he has already bestowed on us.

"Our doctrines" included—and must ever include—the declaration of the law to believers.

[5] Last, but no means least, is Christian perfection. Now don't be put off because you've heard the word "perfection." Wesley didn't endorse a perfectionism that renders people neurotic. He didn't endorse a religious superiority that leaves people snobbish and self-righteous. He did,

however, encourage his people to look to God for deliverance from every vestige of selfism.

Wesley knew, as the church catholic has always known, that selfism is the essence of sin. To be freed from sin profoundly is to be freed from a self-preoccupation that measures everything and everyone in terms of catering to the self and magnifying the self and promoting the self. Since we all need to be freed from such self-preoccupation as we need nothing else, and since all of Christ's people have been appointed to be delivered from it in heaven, why not look to God to be delivered from it now? Why set arbitrary limits to what God can do to free us in this life?

I know what you are going to tell me: you are going to say that any concern with deliverance from selfism is at bottom another form of self-preoccupation. But not so for Wesley. For him Christian perfection was self-forgetfulness, self-forgetfulness that frees us for love of God and neighbour. Self-forgetful love for God and neighbour entails a self-sacrifice that is so thoroughly selfless as not even to be aware of being a sacrifice. "Lost in wonder, love and praise," wrote Charles Wesley. Be sure to underline "lost"; self-abandoned to discerning and doing God's will, self-abandoned to assisting the poor, the lonely, the outcast, the disadvantaged, the spiritually inert.

When Wesley saw the plight of the poor, sick people who first joined his Anglican renewal movement he gathered to himself a surgeon and an "apothecary," and then scrounged the money to pay them. In the first five months of this program his apothecary distributed drugs to 500 people. The drugs cost forty pounds. He raised the money himself. By 1746 he had established London's first free dispensary.

Wesley was distressed at the plight of aged widows. He purchased houses and refurbished them. Would the widows who had to live in them feel themselves demeaned as charity cases much beneath the social position of Wesley himself? Every time he was in the neighbourhood he ate at their table and ate the same food.

When the banks refused to lend money to sobered-up, industrious converts who wanted to start up small businesses, Wesley scrabbled for

"OUR DOCTRINES"

fifty pounds and then handed out small loans. In the first year he helped 250 people make a fresh economic start.

When Anglican officialdom faulted Wesley for advocating Christian perfection he asked the bishops who faulted him, "When you were at Holy Communion this morning, did you pray the Collect, 'cleanse the thoughts of our hearts by the inspiration of your Holy Spirit that we may perfectly love you...'? And when you prayed these words, did you mean them? Then why are you faulting me now?"

May 24th. Most of us associate the date with the birth of Queen Victoria. It's more profound to associate the day with the new birth of the Reverend John Wesley, Anglican clergyman, servant of God, leader of the eighteenth-century Awakening. Because his heart was 'strangely warmed,' the hearts of millions throughout the world have been set on fire to the glory of God, and to the edification of the neighbour, and, not least, to the relief of the sufferer.

17

HOLINESS OF HEART AND LIFE

We can be admitted to the concert hall, any concert hall, only if we have a ticket. The ticket of admission gives us the right to hear the symphony concert. Let us suppose we possess such a ticket. We sit down to listen to the glorious music of the masters—only to discover that we are bored out of our minds, since the music seems much ado about nothing; or worse than being bored, we are jarred, upset, since the concert strikes us as grating, pointless, seemingly endless, an utter waste of an evening we could have spent at something fruitful—and all of this just because we are tone-deaf. The ticket of admission gives us the right to be present; but as long as we are tone-deaf we aren't fit to be present. Regardless of our right to be at the concert, it is only our musicality that fits us for the concert. Without that musicality which fits us for the concert, the concert is merely a huge frustration.

John Wesley insisted that forgiveness of sins gives believing people the right to heaven; but only holiness renders us fit for heaven. Justification (pardon, forgiveness) admits us; sanctification (holiness, new birth) fits us. Justification means that in Christ believers have a new standing

---

* A sermon preached at the annual service honouring Hay Bay Church in Adolphustown, Ontario, the cradle of Methodism in Upper Canada.

with God; sanctification (holiness) means that in Christ believers have a new nature from God.

Just as Martin Luther emphasized massively the believer's new standing with God, so John Wesley emphasized massively the believer's new nature from God. In fact, said Wesley, it was for the sake of restoring sanctification or holiness to the church catholic that God had raised up Methodism.

Wesley was born an Anglican and died an Anglican. He never wanted to be anything other than an Anglican (and had difficulty understanding why anyone else would want to be). He looked upon his people, the Methodists, as having been raised up by God as a renewal movement to restore to Anglicanism specifically, and to the church catholic generally, what had lain dormant for too long. He believed himself commissioned to remind Christians everywhere of God's insistence on holiness of heart and life.

Let's approach the matter from a different angle. Wesley, together with his early-day followers (we are speaking now of the 1740s) joyfully held out a grand truth to any and all: "God can do something with sin beyond forgiving it." He can? What can God do with sin beyond forgiving it? He can unlock its grip upon us; he can get its "hooks" out of us. Never shall I forget one of my greater blunders with respect to spiritual counsel. A man had come to see me for help with his besetting sin (note: besetting sin, not besetting temptation). I listened to him carefully, empathetically (I thought) and then attempted to impart reassurance concerning the forgiveness of God, the mercy of God, the patience of God, the kindness of God. As I spoke I could tell from the expression on the man's face that he regarded my counsel as entirely off-target. Politely he waited until I was finished. Then he said to me plaintively, pleadingly, almost desperately, "Victor, I don't want forgiveness; I want deliverance."

Let us make no mistake. If the church has lost sight of the fact that God can do something with sin beyond forgiving it, then parachurch groups have not. Virtually all parachurch groups have one purpose: the deliverance of those who are in chains at present. Alcoholics Anonymous exists only to facilitate the deliverance of the alcohol-enslaved. So do the other organizations, whether they address wife-battering or drug-addiction or gambling.

Wesley had more to say on this matter. When he looked out over the church-scene of his day he saw a great many church-folk (and a great many more clergy, proportionately) who cavalierly reassured themselves that "of course" their sin was forgiven, even as they were held fast in its grip. Wesley's comment was, "Did you say, 'Of course'? Never say 'Of course'. Don't presume upon forgiveness. After all," he continued, "deliverance from the power of sin is confirmation of our having been forgiven the guilt of sin. Where there is no deliverance, don't be in any hurry to assume forgiveness."

"Then did he mean" (someone wants to object) "that unless we have been delivered from every last manifestation of sin, every last vestige of it, we haven't been forgiven any of it?" We shouldn't push Wesley to such an extreme. He wanted only to startle cavalier, complacent folk who were shallow and presumptuous. Deliverance from sin's grip confirms forgiveness of sin's guilt.

I remain convinced we need to hear and heed Wesley on this matter, for otherwise we shall come to think, whether consciously or unconsciously, that God cannot do anything with sin beyond forgiving it. And what would this be except a licence to sin for the cavalier and despair over sin for the serious? Wesley wanted to move all believers past two pitfalls: cavalier indifference and hopeless despair.

Wesley knew much that the contemporary church has largely forgotten. He knew that the command of God, beating like a big bass drum over and over in Scripture—"You shall be holy, for I the Lord your God am holy"—he knew this to be the root command in Scripture. He also knew that what God commands his people God gives his people. Therefore "You shall be holy, for I the Lord your God am holy" was not only the root command in Scripture; it was also the crowning promise in Scripture.

Because of his knowledge of Hebrew Wesley knew something more: he knew that the root meaning of the word "holy" is "different." In Hebrew the word-group around *kadosh* has to do with difference. God is holy, elementally, in that God is different. God is different from his creation in general, different from any one creature in particular. God is profoundly, *kadosh*, different.

The New Testament Greek word that translates *kadosh* is *hagios*. In the New Testament it is everywhere used of Christians. Christians are said to be *hagioi* (plural). All the English translations here read "saints." Paul writes letters to congregations in a dozen different cities, always beginning his letter, "To the saints in...(Corinth, Philippi, wherever). To be holy, a saint, is simply to be different. Different from what? Different for what? Different from "this present evil age"; different from that "darkness" which is "passing away" (to quote the apostle John); different from "the form of this world" which is "passing away" (to quote the apostle Paul). If Christians are different from this, what are we different for? We are different for the kingdom of God; different for that "new heavens and new earth in which righteousness dwells"; different for intimate acquaintance with Jesus Christ and conformity to him.

Wesley always insisted that if Jesus Christ does not or cannot make the profoundest difference to us and within us, then the entire Christian enterprise is pointless. But it isn't pointless. Our Lord can do within us all that he has promised to us.

Wesley's conviction here was one with the conviction (and experience) of the earliest Christians. Paul wrote to the congregation in Corinth, "Do you not know that the unrighteous will not inherit the kingdom of God? Do not be deceived; neither the immoral, nor idolaters, nor adulterers, nor sexual perverts, nor thieves, nor the greedy, nor drunkards, nor revilers, nor robbers will inherit the kingdom of God. And such were some of you. But you were washed, you were sanctified, you were justified in the name of the Lord Jesus Christ and in the Spirit of our God." "Such *were* some of you." The congregation in Corinth had among its members men and women who had spent years in notorious sin—undisguisable, undeniable, thoroughly degrading, habitual sin. And then they had known release. Now they continued to rejoice in a deliverance for which they would thank the deliverer eternally.

When Wesley spoke of holiness he characteristically spoke of "holiness of heart and life." By "heart" Wesley meant our inner intent, attitude, disposition; by "life" he meant our behaviour, conduct, visibility. He insisted that an inner intent that wasn't matched by outer manifestation was useless posturing, while an attempt at outer manifestation not rooted in inner transformation was crass self-righteousness. Supposed holiness of heart alone dishonoured God in that it was feeble. Supposed holiness of life alone dishonoured God in that it was arrogant. Holiness of heart and life are one as Spirit-quickened intention is fulfilled in Spirit-generated conduct.

We could illustrate this endlessly from the triumphs of grace that early-day Methodists spoke of when they commended their Lord for their deliverance. Yet I think it better to illustrate Wesley's conviction from the little man's own life. Early in his ministry Wesley wrote, "Resentment at an affront is sin, and I have been guilty of this a thousand times." (In our spiritual benightedness today we should likely say, "Resentment at an affront is entirely natural and perfectly understandable." Wesley would reply, "Entirely natural in fallen human nature; perfectly understandable according to fallen human reason—and no less sin for that.")

The man who always knew resentment at an affront to be sin was slandered by Bishop Lavington, an Anglican Church dignitary from Exeter. Lavington poured contempt on the Methodist people many times over, falsely accusing them unconscionably. He maintained that Methodists were stupid, irrational, hysterical, treacherous and politically treasonous. Yet the vilification Lavington heaped on the Methodist people was moderate compared to the vilification he poured on Wesley. Years later Wesley found himself at worship in an Anglican church whose communion service that Sunday was administered by none other than Bishop Lavington. Later the same day Wesley wrote in his Journal, "I was well-pleased to partake of the Lord's Supper with my old opponent, Bishop Lavington. O may we sit down together in the Kingdom of our Father." When he wrote, "I was well-pleased" he was transparently sincere. "Resentment at an affront is sin"—and having been "guilty of this a thousand times," Wesley found himself resentment-free; resentment-free before the man who had slandered him and his people repeatedly; resentment-free before the man who, two weeks later, would be found dead.

How did Wesley think we were to get to the point of "holiness of heart and life"? He always maintained that when the Holy Spirit acquaints us initially with our sinnership we do see it, and rightly view it with horror. In fact we see our sinnership with such starkness as to know that the Saviour is our only hope and help. Having grasped this much of our depravity, and having abandoned ourselves to our Saviour, however, we still haven't grasped the enormity of our depravity. We still haven't comprehended either the scope or the depth of sin in us. Its scope is vast, for it leaves no area of life unaffected. Its depth is unfathomable, for it goes deeper than we can see at present. Then another work of grace is needed, a subsequent work of grace. At this point we can only cry out to God and plead with him to remedy what he has newly acquainted us with about ourselves. A second work of grace is needed? Also a third, a fourth, a fortieth. This ongoing exposure to the roots of our sin, this ongoing awareness of the twists in our twisted heart, this ongoing self-abandonment to God lest our newly-exposed depravity warp us and horrify us one minute longer—this ongoing development is our ever-increasing holiness of heart and life. The key to it all, said Wesley, is singlemindedness. Do we want this more than we want anything else? Is it our one focus, aspiration, craving, preoccupation?

Human depravity is ever so varied. Yet there are three instances that Wesley mentions so very often as to seem like a refrain: pride, anger and self-will. God wrestles down our pride by working humility in us (even if it takes more than a little pain for us to become humble); he dispels our anger (here Wesley meant ill-temper, petulance, irrational rage) by working patience in us; he denatures our self-will by having us hunger to do his will. Wesley gathers all of this up by saying that as God's Spirit discloses new depths and layers and extensions of sin in us, God also works in us a new desire for and a new capacity for self-forgetful love of God and neighbour, for "holiness of heart and life" is finally going to be self-forgetful love of God and neighbour.

HOLINESS OF HEART AND LIFE

Love of God has to be self-forgetful, or else what we call "love for God" is nothing more than a tool for using God, exploiting him. Love of neighbour has to be self-forgetful, or else what we call "love of neighbour" is nothing more than a pretext for self-congratulation.

Needless to say, we cannot will ourselves to be self-forgetful, for the very attempt at willing this fixes us in our self-concern, this time a self-concern with a false religious-legitimisation (a kind of hypocrisy that Wesley abhorred). We become truly self-forgetful and profoundly self-forgetful only as we unselfconsciously "lose" ourselves in God.

Here we come to what I call the mystical aspect of Wesley's "holiness of heart and life." When Wesley speaks of holiness he isn't thinking first of morality; he is thinking first of God's Godness, and our inclusion in that. For this reason when Wesley speaks most deliberately of "holiness of heart and life" he quotes hymn-lines penned by brother Charles, hymn-lines that speak, as the mystics speak, of immersion in God, submersion in God, engulfment in God. Listen to him speaking of ordinary believers like you and me whom God has taken ever so deep into himself:

> Plunged in the Godhead's deepest sea,
> And lost in Thine immensity.

The vocabulary here—"plunged," "deepest," "sea," "lost," "immensity"—it is oceanic imagery that Wesley has to use just because God himself is oceanic, vast, uncontainable—even as Wesley knows that not even oceanic imagery is oceanic enough. No vocabulary can finally do justice to having our petty self-concerns drowned in God's drenching depths. No vocabulary can do justice to a vision of God that is so bright and an experience of God so compelling that words are forever inadequate. Listen to Wesley himself crying out,

> Fulfil, fulfil my large desires,
> Large as infinity,
> Give, give me all my soul requires,
> All, all that is in Thee.

And elsewhere,

> Let all I am in Thee be lost;
> Let all be lost in God.

We shall never understand Wesley until we understand his all-consuming preoccupation with God. God is the environment of his people as surely as water is the environment of fish. It wasn't so much that Wesley was aware of living in God as that he couldn't understand not living in God. With his last breath he held out to the simplest believer a heart-drenching, self-oblivious, horizon-filling love. He knew what it is to be drawn so close to the fire of God's love that the flames simultaneously consumed sin, cauterized sin's wounds and consummated love's longing.

Was all of this nothing more than an idiosyncratic, psycho-religious quirk in Wesley? On the contrary, he insisted that Scripture speaks over and over of the many who have heard and seen what cannot be uttered. Then whether ancient or modern, whether enjoyed by many or few, is it all nothing more than a privatized religious "trip" utterly devoid of sacrificial service to the neighbour? On the contrary, it will always bear fruit in love of the neighbour. See Wesley himself, 80 years old, trudging with numb feet through icy slush on four successive bitter winter mornings as he goes from house to house. He is soliciting money for his beloved poor. He keeps begging until a "violent flux" (as he spoke of it in eighteenth-century English; today we'd say, "uncontrollable diarrhea") forces him to stop. By now he has garnered 200 pounds. Why does he freeze himself half to death, at age 80, sick as well, on four successive winter mornings? Because his heart's been broken at the predicament of people who are colder, hungrier, sicker than he is.

Wesley's conviction that the deeper layers of our heart-condition must be dealt with as we are made aware of them; his familiarity with the scorching fire of God's love that sears and saves in the same instant; his self-forgetful immersion in the miseries of others as he brought them a joy they were going to find nowhere else: it's all gathered up in his oft-repeated expression, "holiness of heart and life."

In 1784, at 81 years of age, he was still saying, " Can you find... anything more desirable than this?"

HOLINESS OF HEART AND LIFE

And when William Losee came from upstate New York in 1790 to establish Methodist societies in Ontario he came because he knew—as his spiritual descendants came to know—that there wasn't, there isn't, and there never will be "anything more desirable than this."

18

"THE DUTY OF CONSTANT COMMUNION"

The fifth of the Ten Commandments tells us that we are to honour our father and mother in order that our days may be long in the land that the Lord our God gives us. Most immediately we are to honour our biological father and mother, those who begat us and bore us and gave us life, and whose wisdom, faithfulness and encouragement helped us past pitfalls when we were less than mature.

Lutheran Christians ever since Martin himself have believed that God intends a wider application of the fifth commandment. Lutherans have always believed that "Honour your father and mother" also means "Honour all—however long dead—whose wisdom, faithfulness and encouragement now assist you, inspire you, make you wise; in short, honour all whose wisdom, faithfulness and encouragement continue to help you past pitfalls in your discipleship since your faith isn't yet mature." If our Lutheran friends are correct, then we obey the fifth commandment as we honour our foreparents in faith.

One such foreparent of all Christians is John Wesley. He can help us past many pitfalls that surround us and concerning which we need help, since our faith is less than mature. Today we are going to honour him by taking to heart his convictions concerning Holy Communion.

In 1787, when Wesley was 84 years old, he wrote a tract called, "The Duty of Constant Communion." His 1787 tract was a re-write of the tract he had penned fifty-five years earlier in 1732. "Five and fifty years ago," he tells us in that English style which is archaic in the twenty-first century, "Five and fifty years ago the following discourse was written for the use of my pupils at Oxford… I then used more words than I do now. But I thank God I have not yet seen cause to alter my sentiments in any point which is therein delivered." (He means that what he believed in 1732 he still believed in 1787.)

Immediately Wesley says that while he isn't surprised at people who don't fear God being indifferent to Holy Communion, he finds it incomprehensible that many who do fear God are infrequently found at the Lord's table. When he asked these people why they shied away from Holy Communion they quoted Paul's word in 1st Corinthians 11:27: "Whoever… eats the bread or drinks the cup of the Lord in an unworthy manner will be guilty of profaning the body and blood of the Lord." In Wesley's era God-fearing people were absenting themselves from Holy Communion inasmuch as they regarded themselves unworthy and didn't want to incur the judgment of God.

It still happens. On the first communion Sunday of my first pastoral charge I stepped into the sanctuary to begin worship only to find that the congregation had segregated itself, some worshippers sitting on one side of the sanctuary, other worshippers on the other side. I asked what this meant and was told that on communion Sundays the congregation divided itself into those deeming themselves worthy and those unworthy. I was appalled, and immediately had everyone sit together. Whatever Paul meant by "eating and drinking unworthily" he didn't mean that.

Let us be sure we understand something crucial. God is free; God is sovereign; therefore God can meet us anywhere at any time in any manner through any means. Nevertheless, he has promised that he will invariably meet us—unfailingly meet us—through Scripture, sermon and sacrament. In other words, while we may be overtaken by God at any

THE DUTY OF CONSTANT COMMUNION

time by any means (surprised by God, that is) we know that we shall find God for sure, *every* time, at Scripture, sermon and sacrament. Therefore we must never absent ourselves from these. When well-intentioned yet misguided people told Wesley they absented themselves from Holy Communion lest they endanger themselves through partaking "unworthily," he told them they were endangering themselves far more by not partaking at all. And then he told them why they were at spiritual risk for not partaking at all.

I:—In the first place, Wesley reminded them, it is the Lord's command that we come to his table. "Do this in remembrance of me. Do it." It's an imperative, not a suggestion. Jesus Christ commands us to come to his table. It is therefore the obligation of everyone who believes in him to obey him and come. Not to come is simply to defy and disdain the one we call "Lord." But to call Christ "Lord" is to obey him, at least to want to obey him, to be eager to obey him. How can we call upon him as Lord, admit that he who is Lord is also our Justifier, yet continue to regard ourselves as unworthy? More to the point, he hasn't commanded us to come if first we deem ourselves worthy; he has simply commanded us to come.

Then Wesley adds a footnote. On the eve of his death Jesus told his followers that he wouldn't call them servants, since a servant merely obeys without being admitted intimately to the mind and heart of the servant's master. Rather because he himself, continued Jesus, because he has drawn his followers most intimately into his mind and heart he calls them servants no longer but friends. (John 15:15) "Now," says Wesley, "if our Lord draws us so intimately into his mind and heart as to call us friends, surely we can't turn down his final request. What friend turns down his dying friend's final request?"

There is another point, not made by Wesley, yet too important for us not to mention. In the ancient world the word "friend" was rich with several meanings. In Israel "friend" had a special meaning; it meant "best man" at a wedding. In Rome "friend" had a special meaning too; it meant "someone intensely loyal to Caesar." No one can imagine the best man at a wedding failing to do what the bridegroom has asked him to do. No one can imagine a Roman soldier publicly declaring his utmost loyalty to Caesar and then publicly refusing to do what Caesar asks of him.

"Absent ourselves from Holy Communion, for any reason?" Wesley asks; "Don't we know what the word 'friend' means?"

II:—In the second place, says Wesley, Holy Communion is more than just God's command; it is also God's provision for our spiritual need. To be sure, Christians are sinners who have come to faith and repentance through the incursion of God's Spirit. Yes, we have passed from death to life, from darkness to light, from bondage to freedom, from guilt to acquittal, from shame to glory. Nevertheless, sin still dogs us. Our glory isn't without some tarnish; our freedom isn't without niggling habituation. Yes, we live in the light of him who is light; still, that darkness which our Lord has overcome hasn't yet been wholly overcome in us. Or as Martin Luther used to say, "In putting on Christ in faith we have also put on the new man (woman); the old man is therefore put to death; but the stinker doesn't die quietly." In other words, however strong our faith, in fact it is weak. However mature our discipleship, we have not yet graduated. However resilient we think we are in the company of our Lord, we are yet frail and fragile and faltering. Therefore we can't afford to pass up any provision God has made for us in our need of greater deliverance. For this reason Wesley speaks of Holy Communion as "a mercy of God to man." Quoting Psalm 145:9 ("God's mercy is over all his works") Wesley reminds us that however God deals with us—whether gently or roughly, whether starkly or subtly, whether suddenly or slowly—whatever God does to us and with us he does ultimately just because he is *for* us. Therefore everything God does to us and with us is finally an expression of God's mercy. In light of this, who is so foolish as to absent herself from the most dramatic representation of that mercy, Holy Communion?

Wesley never hesitated to be blunt. Because partaking of the Lord's Supper is a command of God, he said, to spurn it is to announce that we have no piety; and because partaking of the Lord's Supper is a mercy of

God, to spurn it is to announce that we have no wisdom. Piety, Wesley had learned from John Calvin, is the love of God and the fear of God. To be without piety is therefore ultimately to be insensitive to God. To be without wisdom is simply to be fools.

Fools? Yes, says Wesley as he develops a theme that runs like a thread through all his writings. The theme is this: none but the holy are finally happy. He insists tirelessly that God has fashioned us for happiness. Not for superficial jollity or frivolity or sentimentality, but certainly for deep-down contentment, joy, happiness. Let's not forget that the Greek word *makarios*, rendered "blessed" in most English translations of the beatitudes ("Blessed are those who hunger and thirst after righteousness, for they shall be filled," etc.); the Greek word *makarios* also means "happy" (in both ancient Greek and modern Greek). Of course. How could we ever be blessed—by God himself—and finally be miserable?

To be sure, there is no end to the pleasure we can find in nature; no end to the pleasure we can find in culture; no end to the pleasure we can find in our own bodiliness and our intellectual life. Nonetheless, there is one delight that all of this can't give us: our "enjoyment" of God, in Wesley's words. Wesley insists there is one throbbing pleasure that God's children know and unbelievers can't know: "delight in God."

Now, says the indefatigable man, only as we are holy are we profoundly happy. Yet we can't render ourselves holy. Holy Communion is one of God's provisions to render us holy. To absent ourselves from it is to cut ourselves off from that blessedness which is our greatest happiness.

III:—In Wesley's day (the 1700s) as in our day people put forward a variety of reasons as to why they don't or even shouldn't come to the Lord's Supper. We need not suspect these people of insincerity; the reasons they put forward aren't excuses offered lamely. Those who absent themselves from the Lord's Supper are sincere, says Wesley—and they are sincerely wrong.

One reason put forward: "I have sinned, and therefore I am not fit to communicate." Wesley said this was nothing short of ridiculous, however well intentioned. While sin is a violation of the command of God, we don't atone for violating the command of God by violating another command (to communicate). Nobody atones for the sin of theft by committing the sin of murder. If we have sinned (better, since we sin) there is all the more reason for betaking ourselves to Holy Communion where we shall find—for sure—in the words of Wesley, "the forgiveness of our past sins" and "the present strengthening and refreshing of our souls"—and all of this because Jesus Christ our Lord has already atoned for us.

Another reason put forward for not attending Holy Communion: "I can't live up to the promise made in the communion service to remain Christ's true follower." Wesley agrees: none of us can live up to the promise. At the same time, he tells us, none of us lives up to any of the promises we make anywhere in life. But this is no excuse for not making a promise. Do we refuse to get married (with the promise marriage entails) on the grounds that we are never going to be the perfect spouse?

Another reason put forward. "Frequent partaking of the Lord's Supper will diminish our reverence for the sacrament." "What if it did?" says Wesley; "Would this render null and void the command of God?" Needless to say, it is Wesley's conviction that frequent communion, so far from diminishing our reverence for the sacrament, will only increase it.

Another reason is advanced for not coming to the Lord's Table: "I have come so very many times already, and I don't feel I have benefited in any way." Here Wesley replies in two instalments. In the first place, the issue that can't be dodged, he repeats yet again, is the command of God. God insists that we honour him and his will for us by bringing ourselves and whatever faith we have to that table where we can meet him for sure. In the second place, we have benefited from regular attendance at the Lord's Supper regardless of how much or how little we may feel. Even when we feel nothing, says Wesley, we are being "strengthened, made more fit for the service of God, and more constant in it." What's more, he continues, not only have we benefited where we feel we haven't, but also the day comes when feeling catches up to fact; what has been real in our hearts, albeit hidden in our hearts, is now manifested within our hearts so as to leave us without complaint concerning feeling.

The most telling objection to frequent communion came from those who trembled before Paul's word in 1st Corinthians 11. "Whoever eats the bread or drinks the cup of the Lord in an unworthy manner will be guilty of profaning the body and blood of the Lord." What is the unworthiness that Paul has in mind? It isn't an extraordinary, inner, personal unworthiness. Then what is it? The clue to it is given two verses later: "For anyone who eats and drinks without discerning the body—i.e., the body of Christ, the congregation—eats and drinks judgment upon himself." We must recall the situation in Corinth. The congregation there was a mess. Party-factions were fragmenting the congregation. One man was involved in open incest and no one seemed to care. Parishioners preferred religious "glitz" to spiritual profundity. Boasting had supplanted cross-bearing. Within the congregation there flourished bitterness, lovelessness, self-exaltation, superficiality and sleaze. Paul said it had to end. The Corinthians had lost sight of the fact that the congregation is Christ's body. Currently the body in Corinth appeared hideous. Anyone who came to the Lord's Supper without discerning this, said Paul, was in a sorry state herself.

In other words, when we come to Holy Communion we must understand that because the congregation is Christ's body, we must be determined to ensure that it exhibits itself as Christ's body, lest the watching world pour contempt upon him who is the head of the body, Christ Jesus himself. To eat and drink worthily is simply to come to the Lord's Supper determined to live together as a congregation so as to bring honour to the congregation's Lord. Therefore let all who have resolved to do this never absent themselves from the service.

It is only fitting that we let John Wesley himself have the last word. When he has finished telling us why we must come to Holy Communion, and come constantly; when he has finished replying to the well-intentioned but groundless reasons that people advance for not coming, he then concludes his tract, "If any who have hitherto neglected [Holy Communion] on any of these pretences will lay these things to heart, they will, by the grace of God, come to a better mind, and never more forsake their own mercies."

CONCLUSION

JOHN WESLEY: A GIFT TO THE UNIVERSAL CHURCH

PROLOGUE

Although John Wesley is readily acknowledged as the eponym of all things Methodist and as an eighteenth-century evangelist, fewer people appreciate his contribution to the church catholic. Indisputably he was the most significant Anglican thinker of his era, rooted in the English Reformation yet influenced by the Puritans. He was possessed of an idiosyncratic yet biblical eschatology of loving (alongside the Reformed community's eschatological emphasis of knowing God and the Roman Catholic's of seeing God). No sycophant of modernity, Wesley was steeped in Patristics, albeit preferring the Eastern Fathers to the Western. Insisting that he and the Anglicanism he cherished (the Book of Common Prayer he deemed unambiguously Protestant) were children of the Wittenberg-Geneva restoration, Wesley nevertheless recognized the spiritual riches of the Counter-Reformation mystics, and he insisted as well that his people school themselves in them. Knowing that evangelistic zeal must be matched by a passion for holiness lest spiritual neonates fail to thrive, he oriented his characteristic "social holiness" to Britain's most despised and neglected. Ever upholding the universality of the body of Christ, he maintained the Eucharist to be

God-appointed *viaticum*, that "food for the journey," neglect of which could only attest one's folly in neglecting God's provision and could attest no less one's disobedience in trifling with God's commandment.

INTRODUCTION

The most casual glance at Wesley's "Catholic Spirit" attests his rejection of doctrinal indifference.[1] Truth matters, and theological truths (statements) that point to and that commend Truth (the operative reality of Jesus Christ) are not to be trifled with, let alone traduced. At the same time, Wesley was aware that his Shepherd had sheep of other folds. In light of such diverse sheep-folds, he gratefully adopted (and zealously adjusted) the work of Eastern Fathers and of Roman Catholic Counter-Reformation mystics. His magnanimity is evident in his "olive branch," "A Letter to a Roman Catholic."[2] When nephew Samuel Jr. became a Roman Catholic, thereby rendering his father, Charles, apoplectic, John calmly wrote Samuel:

> Whether of this church or that I care not: you can be saved in either or damned in either … and except you be born again you cannot see the kingdom of God … Let the Spirit of God bear witness with your spirit that you are a child of God, and let the love of God be shed abroad in your heart. … Then, if you have no better work, I will talk with you of transubstantiation and purgatory.[3]

Wesley consistently maintained he was Protestant, and a Church of England Protestant. Consistently he discountenanced both the "Romish" error and the latitudinarianism that blunted the cutting edge of the

---

1. John Wesley, *The Works of John Wesley* (vol. 1; bicentennial ed.; Nashville: Abingdon, 1984), 79–95.

2. John Wesley, "A Letter to a Roman Catholic," in *John Wesley* (ed. Albert C. Outler; New York: Oxford University Press, 1964), 493 ff.

3. Kenneth G. Newport and Ted A. Campbell, eds., *Charles Wesley: Life, Literature & Legacy* (Peterborough, U.K.: Epworth, 2007), 134.

gospel.[4] Still, he wanted the sole stumbling block to faith to be the affront of the gospel, never the affront of a narrow or bigoted spirit.

Not least, Wesley insisted on one condition only for those desiring admittance to the Methodist Society: "A desire to flee from the wrath to come, to be saved from their sins."[5] In many respects, then, Wesley remains a model of gospel catholicity and of ecumenical magnanimity.

ESCHATOLOGY

In accord with all New Testament writers, the apostle Paul maintains that in Jesus Christ "the end of the ages" has come (1 Cor 10:11). Since the *eschaton* is upon us now, Christians look not for its arrival but rather for its final, full manifestation. Different families in the church catholic, however, emphasize different aspects of the *eschaton*.

The Reformed family emphasizes an eschatology of knowing: we are going to know God in such a way as to render doubt impossible. From John Calvin to Karl Barth, the Reformed family has underlined the cruciality of a proper knowledge of God and of the conditions of such knowledge; this includes, for example, the belief that since God alone knows God, we can know God only as we are included (by grace) in God's self-knowing. Although at present we know "in part," the day has been appointed when "in part" will disappear and all noetic distortions remedied.

The Roman Catholic family, on the other hand, emphasizes an eschatology of seeing. This is no surprise in light of the emphasis that Roman Catholicism customarily places on seeing, in that the visible is accorded a place in Rome's ethos that Protestants reserve for the audible. In line with the accent on the visual are the visions that Roman Catholics have and whose fruitfulness has appeared in new orders, missions, and educational institutions.

In their eschatology of seeing, the Roman Catholic family avers that

---

4. Not infrequently Wesley speaks of the "Romish delusion." See, e.g., his *Works*, vol. 1, 128–129.

5. Wesley, *Works*, vol. 9, 70.

God's people have been appointed to the Beatific Vision. We are going to see God: see God in God's inherent beauty, the beauty of God (according to Scripture) being one aspect of the glory of God.

And the Methodist family? Wesley's eschatology is an eschatology of loving. We are going to love as we have been loved by a Father who spared not his Son and therein spared not himself in the course of sparing us. Love divine, all other loves excelling, will finally love every last vestige of unlove out of us, and we shall be transported, "lost in wonder, love and praise."[6]

A major indication of Wesley's love-eschatology is found in his sermon, "The Almost Christian," a tract not about the "almost" Christian but about the nominal Christian (who may be far from "almost persuaded"). In Part I of the sermon, Wesley discusses the spiritual deficits of those who have substituted nominal Christianity for self-abandonment to the Saviour. He concludes, to no one's surprise, that nominal Christians are marked by lack of faith. In Part II, Wesley announces immediately what marks "altogether Christians," those who cling to the Son and who are born of the Spirit. Such people are marked not by faith (which is what we expect him to say) but by love.[7]

It is pointless to say that Wesley has unconscionably jettisoned justification by faith for justification by love. Everywhere he insists on justification by faith (as we shall see shortly), and justification by faith alone, necessarily by faith alone. Along with the Protestant Reformers, Wesley insists that although faith includes understanding (or else the deity we worship is an idol) and assent, faith becomes such only at the point of trust as the sinner entrusts oneself to the only Saviour one can ever have. To be sure, having contrasted the unbeliever's lack of faith in God with the believer's love for God, Wesley immediately goes on to expound the nature of faith. Still, the Wesleyan trajectory is evident.

In his celebrated "Catholic Spirit," Wesley pleads for a love that is

---

6. Charles Wesley, "Love divine, all loves excelling," in John Wesley, *Works*, vol. 7, 546.

7. Wesley, *Works*, vol. 1, 131–141.

neither spineless sentimentality nor affectionless admonition. In this regard he writes, "Love me with a love that is patient if I am ignorant and out of the way, bearing and not increasing my burden." If, continues Wesley, you, a believer, find me, a believer, sinning, love me so as to recognize that I sinned "in sudden stress of temptation."[8]

Wesley's eschatological love-orientation is evident in the space he gives to the exposition of his favourite epistle, 1 John. Whereas Reformed Protestants have returned again and again to Paul's epistle to the Romans whenever the church was staggering and needed to be strengthened and to be stiffened, Wesley turns to John's first letter. His exposition of 1 John, a small epistle compared to Romans, is at least half the size of his exposition of Romans.[9]

Always to be remembered in the context of Wesley's eschatology is his understanding of Christian perfection. Characteristically his "Christian perfection" is not utter sinlessness or faultlessness or flawlessness. (He points out in his *A Plain Account of Christian Perfection* that the godliest never get beyond needing the intercession of the atonement.)[10] Christian perfection is perfection in love (recall the Anglican collect for Holy Communion, "that we may *perfectly love* Thee"). It is the removal of every last impediment to unobstructed loving. He insists that God's people have been appointed to a single-minded, self-forgetful love of God and of neighbour.

Then is Wesley's eschatology merely one among three (at least), one alongside several others? Or is an eschatology of love the substance, the integration, and the crown of all others? Tirelessly, Wesley reminds us that the great commandment is that we are to love profligately both God and neighbour. To be sure, faith is a form of knowing, and faith knows God without any weakening of "know" at all. Still, the great commandment is not that we understand God on the grounds that God is

---

8. Wesley, *Works*, vol. 2, 91.

9. John Wesley, *Notes on the New Testament* (Wakefield, U.K.: William Nicholson and Sons, 1972).

10. John Wesley, *A Plain Account of Christian Perfection* (London: Epworth, 1952), 43.

intelligible intelligence. We are to love God on the grounds that God *is* love (1 John 4:8); love is all God is. Yet since the "root commandment" of Scripture is "You shall be holy as I the Lord your God am holy" (Lev 19:2), the Great Commandment to love is the content of the "root commandment" to be holy. Since Wesley was Puritan-informed and was therefore aware that all God's commands are "covered promises," both commandments are fulfilled in what Wesley called "the great, overarching promise of Scripture"; namely, the salvation at God's hand that is nothing less than the transmogrification of women and of men whose knowledge of God is the apprehension of love and whose sight of God is the beholding of love.

In 1770, Wesley was shocked to hear of the premature death of his younger friend and fellow evangelist, George Whitefield. At a memorial service for Whitefield, Wesley commented, tersely and tear-choked, on the love that Whitefield had awakened in him: "Can anything but love beget love?"[11] Only love can beget love. Just as surely, Methodists since Wesley have always known, ultimately love begets love and nothing else. Wesley's is an eschatology of love.

THEOLOGY

The myth shows no sign of evaporating—the myth, that is, that compared to the Reformed or Lutheran traditions the Methodist tradition is theologically effete. In fact, Wesley expected (unrealistically, perhaps) that his lay preachers, like him, would study five hours per day. He maintained the most important subject for the preacher to study was Scripture, and after that, logic—since a self-contradicted preacher will never utter a coherent message, and the preacher's utterance ought to reflect the consistency of God's action and speech. All the*ology* has to be *logic*ally rigorous or else it does not help the would-be preacher and cannot be communicated in any case.

Then what theology informed Wesley and will continue to inform those who bear his name? Wesley was thoroughly acquainted with

---

11. Wesley, *Works*, vol. 2, 338.

seventeenth-century Anglican thought; he read the sixteenth-century continental Reformers; he cherished the English Reformers (Ridley, Latimer, Tyndale, and Cranmer, the lattermost's Book of Common Prayer being, Wesley insisted, the finest liturgical vehicle the church catholic had ever seen.)

Regularly I point out to my students passages in Wesley where the vocabulary and the word-patterns come straight out of Calvin's *Institutes of the Christian Religion*. (It should be noted here that Wesley always insisted he agreed without reservation with the Genevan Reformer's understanding of Total Depravity, and was only a "hair's breadth" from Calvin on several other matters.)[12] It was while Wesley heard read at worship the preface to Luther's commentary on Romans that he came to faith; it was while Charles was reading the text of Luther's commentary on Galatians that Methodism's major poet came to faith. When Wesley published his *Christian Library*, a fifty-book collection he edited and expected Methodists to read, thirty-two of the fifty volumes were by Puritan divines.

Wesley's studies at Oxford found him meticulously apprised in the patristic scholarship for which the university was reputed. Wesley knew the church fathers thoroughly, and, although a son of the Western church, he was critical of Augustine, the chief Western thinker, always preferring the Eastern Fathers whose outstanding representative was Athanasius.

Even though Wesley was sharp in his criticism of what he observed concerning the Eastern Orthodox congregation in London,[13] he remained indebted to outstanding Eastern Fathers such as Ephrem the Syrian (ca. 306–373) and Macarius (ca. 300–391). In fact, Macarius was the Eastern thinker whose *Spiritual Homilies* underlie Wesley's understanding of sanctification.

Then is Wesley's theology a hodgepodge, little more than a grab-bag

---

12. Wesley, *Works*, vol. 2, 184.

13. Thomas Jackson, ed., *The Works of John Wesley* (vol. IX; repr., Grand Rapids: Zondervan, 1958–1959), 216–217.

through which he runs his fingers, retaining whatever his hand happens to grasp? On the contrary, there is a profound, coherent theology that Christians who bear his name have found compelling; it is a theology that admits many ingredients just because it disdains no one. Yet it is stamped ultimately by Wesley's genius as he forged a theology that, as he maintained and as those after him have acknowledged, is formed, is informed, and is normed by the substance and the logic of "the general tenor of Scripture," as he customarily put it. For instance, although some biblical texts might be read as supporting predestination, the "general tenor"[14] of Scripture may not be read in this way; neither does the "general tenor" permit us to deny that God's mercy is over *all* his works, an eternal decree of reprobation thereby ruled out. The "general tenor of Scripture" forbids us to narrow the idea that "God desires *all* to be saved" into "God desires *some*."

Wesley's theology is catholic (i.e., non-sectarian). At its centre, he upholds the three "grand doctrines," without which the gospel is neither needed nor effective: original sin, justification by faith, and holiness ("present, inward salvation").[15] He endorses the Vincentian Canon: what has been believed by all Christians, at all times, in all places.

To be sure, Wesley wrote no tome of systematic theology. Neither did Luther, however, and no one disputes Luther's theological singularity and profundity. Nevertheless, Wesley thought systematically, as an examination of his *corpus* on any topic shows.

---

14. Wesley, *Notes on the New Testament* (Wakefield, U.K.: William Nicholson and Sons, 1872), Rom 12:6.

15. Jackson, *Works of John Wesley*, vol. XII, 246. Wesley insisted that the denial of original sin renders all Christian doctrine incoherent. He makes this point repeatedly in his tract, "The Doctrine of Original Sin, according to Scripture, Reason and Experience," in Jackson, *Works of John Wesley*, vol. IX. It is Wesley's single largest tract.

JOHN WESLEY: A GIFT TO THE UNIVERSAL CHURCH
TRADITION

Amnesia, G. K. Chesterton has written, is distressing not because someone cannot remember where she left her umbrella; amnesia is distressing because the amnesiac, lacking all memory, does not know who she is; that is, the person devoid of memory lacks an identity. Lacking an identity, she does not know how she ought to behave and therefore cannot be trusted.[16] Wesley was aware that a denomination or a congregation without Christian memory is a denomination or a congregation that can never be trusted.

The idea of Christian memory is more often called "tradition" by the church. Yet tradition, the received wisdom of the church, is never to be confused with traditionalism, the mindless absorption of all aspects of Christian history, many of which contradict the gospel and therefore should be jettisoned. Tradition, said Chesterton once again, is simply enfranchising the departed: the dead are permitted to vote. Wesley too insisted that the dead are permitted to vote; at the same time he insisted no less emphatically that the dead must not be permitted to veto. For this reason, he cherished Christian memory without sacralising it so as to elevate it above Scripture and therein to denature the gospel.

Insisting on the necessity of Christian memory, Wesley eschewed theological novelty. The theologically novel is *ipso facto* heretical. Since God has never left himself without witnesses, Wesley finds salvifically memorable many aspects of Christian history contemporary evangelicals set aside too readily. Evangelicals frequently assume they are the first generation of Christians to face the challenges they have recently identified, not realising that little is new in church history and that the challenges besetting the church today have been faced and fought several times already in the centuries between antiquity and contemporaneity.

To be sure, Wesley never uses the word "tradition," since the first of the *Edwardian Homilies* (one of Anglicanism's theological benchmarks)

---

16. Although Chesterton makes similar points in many works, for a protracted discussion of the place of tradition, see *Orthodoxy* (New York: Dover, 2004) and *The Everlasting Man* (New York: Dover, 2007).

speaks of "the stinking puddles of men's traditions." He prefers "Christian Antiquity."[17] In this connection, Wesley always sees Patristics as amplifying Scripture and resolving ambiguities in Scripture. To this end he writes, "The esteeming of the first three centuries, not equally with but next to the Scriptures, never carried any man (*sic*) into dangerous errors, nor probably ever will."[18]

There are other aspects of tradition that Wesley, a Protestant who never hesitated to speak of "the Romish delusion," nonetheless finds in Rome. For instance, eight of the books listed in his *Christian Library* are by Roman Catholic mystics of the Counter Reformation, the Counter Reformation being Rome's implacable opposition to the "Lutheranism" claiming vast tracts of Europe in the sixteenth century. Admittedly, he read Roman Catholic mystics critically, red pen poised at all times (the way he read everyone). Nevertheless, always honouring God's command to "plunder the Egyptians" (Exod 3:22), he recognized in them an immersion in God whose experience and vocabulary were one with a biblical mysticism unashamed to speak of transport, of rapture, of vision, and of audition; unashamed to speak of revelations, of visitations, and of hearing and of seeing what may not be uttered; and unashamed of Daniel's trance, of Paul's man from Macedonia, and of Isaiah's lip-seared prostration in the temple. Wesley knows that the Christian tradition has never lacked people for whom God's mediated immediacy is intimate and is intense in equal measure. Wesley is always aware that there is nothing more pathetic, useless, and dangerous than individual, congregation, or denomination devoid of Christian memory.

---

17. For an amplification of Wesley's understanding here, see Ted A. Campbell, *John Wesley and Christian Antiquity* (Nashville: Abingdon, 1991).

18. Jackson, *Works of John Wesley*, IX.

JOHN WESLEY: A GIFT TO THE UNIVERSAL CHURCH
PROTESTANT CONVICTIONS

Lest anyone think that Wesley was in truth what he was often accused of being, a crypto-Jesuit, it must be added immediately that Wesley upholds both the formal and the material principles of the Magisterial Reformation. Wesley's endorsement of the formal principle, *sola scriptura*, is evident explicitly and implicitly throughout the thirty-five volumes of his *Works*. Characteristically he asserts he is *homo unius libri*, a man of one book.[19] He never means he reads one book only. (Five paragraphs after describing himself as *homo unius libri*, he quotes Homer's *Iliad* in Greek.) "One-book only" bibliolatry he pronounces "rank enthusiasm; you are then above St. Paul,"[20] who asked Timothy to bring him books. He means rather that one book is the unmodified norm of Christian faith and conduct. In a letter to a critic, he maintains, "I receive the written Word as the whole and sole rule of my faith."[21] The four young men who birthed Methodism at Oxford "had one, and only one rule of judgement with regard to all their tempers, words and actions; namely, the oracles of God"[22] ("oracles" being a term he borrowed from Calvin). On the matter of Scripture, Wesley is incontrovertibly Reformational.

Similarly Wesley insists on the material principle of the Reformation, justification by faith. In a sermon he expostulates that justification by faith is the "the very foundation of our Church [i.e., Anglican] ... and indeed the fundamental [doctrine] of the Reformed Churches."[23] In the minutes of the second Methodist Conference (1745), he states categorically that where justification is not upheld the church does not exist.[24] In the face of detractors, he maintains he has extolled justification by

---

19. Wesley, *Works*, vol. 1, 105.
20. Jackson, *Works of John Wesley*, vol. VIII, 315.
21. For a cogent discussion of Wesley's understanding of Scripture, see Scott J. Jones, *John Wesley's Conception and Use of Scripture* (Nashville: Abingdon, 1995), as well as Jones, "The Rule of Scripture," in *Wesley and the Quadrilateral* (W. Stephen Gunter et al.; Nashville: Abingdon, 1997).
22. Jones, *John Wesley's Conception and Use of Scripture*.
23. Wesley, *Works*, vol. 4, 395.
24. Wesley, Works, vol. 10, 126–127.

faith from the day of his evangelical awakening: "I believe justification by faith alone as much as I believe there is a God. ... I have never varied from it, no, not an hair's breadth from 1738 to this day."[25] Always suspicious of Quakerism for several reasons, he declares, "I have not known ten Quakers in my life whose experience went so far as justification." (He means he has not met any.)[26]

Wesley's elaboration of justification sufficiently attests his agreement with the Reformers. He concurs with them concerning "the imputation of Christ's righteousness," while noting that Scripture nowhere uses the expression.[27]

ZEAL FOR EVANGELISM

Although Wesley was a gifted patristics scholar and the most important Anglican thinker in the eighteenth century, we remember him today primarily because he was an evangelist. Contemporary evangelism, however, appears to differ from his in several respects. Our concern with evangelistic techniques, programs, and "Ten Effective Steps" he would regard as manipulation at best and as unbelief at worst.

Wesley's evangelism presupposes three pillars: predicament, penalty, and provision. Humankind's predicament is bleak: the unrepentant sinner "abides in death ... lost, dead, *damned already*"[28] (emphasis Wesley's). There is nothing in Wesley of modernity's psychologizing of the human predicament; namely, we feel guilty (without being guilty), anxious, nervous, and frustrated. Neither is there any existentializing of the human predicament: through our sin we have alienated ourselves from God, from others, and from self.

---

25. Jackson, *Works of John Wesley*, vol. X, 349. Wesley makes the same point in his *Works*, vol. 4, 147. For Wesley's single most sustained treatment of justification, see his *Works*, vol. 1, 182–199.

26. John Wesley, *The Letters of John Wesley* (ed. John Telford; vol. 7; London: Epworth, 1931), 26. For a more sustained discussion of Wesley's assessment of Quakerism, see his "A Letter to a Person Lately Joined with the People Called Quakers," in Jackson, *Works of John Wesley*, vol. X, 177–188.

27. Wesley, *Works*, vol. 1, 458.

28. Wesley, *Works*, vol. 1, 151.

Wesley insists, rather, that we are alienated from God, from others, and from self not on account of our sin but on account of *God's judgment* on our sin. We have not sashayed or wandered out of Eden; we have been *expelled* by a judicial act of God.

The penalty for our primal disobedience is God's condemnation. Such condemnation is not reserved for the future; it is operative now. The Day of Judgment will merely render undeniable that truth of which the condemned are now culpably ignorant.

In light of the foregoing predicament and penalty, the divinely-wrought provision is the atonement. Before sinners can repent and "return home," provision must be made for them wherein the barricade to their return is removed. Before we can be reconciled to God, God must be reconciled to us. It is little wonder Charles Wesley exults:

> My God is reconciled,
> His pard'ning voice I hear.
> His blood atoned for all our race,
> And sprinkles now the throne of grace.[29]

Neither is it surprising that Charles Wesley characteristically speaks of someone's coming to faith as "she received the atonement." He typically gathers up predicament, penalty, and provision in his pithy hymn:

> Who hath done the dreadful deed,
> Hath crucified my God?
> Curses on his guilty head,
> Who spilt that precious blood.
> Worthy is the wretch to die;
> Self-condemned, alas, is he! –
> I have sold my Saviour, I
> Have nailed him to the tree.

---

29. Charles Wesley, "Arise, my soul, arise," in John Wesley, *Works*, vol. 7, 324–325.

> Yet thy wrath I cannot fear,
> Thou gentle, bleeding Lamb!
> By thy judgement I am clear,
> Healed by stripes I am:
> Thou for me a curse wast made,
> That I might in thee be blest;
> Thou hast my full ransom paid,
> And in thy wounds I rest.[30]

Methodist hymnody sings about the atonement more than about anything else.

PASSION FOR HOLINESS

The "predestination/election" word-group occurs approximately fifteen times in Scripture, and Christians have fought fiercely over its meaning. The "holy/sanctity" word-group occurs 833 times, yet Christians have paid far less attention to it. Wesley, however, insists that holiness or final, full salvation is the grand promise of Scripture and the overarching theme of Scripture; it is the *raison d'être* of Methodism, the latter raised up by God "to spread scriptural holiness throughout the land."[31] (In every class, I tell my students that Scripture is preoccupied with holiness. In the wake of our denial of God's holiness, he reaffirms it; in the wake of our contradiction of ours, he reestablishes it. The ultimate purpose of the cross is not that we are forgiven but that we are rendered holy, forgiveness being necessary to the restoration of our holiness.)

In addressing this topic, Wesley characteristically speaks of "holiness of heart and life."[32] By "heart" Wesley means our inner intent, our atti-

---

30. Charles Wesley. "Glorious Saviour of my soul," in John Wesley, *Works*, vol. 7, 337–338.

31. For an exposition of this programmatic term, see Wesley, *Works*, vol. 1, 159–182.

32. This expression is found *passim* in Wesley. For an amplification of his "holiness of life arising from holiness of heart," see his *Works*, vol. 3, 75.

tude, and our disposition; by "life" he means our behaviour, our conduct, and our visibility. He insists that inner intent unmatched by outer manifestation is useless posturing, whereas an attempt at outer manifestation not rooted in inner transformation is crass self-righteousness. Supposed holiness of heart alone dishonours God in that it is feeble. Supposed holiness of life alone dishonours God in that it is arrogant. Holiness of heart and life are one as Spirit-quickened intention is fulfilled in Spirit-generated conduct.

Every day in his public ministry, Wesley interacted with people whose addictions had held them fast for years. In the face of their enslavement, he insisted, in effect, that God could do something with sin beyond forgiving it. Specifically, God could not only release them from sin's guilt (justification, forgiveness), but God could also release them from sin's grip (sanctification, holiness).[33] Beyond being pardoned, his people needed to be delivered.

Lest we forget Wesley's eschatological orientation, we need to hear him say again, "Justification gives us the right to heaven; holiness makes us fit for heaven."[34]

A ticket gives someone the right to the symphony concert; her musicality, however, renders her fit for the concert. What's the point of being admitted to the concert if one is tone-deaf and finds the world-class violinist a screechy scourge? What's the point of being admitted to that realm where God's will is done perfectly if one has never relished doing it at all?

Wesley was anything but naïve as to the grip wherewith sin throttles people. We need the company and the wisdom of fellow-believers,

---

33. Holiness of heart and life is intimately related to freedom from sin's guilt and grip. For an amplification of the latter see, e.g., Wesley, *Works*, vol. 1, 122–124; vol. 2, 120.

34. Wesley, *Christian Perfection*, 31. Wesley makes the same point in "On the Wedding Garment," in his *Works*, vol. 4, 144. He expected this written sermon (March 1790) to be his last, his pronouncement here concerning the relationship of justification to holiness being his final word to the Methodist people. (He lived another year and penned another five sermons.)

especially of those whose present deliverance will spare us paralyzing discouragement. In this context Wesley utters his famous "No holiness but social holiness."[35] By "social" he does not mean, contrary to the misunderstanding of liberal churchmanship, that "social holiness" is another term for a program of leftist social transmutation. He means, rather, precisely what the parachurch groups that have arisen from his ethos and that exist to facilitate a great deliverance (the "Anonymous" groups assisting the addicted of all sorts) have long known: the habituated (all sinners are such) need each other in order to escape their prison.

KINGDOM VISIBILITY

Repeatedly Wesley asked whether Britain could be called "Christian" in light of social inequities so extreme as to be iniquities. Repeatedly he challenged distillers on account of the damage their "liquid fire" fostered, rich horse moguls whose grain-devouring steeds deprived the needy of bread, and even tea-drinkers whose carriage-trade habit left them with insufficient funds for the poor. (See his "A Letter to a Friend Concerning Tea," 1748.)[36] "I love the poor,"[37] Wesley reminded sobered, industrious, thrifty Methodists whose social ascendancy distressed him.

Aware that the disadvantaged are more frequently and seriously ill than are the privileged and are more remote from medical intervention, Wesley scrounged money to employ a surgeon and an apothecary. (In the first five months alone drugs were distributed to 500 people.) In 1746, he established London's first free pharmacy. Haunted by the banks' refusal to lend his people money for start-up business loans, he scrabbled fifty pounds for the first wave of entrepreneurs, these people in turn lending

---

35. In this connection Wesley averred, "'Holy solitaries' is a phrase no more consistent with the gospel than holy adulterers." In Jackson, *Works of John Wesley*, vol. XIV, 321. For the same point, see Wesley, *Works*, vol. 1, 533–534.

36. In Jackson, *Works of John Wesley*, vol. XI, chap. LI.

37. John Wesley, *The Letters of John Wesley* (ed. John Telford; vol. 3; London, Epworth, 1931), 229.

to others so that 250 were helped in the first year. The school he developed for the children of Kingswood coal miners operates to this day.

Although some Christian advocates of a quasi-Marxist "social justice" like to claim Wesley as progenitor, he never vested confidence in a putative proletarian wisdom or virtue. Always concerned with the Kingdom of God, he regarded a philosophically-defined "justice" as no better, no more God-honouring, and, not least, no more just than the privilege it attempted to replace, as the French Revolution would shortly make plain. The scars he bore on his face and on his forehead reminded him every day of what Methodists could expect from mobs whose passions had not yet been reoriented by the gospel. If anyone needed to be informed, a survivor of the Wednesbury riots (1743) could help. For at Wednesbury, Methodists had been assaulted, their services violated, their homes torched, and their women raped. (Wesley's non-vindictiveness attests his Lord's triumph within him, for he visited the town thirty-three times and preached there at age 87, in 1790.)[38]

An able Hebraist, Wesley knew that the primary meaning of *mishpat* is "judgement"; secondarily it means "justice" as that human act quickened by God's judgement, which judgement aims at restoration (*shalom*) and is therefore replete with mercy. "Justice" in the Aristotelian (philosophical) sense—one gets what one deserves (and no more)—was not a determination of Wesley's understanding or ethos. Always nervous about the clamour for social justice in Revolutionary France where unjust savagery of the right would soon give way to unjust savagery of the left, Wesley-the-Tory held up the reign of God, not politically correct ideology, as the operative reality whereby a fallen creation is assimilated to the "new heavens and new earth in which righteousness dwells" (2 Pet 3:13).

---

38. For a depiction of the incidents referred to above and a comprehensive exploration of this assault on the Methodist people, see J. Leonard Waddy, *The Bitter Sacred Cup: The Wednesbury Riots 1743-44* (Madison, N.J.: World Methodist Historical Society, 1976).

MERCY IMMENSE AND FREE
EUCHARISTIC WORSHIP

Anglicans in Wesley's era received Holy Communion three times per year: Christmas, Easter, and Pentecost. Throughout his adult life, Wesley received Holy Communion on average 4.5 times per week. The Lord's Supper is an "instituted" means of grace, "instituted" signifying that in this Christ-mandated rite Jesus has pledged himself to his people *unfailingly*.[39]

Wesley was always astounded that some people who genuinely (claim to) fear God are indifferent concerning Holy Communion.[40] For him the grounds of "constant communion" (his unaltered vocabulary in 1732 and fifty-five years later in 1787) were twofold: one, God commands it; two, we need it.[41] Since Holy Communion is God's command and is therefore to be obeyed, neglecting it means we have "no piety." Since Holy Communion is God's provision and is therein a mercy, neglecting it means we have "no wisdom." Not surprisingly, then, Wesley's realism concerning the nature and efficacy of the Lord's Supper is notable: "What better way of *procuring* pardon? ... You have an opportunity of *receiving* his mercy" (emphasis mine). The Eucharist conveys the mercy it attests. When absentees advanced reasons why they should not communicate, Wesley's stern response was that they should not add disobedience to disobedience, no reason, however piously cherished, overturning God's precept and provision.[42]

Those who asserted "We don't feel any different for having been to the Lord's Table," Wesley dealt with at greater length. Drawing on his pastoral wisdom, he averred that if evaders simply obeyed, they would find affect catching up with act. Not finished with those who claim to be affect-deficient, Wesley maintained that at the Lord's Table, Christ meets them in person with a fivefold "benefit": they are strengthened "insensibly," made more fit for the service of God, made more constant

---

39. See, e.g., Wesley, *Works*, vol. 1, 378–397.
40. Wesley, *Works*, vol. 3, 428.
41. Wesley, *Works*, vol. 3, 428.
42. Wesley, *Works*, vol. 3, 435.

in the service of God, kept from backsliding, and spared many temptations.[43] Undeniably it is Wesley's conviction—together with that of the church catholic—that at the Lord's Table one receives Christ himself.

Not relenting at all, Wesley warns, "No man *(sic)* who does not receive it as often as he can has any pretence to prudence"[44]; and such a person, Wesley insists, lacks self-perception. In short, unless we frequent the Lord's Table, we are deficient in piety, in prudence, in obedience, and in perception of our need of mercy.

One more aspect of Wesley's understanding must be highlighted. Whereas the Reformed tradition maintains that Holy Communion is a "confirming" sacrament, ever since June, 1740, Wesley maintained it to be "converting" as well.[45] The Lord's Supper not merely confirms and strengthens in faith those already possessed of faith; it may also bring to faith the unbeliever whose dark night ends at the communion rail.

EPILOGUE

We should not equate Wesley's contribution with his theological legacy, with "our doctrines" (as he liked to say), or even with his broader intellectual influence. The gift of John Wesley is given anew, rather, as the people who name him embody his spirit; given again as his descendents exemplify the ethos of those whose work and whose witness fuelled the conflagration spreading throughout England and the New World. Even though it would be unfair to restrict "descendents" to Methodist preachers, it remains that Methodism, then and now, is conveyed not by a liturgy, by a curia, by a bureaucracy, or even by a hymnody, but, chiefly, is conveyed, as Methodist icon Hugh Price Hughes (1847–1902) insisted, by its preachers. Concerning these preachers, historian Dee Andrews has written that their service to the gospel, in early-day American Method-

---

43. Wesley, *Works*, vol. 3, 437.
44. Wesley, *Works*, vol. 3, 439.
45. Wesley, *Works*, vol. 19, 158.

ism, required "not only a gambler's nerves and a dancer's endurance but also the cunning of a hunter and the courage of a soldier."[46] She does not exaggerate, for of the first 737 Methodist ministers in America, one-half died before they were thirty years old. Two-thirds did not live long enough to serve twelve years. Vocation meant immolation. Not the least of Wesley's gifts to the wider church is selfless service to the Master, voiced by the apostle Peter and offered up by Methodist preachers, "We have left everything and followed you" (Mark 10:28 RSV).

---

46. Dee Andrews, *The Methodists and Revolutionary America, 1760–1800* (Princeton: Princeton University Press, 2002), 234.

Index

aesthetics, 76, 91
abortion, 210
Act of Uniformity (1662), 225
affluence, temptation of, 41–42
African Methodist Episcopal Church, 140
After Modernity, What? (Oden), 206
Agenda for Theology (Oden), 206
Alcoholics Anonymous, 115–116, 244, 276
alcoholism, 21–22
Aldersgate awakening/heartwarming, 20, 32–35, 37, 42, 61, 76, 85, 128–129, 219, 234–235
"Almost Christian, The" (Wesley), 19, 219, 264
Ambrose, 38, 196, 209
Ancient Christian Commentary on Scripture (Oden), 204–205. 207, 208
Andrews, Dee, 279–280
anger, 105, 248
Anglican Church (Canada), 141, 173
Anglican Prayer Book, *see* Book of Common Prayer
Anglicanism, 11, 18, 32, 34, 63–64, 75, 86, 92–93, 130, 131, 138, 141, 155, 160–161, 173–176, 177, 185–186, 201, 211, 216, 226, 233, 235, 240–241, 244, *see also* Church of England
Anglo-Catholicism, 92
Annesley, Dr Samuel, 30, 225, 226
antinomianism, 61, 62–64, 80–82, 86n2, 101–102, 103–104, 111–112, 129
Aquinas, Thomas, 12, 38, 152, 209
Arianism, 64, 78, 144, 216, 220, *see also* Arius; Council of Nicaea
Aristotle, 152, 277
Arius, 144, *see also* Arianism; Council of Nicaea
Arminian Magazine, 143
Arminianism, 143–152, 208, 220, *see also* Arminius
Arminius, Jacob, 144–152, 208, *see also* Arminianism
arrears of sin, 56, 109–110
Articles of Religion (Methodist), 176
arts, the, 141, 177
assurance, 48, 52–53, 62
Athanasisus, 38
Athanasius, 21, 144, 196, 209, 267
atonement, 12, 36, 67–69, 107, 112, 113, 125, 145, 151, 169–170, 196, 220, 257–258, 273, *see also* limited atonement
Augustine, 21, 38–39, 149, 152, 205, 208, 209, 210, 267
"Awake, Thou That Sleepest" (Wesley), 219

Baius, Michael, 152
Bañez, Domingo, 152
bands, 25–26, 96, 128, 138
baptism, 39, 201, 211–212, 218, 233
Barth, Karl, 12, 38, 210, 263
Basil the Great, 38, 209
Belgic Confession, 148–149
beliefism, 62
Beza, Theodore, 147, 149
Bible, *see* Scripture

Bible Christian Church of Canada, 139–140
Biel, Gabriel, 69
Birney, Earle, 177
Black, William, 139
Bland, Salem, 141
Book of Common Prayer, 31, 92, 131, 227, 234, 261, 267
Booth, Catherine (Mumford), 189–200
Booth, Herbert, 198
Booth, William, 183–202
Bourignon, Antoinette, 124
Briggs, William, 142
British Methodist Episcopal Church, 140
British Wesleyans, 139
Brother Lawrence, 124
Brown, George, 179
Bullinger, Heinrich, 13
Bultmann, Rudolf, 206, 210
Burrows, Eva, 201

Calvinism/Calvinist theology, 36, 37, 54, 56–57, 61, 62, 63, 65, 72–74, 92–93, 102n3, 103, 109, 113, 124nn22&24, 129n29, 138, 145, 147, 148–152, 171, 177, 184, 187, 209, 220, 239, 257, 263, 267, 271, *see also Institutes of the Christian Religion* (Calvin)
Cardinal Bellarmine, 150
"Case of Reason Impartially Considered, The" (Wesley), 88
"Catholic Spirit" (Wesley), 214, 218–219, 262, 264–265
catholicity, of the church, 11, 19–20, 35–36, 67, 92–93, 109, 120, 129n30, 130, 138, 161, 240, 244, 261, 279; of education/learning, 92–94; of space, 93; of spirit, 218–219, 22; of theology, 68, 92, 220, 268; of time, 93
Chalmers, Thomas, 115, 116
Charles II (King), 226
Charterhouse School, 30
Chesterton, G. K., 90, 269
Chown, Samuel 141
Christ alone, 32–33, 72, 82, 148, 234
Christian antiquity, 31, 93, 104, 207, *see also* Church Fathers
Christian Guardian, 176

Christian Library (Wesley), 20, 109, 267, 270
Christian Mission, The, 199
Christian perfection, *see* sanctification
Christian Perfection (Law), 110
"Christian Perfection" (Wesley), 47–48
Christianity Today, 206
Christology, 39, 64, 67, 70, 75, 123, 144
Chrysostom, John, 38, 209
Church of England, 29, 31, 34n4, 63, 137, 139, 140–41, 176, 184–186, 225, 262. *See also* Anglicanism
Church Fathers, 21, 30–31, 35, 38, 86, 90, 93, 104, 119, 129–130, 137, 148–149, 196, 204–212, 219–220, 262, 270, *see also* Christian antiquity
church government, 183–188
Church of the Nazarene, 142
Church of Scotland, 140, 173, 176

Cicero 74–75, 77n54
circuits, 172–173, 186–187, 191, 193–194, 197
circuit meetings, 187
circumcision, 211–212
"Circumcision of the Heart, The" (Wesley), 61, 75–76, 138
classes, 25, 128, 138, 185–186
class leaders, 187
Clergy Reserves, 173, 175
Colonial Advocate, The, 174
commands/commandments of God, 22, 26, 49–50, 55, 80, 88, 97, 150, 179, 255–258, *see also* covered promises; root command of Scripture; Ten Commandments
Commentaries (Blackstone), 172
Commentaries (Calvin), 56, 148
Commentaries (Wesley), 73–74, 76
Commentary on Galatians (Luther), 61, 123, 267
Commentary on Romans (Luther), 20, 32, 61, 267
congregationalists, 184
Congregational Union of Canada, 18, 140, 207
conscience, 50, 155 187, 225, 231
Co-operative Commonwealth Federation, 141
Coughlan, Laurence, 139

INDEX

Council of Nicaea, 144
Council of Trent, 101, 130n32
Counter-Reformation, 21, 86, 92–93, 124, 261, 270, *see also* Roman Catholicism
covered promises, 22–23, 97, 107, *see also* commands/commandments of God
Cranmer, Thomas, 267
cross, the, 12, 19, 69, 127, 151, 169–170, 236, 274, *see also* atonement
cross-bearing, 55–56, 102, 259, *see also* discipleship
Cummin, Alexander, 188

Declaration of Indulgence (1672), 226
Deed of Declaration (1784), 184
depravity, 33, 50, 68–69, 113, 145–146, 196, 220, *see also* Total Depravity
discipleship, 41, 47, 55–56, 62, 64, 102, 105–106, 110–111, 118–119, 172, 217, 231, 238–239, 253, 256, *see also* cross-bearing
Dissenters, 137, 155, 177, 186–187, 225–226, *see also* non-conformists
district meetings, 187
Doctrinal Standards in the Wesleyan Tradition (Oden), 211
doctrine, 40, 214
Donald N. and Kathleen G. Bastian Chair of Wesley Studies, 142, 213, 221
double predestination, 145, 197, *see also* predestination
Dudek, Louis, 177
Duty of Constant Communion, The (Wesley), 253

Eastern church, 19–20, 21, 38–39, 128–129, 204–205, 208, 209, 211
Eastern Orthodoxy, 19, 21, 267
Ecumenical Councils, 210
Edwardian Homilies, 92, 269
Edwards, Jonathan, 12, 86, 118, 143–144
elect/election, 12, 208, 274
Elizabeth I (Queen), 93
English Reformation, 261, *see also* Reformation
Enlightenment, the, 48, 91–92, 172
enthusiasm/enthusiasts, 20, 39, 46–49, 54–56, 63, 82, 87–88, 105, 11, 113, 126, 184

Ephrem the Syrian, 267
epistemology, 49–50, 54, 144–145
Epistle to the Romans (Luther), 32–33, 234
Erasmus, Desiderius, 178–179
eschatology, Calvinist/Reformed, 19, 263; Roman Catholic, 18, 263–264; Wesleyan, 19, 81–82, 122, 211, 215–216, 263, 264–265, 275
Essay Concerning Human Understanding (Locke), 182
ethics, 70–71, 91, 102, 112, 209
Eucharist, 31, 92, 128, 261–262, 278, *see also* Holy Communion; sacraments
Evangelical Association, 140
Evangelical Awakening/Revival, 30, 47, 48
evangelical poverty, 41
evangelism, 34, 141, 202, 231, 272
Eversfield, Stephen, 188
Examination of Perkins' Pamphlet (Arminius), 150
extra nos, pro nobis, 39, 67–68, *see also* in nobis

faith, and antinomianism, 62–63; and Arianism, 144; assurance of, 56, 62, 137, 156; and atonement, 12; binds us to Christ, 235–236; and catholic love, 218–219; of the church universal, 91, 207–209; in Christ, 32–33, 62, 63, 67, 76, 217; and Christian Perfection, 109–109; and the creeds, 209; and discipleship, 118–119; and doctrine, 214; as dynamic, 114; and education, 230; essentials of, 218; and faith alone/ *sola fide*, 61, 102; and the gospel, 40, 47; by grace/as gift of God, 33, 34, 46, 61, 69, 86, 137–138, 145–146, 220, 238; and inbred sin, 106; and human affirmation and activity, 69; and humanism, 91; and knowing the Father, 145; and the law, 60, 63–64, 71; and limited atonement, 151; and loving God, 19; and moralism, 34, 61, 157; and mysticism, 33, 61, 123–124; and nominal Christianity, 219; and obedience, 62; and preaching, 30; and predestination, 150, 151; price of, 219–220; and prosperity, 128; and reason, 86, 88, 89–91; as relationship, 41, 114; and repentance, 13, 105–106; and restoration of *imago*

dei, 67–68, 116–117; and righteousness, 150; and sacraments, 201–202, 253–258; and sanctification/holiness/holy living, 37, 61, 102, 109, 138, 196; and self-abandonment, 83; and the Spirit, 146; and stewardship, 42; witness to, 223; and witness of the Spirit, 234, *see also* justification by faith
faith alone, 20, 35, 61, 102
Fall, the, 23, 36, 39, 66–69, 79, 81, 90, 102, 133, 144–145, 151, *see also* depravity; Total Depravity
Family Compact, 173, 175, 178
fanaticism, *see* enthusiasm
Farther Appeal to Men of Reason and Religion, Part II, A (Wesley), 75
Fénélon, François, 124
Flavelle family, 141
Fletcher, John, 196
forgiveness, *see* atonement; faith; justification by faith; repentance
formalism, 39, 46
freedom, and Christian Perfection, 102–103; of God, 125, 254; and "graced willing," 151–152; vs. liberty, 66, 132; to obey Christ, 66; and sanctification, 103–105; and self-forgetful love of God and neighbour, 97, 115; from self-preoccupation, 240
Free Church tradition, 216
Free Methodist Church, 140, 142
Frei, Hans, 206
French Revolution, 180, 277
Freud, Sigmund, 90, 91
fruits of class membership, 25–26
fruits of the Spirit, 565

General Spread of the Gospel, The (Wesley), 133
Gerhardt, Paul, 233
Gill, John, 103
Globe (Toronto), 179
glory of God, 72–74, 111, 241
godliness, 62, 82, 102, 138
Gomarus, Franciscus, 152
Gooderham family, 141
gospel, and assurance, 231; and discipleship, 128; and evangelism, 145; free to all, 143, 146; and hymns, 30, 156–157; and humanistic learning, 180; of justification, 85; and *logos*, 88; vs. moralism, 235; and mysticism, 120–121; preached, 155; promise of, 23; promise of freedom, 97; and Prosperity Gospel, 118; and release from power of sin, 37–38, 42, 237; spirit of, 23; and social elevation, 40–41
grace, Arminius on, 148–152; and belief, 33; and Christian perfection/sanctification, 37, 103–106, 108–120; and deliverance from power of sin, 247; and Eastern Church, 39; efficacy of, 197; fasting as a means of, 21; grace alone, 34; and hymns, 156–157; and mysticism, 125; as presence of Christ, 40; prevenient, 68–70; and reason, 86, 88, 90–91; and repentance, 13, 36; 39–40, 50, 61, 149; and sacraments, 212; sovereignty of, 231; state of, 39; subsequent work of, 248; and thankfulness, 40, *see also gratia operans/ co-operans*; justification by faith; sanctification
grace alone, 34, 61
gratia operans/co-operans, 149, 208
Great Ejection, the, (1662), 219, 225
Gregory the Great, 38, 209
Gregory of Nazianzus, 38, 209, 211

hagios, 246
Heidelberg Catechism, 149
Herberg, Will, 210
heresy, 93, 105, 144–145, 146, 149, 209–209
higher education, 88, 91–92
holiness, *see* sanctification
Holiness Churches, 12, 121
Holy Club, 30, 31, 137
Holy Communion, 26–27, 31, 32, 129, 131, 137, 138, 186, 191, 201–202, 233–234, 241, 247, 253–259, 278–279, *see also* Eucharist; sacraments
Holy Spirit, 12, 21, 34, 38, 45–57, 71, 85–86, 102n3, 105, 112, 114, 125, 126, 127, 131, 145–146, 148, 156, 164, 169–170, 196, 198, 201, 208, 212, 218, 231, 237–238, 241, 246, 247, 248, 256, 264

INDEX

homoousion, 38, *see also* Athanasius
Homer, 271
Hopkey, Sophia, 32, 234
Hughes, Hugh Price, 195–196, 279
humanism, 30–31, 91–92, 146–147, 148, 152, 178–179, 180, 226–227, *see also* Enlightenment; Renaissance
humility, 33, 34, 55, 61, 114, 116, 138, 248
hymns/hymnody, 12, 30, 126, 139, 166–169, 198, 274

imago Dei, 66–67, 86, 116–117
Imitation of Christ (à Kempis), 110
imputed obedience, 62
incarnation, the, 12, 52, 69, 71, 73, 76, 88, 144, 164–165, 216
Industrial Revolution, 40–41
infralapsarianism, 152
in nobis, 39, 67–68, 71, *see also extra nos, pro nobis*
Institutes of the Christian Religion (Calvin), 37n11, 48, 54, 102n3, 124, 220n3, 267
itinerant ministers/evangelists, 11, 140, 153, 162, 185–186, 193, 197

James II (King), 29
Jerome, 38
John Wesley's Scriptural Christianity (Oden), 211
Jones, Peter, 140, 175
judgment, 12, 102, 132, 150, 192, 217, 218, 254, 259, 273
Judgment Day, 273
Junius, Franciscus, 152
justification by faith, 20, 34–37 47–58, 62, 85–94, 104–134, 138, 179–182, 202, 217, 235–236, 264, 268, 271–272, *see also* grace

kadosh, 246
Kempis, Thomas à, 110, 229
kenosis, 12
Kierkegaard, Soren, 52, 212
Kilham, Alexander, 186–188, 199
kingdom of God, 24, 94, 106, 219, 246, 247
kingdom of heaven, 201
Kingswood School, 24, 277
Latimer, Hugh, 267
latitudinarianism, 218, 262

Lavington, George (Bishop), 247–248
law, and antinomians, 81–82; convicts of sin, 239; and creation, 79; delight in, 77; dependent on God's will, 79; disclosure of God's nature, 73–74; eternal, 77; and Epistle to the Romans, 82–83; express resemblance of God; and the Fall, 79; and fitness of all things, 80; of God, 59–84, 113–134, 238–242; God's intent for all creation, 79; goodness of, 81; and gospel, 64, 74; to guide believers, 239; and holiness as a gift of God, 183; and holiness of God, 77–78; implies Jesus Christ, 80–81; Jesus Christ as substance of, 65, 66, 72–73, 75, 81; just, 78–81; love of, 75; and love of neighbour, 75; as Mediator, 82; moral, 66–67, 70–71, 81; and moralists, 82; Mosaic, 65; natural, 69–70; nature of, 71–77; orders society, 239; "original" of, 71; properties of, 77–82; re-inscription of, 67–70; righteousness the fruit of, 82; the Torah and Jesus Christ, 82–83; transcript/efflux of God, 80; upheld by faith, 238, *see also* commands/commandments of God; Ten Commandments; Torah
Law, William, 110
"Law Established through Faith (I), The" (Wesley), 64
"Law Established through Faith (II), The" (Wesley), 64
lay delegates, 187
lay preachers, 160–161, 266
legalism, 22, 233, 235, 237
"Letter to a Friend Concerning Tea, A" (Wesley), 276
"Letter to a Roman Catholic, A" (Wesley), 262
Levellers, 24
Lewis, C. S. 93, 117
liberty, 66, 132–133
Life and Diary of David Brainerd, The (Edwards), 118
limited atonement, 12, 138; *see also* atonement
liturgy, 31, 174, 209, 226, *see also* worship
loans to start businesses, 24, 276–277
Loci Communes (Melanchthon), 178
Locke, John 20, 172

Loescher, Valentius, 37
logos, 76, 88–89
Lord's Supper, *see* Eucharist; Holy Communion,
Lopez, Gregory, 124
Losee, William 139, 251
love for God and neighbour, 18, 23, 42–43, 75, 97, 107–108, 111, 115, 240–241, 248–249
Lutheran theology/Lutheranism, 2, 19–20, 27, 32–44, 61–62, 64, 65, 101–102, 103–105, 118n13, 123, 124n22, 134, 146–47 178, 187, 209, 234, 235, 239, 244, 253, 256, 268.

Macarius, 124, 267
McGuire, Dolly 17
Mackenzie, William Lyon, 174
Maddox, Randy, 62n8, 129n28, 131
mainline Protestantism, 203
Marx/Marxism, 90, 91, 277
Massey family, 141
Maxfield, Thomas 103–104
Melanchthon, Philip, 12, 109–110, 178–180, 239
mercy, 12–13, 20, 26–27, 42, 68, 150, 170, 192, 198, 216, 231, 244, 256–257
metaphysics, 70–71, 91, 152
Methodist Book Concern, 177
Methodism, Canadian, 140–142
Methodist Church (Canada, Newfoundland, Bermuda), 139–140
Methodist Church of Canada, 139
Methodist Episcopal Church of Canada, 139–140
Methodist Episcopal Church (U.S.A.), 139
Methodist New Connexion, 188–192, 195, 197–202
Methodist New Connexion Church in Canada, 139, 189
Methodist Times, The, 195–196
mishpat, 277
mission to Georgia, 31, 137, 156
missionary work, 140, 142
modernity, 93, 204, 207, 272
Molina, Luis de, 124, 152
Moral and Political Philosophy (Paley), 172
moralism, 33, 61, 66, 75–77, 80, 102–134, 137–138, 249

Moravians, 32, 62, 128
Mountain, Jacob (Bishop), 173
mysticism, 21, 33–34, 61, 85, 92–93, 106, 120–130, 137–138, 261, 270

neo-orthodoxy, 210
neo-Platonism, 211–212
Nelles, Samuel, 141
Newman, John Henry 12, 210
new birth, 37, 236–237, 241, 243–244
New Itinerary, The, 188
New Testament, 59–60, 72, 82–83, 138, 150, 246
Niebuhr, H. Richard, 206, 210
non-conformists, 175, 225–226, *see also* Dissenters
Notes on the New Testament (Wesley), 59–60, 72–73, 76, 83, 117, 126

obedience, to Christ, 34, 62, 65, 77, 109–110, 239; to God, 33, 49, 61, 106
obscurantism, 88–89, 92
Oden, Thomas C., 203–212
Old Testament, 82, 117

On the Fall of Man (Wesley), 133
On Patience (Wesley), 109, 114, 116
"On Perfection" (Wesley), 47–48, 107
On Sin in Believers (Wesley), 104, 105
One Hundred Preachers, Conference of, 184, 186, 187, 188
"One Thing Needful, The" (Wesley), 94
"Original, Nature, Properties and Use of the Law, The" (Wesley), 64
original guilt, 21, 38
original sin, 21, 35–36, 38, 50, 124, 148, 201, 268
Outler, Albert, 11, 113n10, 120n14, 210
Oxford Institute of Methodist Theological Studies, 11, 101
Oxford University, 20, 30, 86–87, 137, 156, 160, 164, 196, 205, 206, 219, 220, 230, 233, 254, 267

Packer, J. I., 206
Parables of Kierkegaard (Oden), 212
parachurch ministries, 244–245, 276
Pascal, 121, 124, 126
pastoral care, 210, 227, 231

INDEX

Pastoral Theology: Essentials of Ministry (Oden), 207
Patristics, *see* Church Fathers
Pelagianism, 34, 102, 109, 148–149, 151, 208, 220, *see also* semi-Pelagianism
Pentecost, 17, 31
Pentecostal Churches, 12
Perkins, William 150–151
Pierce, Lorne 142
pietism, 11, 208
Plain Account of Christian Perfection, A (Wesley), 47–48, 87, 102, 110, 120–122, 126, 265
poetic influences on Charles Wesley, 164
Polkinghorne, John, 88–89
poor, ministry to, 18, 23, 25, 31, 128, 137, 140–141, 190, 220, 240, 250, 276
positivism, 91
practical divinity, 12
Praedicatio verbi Dei verbum Dei est, 13
prayer, 26, 97–98, 112, 238, 131, 154, 194, 208, 218, 236, 241
preaching, 11, 12, 13 18, 20, 24, 30, 40, 45–46, 47, 48, 63, 64, 85–86 87, 118, 157, 160–163, 171, 172–173, 175, 184, 188, 190–191, 193, 195–197, 214, 219–220, 225–226, 230–231, 235, *see also* women preachers
predestination, 36, 102n3, 138, 143, 145–146, 147, 150–152, 205, 208, *see also* double predestination
Preface to the Epistle to the Romans (Luther), 32, 61, 234
Presbyterians, 173, 176, 187, 207, 210, 213
Presbyterian Church in Canada, 18, 140, 208
pride, 41, 87, 105, 103, 111, 115, 116, 130, 162, 248
Primitive Methodist Church, 139–140, 193
Primitive Physic (Wesley), 23
Primitive Remedies (Wesley), 122
Progress of Liberty Amongst the People Called Methodists, The (Kilham), 187
psychology, 13, 46, 91, 111, 115, 210, 272
public education, and Melanchthon, 178–179; Methodist effect on, 141; and Ryerson, 141, 178–180
publishing, 142
Puritanism, 30, 57, 92–94, 97, 107, 109–110, 137–138, 155, 184, 187, 196–197, 211–212, 214, 217, 219, 220, 225–226, 229, 231, 239, 261, 266, 267

Quakers, 34–35, 193, 201, 272
quarterly meetings, 186

Rack, Henry, 153
Radical Obedience: The Ethics of Rudolf Bultmann (Oden), 2067
Railton, George Scott, 199
Ramus, Petrus, 152
rationalism, 76, 89–90
reason, in economy of grace, 89; and enthusiasm, 87; and the Fall, 90; false reasoning, 88; gift of God, 88; God-ordained tool, 86; and the Gospel, 90; and grace, 90–91; handmaid of faith, 89; and *imago dei*, 86; and the incarnation, 88; and logic, 88, 266; and the *logos*, 89; and loving God with mind, 88; and nature, 89
reconciliation, 12, 51, 53, 66–67, 69, 273
Reformation, the, 21–28, 34, 37–44, 56, 91–94, 123–134, 137–142, 146–152, 178–182, 208–212, 217, 226, 261, 271, *see also* English Reformation
Reformed churches/tradition, 34, 147, 263, 265, 271, 272, 279
Reformers, 13, 34, 50, 66, 68–69, 92, 109, 145, 148, 196, 201, 208, 211, 219–220, 264, 266–267, 272
regeneration, 104, 141, 149, 201, 212, 236–237, *see also* new birth; sacramental efficacy/regeneration; sanctification
Religious Affections (Edwards), 86
Remonstrants, 146, 147
Renaissance, 30–31, 91–92, 152, 226
repentance, 13, 36, 55, 105–107, 119, 150, 160, 256
Repentance of Believers, The (Wesley), 105–106
Requiem: A Lament in Three Movements (Oden), 206
"Review of a Sermon, Preached by the Honourable and Reverend John Strachan" (Ryerson), 174–175
righteousness, of Christ, 57, 62, 82–83, 114, 220; and creation, 24; by faith, 150;

as fruit of law, 82; of God, 217; as ground of justification, 62; and Holy Spirit, 47; imputed, 62; inherent, 62; inward and outward, 107; and *kadosh/hagios*, 246; and kingdom of God, 246; and *makarios*, 257; and moralism, 76; and romanticism, 46; works, 33, 62, 125, 217, *see also* self-righteousness
Roberts, Charles G. D., 177
Roberts Wesleyan College, 85
Romans 7, interpretations of, 60–61, 74, 77–78, 148–149
Romans 9, interpretations of, 149–150
Roman Catholicism, 18, 19–20, 21 38–40, 41 86, 92–94, 118n13, 122, 124, 134, 122–134, 146–147, 151, *see also* Counter-Reformation
root command of Scripture, 22, 97, 245, 266, *see also* sanctification
"Rules of the Band Societies" (Wesley), 25n3, 26, 97–98
Rules and Exercises of Holy Living and Holy Dying (Taylor), 110
Ryerson, Egerton, 17, 141, 171–181
Ryerson, George, 175
Ryerson Press, The, 177

sacramental efficacy/regeneration, 201, 211–212
sacraments, 62–84, 146–152, 201–202, 210, 254–260, *see also* baptism; Holy Communion
St. Bartholomew's Day massacre (1572), 219
Salvation Army, 142, 196, 198–199, 201–202
"Salvation by Faith" (Wesley), 33, 219, 220
sanctification, and awareness of inward/ inbred sin, 105–106, 118–119; degrees of, 107, 112; as deliverance from habituation of sin, 21–22, 37, 42, 96–97, 161, 247, 275; as deliverance from power of sin, 32, 37, 95–97, 104, 129, 130, 138, 161, 237, 240, 244–245, 246; and discipleship, 47, 102, 110, 119; as a doctrine, 39–40; entire, 104n4, 107, 108, 111,114, 115, 118, 130; eschatological reality of, 122, 129n30; fits Christian for eternal blessings, 43, 104, 111, 117, 243–244, 275; and godliness, 78, 138, 140–141, 151; grand deposit/pearl of Methodism, 108, 120, 129, 196, 244, 274; growth in grace, 111, 112, 117; gradual and instantaneous, 120n16; integrates will and affections, 116–117, 131–132; and holiness of heart and life, 21, 22, 96–97, 244, 246–249, 250, 274–275; holiness as root commandment of Scripture, 22–23, 97, 245, 266; as instantaneous work of God, 106; and inward and outward righteousness, 105, 107, 110, 120, 268; and justification, 111n9, 117, 129n30, 130, 243–244; as justification and sanctification together, 104; Magisterial Reformers' understanding of, 130; new nature from God, 244; as organizing principle of Wesley's theology, 105; Patristic understanding of, 130; perfection in love, 23, 115; promise of Scripture, 274; Puritan understanding of, 130; as restoration of God's image, 39, 66–67, 102, 116–117; and self-forgetful love of God and neighbour, 23, 42, 97, 107, 240, 248–249, 264, 265; and *simul totus peccator simul totus iustus*, 101, 108, 109, 131; social holiness, 96, 261, 276; and *sola fide*, 102; as testimony of the Spirit, 112, 114; as third use of the law, 109, 239; as transformation, 39, 102, 129, 196–197, 266, 275; and works righteousness, 62
Scholasticism, Protestant, 39
scholastics, 69, 151–152
science, 20, 88–89, 141, 177, 179
scientia media, 152
shalom, 277
Scotus, Duns 152
"Scriptural Christianity" (Wesley), 211, 219–220
Scripture, *passim*
Select Societies, 138
selfism, 97, 239–240
self-abandonment, 83, 97, 99, 115, 240
self-examination, 49–50
self-forgetfulness, 18, 34, 42, 97, 114–115, 129, 240, 248–249, 250
self-perception, 50

INDEX

self-preoccupation, 23, 97, 115, 217, 239–240, 249
self-righteousness, 33, 156, 217, 239, 247, 275
self-will, 105, 248
semi-Pelagianism, 34, 64, 144, 151, 208, *see also* Pelagianism
Serious Call to the Devout and Holy Life, A (Law), 110
Sermons on Several Occasions (Wesley), 33, 45–46, 47, 48, 59
"Showing Charity to Repentant Sinners" (Wesley), 160
Simon, Menno, 209
simul totus peccator simul totus iustus, 101, 109, 131
small group ministry, 25, 26, 95–99
Social Gospel movement, 141
social holiness 96–100, 141
Societies, 25, 64, 97–98, 138, 185–186, 251, 263
Society of Friends, *see* Quakers
Society for the Protection of Aboriginal Inhabitants of the British Dominions, 140
Socinianism, 148, *see also* unitarianism
sola fide, *see* faith alone
sola scriptura, 271
soteriology, 34, 38, 64, 138, 144
Spiritual Homilies (Macarius), 267
Spurgeon, C. H., 118
Standard Church, 142
Stevens, Wallace, 93–94
stewards, 185–186
stillness, 62–63, 128
Strachan, John (Bishop), 173–174, 177, 180
Streetsville Methodist Church/Streetsville United Church, 181
Suarez, Francisco, 152
subjectivism, 39, 48–49, 55, 216, 232
supralapsarian, 15, 152
systematic theology, 12, 178, 209–210, 268
Systematic Theology (Oden), 209

Taylor, Jeremy, 110
Ten Commandments, 70, 81, 253, *see also* commands/commandments of God; Torah

Theresa D'Avila, 121, 124
Thirty-nine Articles of Religion (Church of England), 92, 177
Torah, 65, 71, 82–83
Torrance, T. F., 89n5
Total Depravity, 33, 36, 50, 68–69, 101, 113, 145–146, 196, 220, 267, *see also* depravity; the Fall
tracts, purpose of, 45–46, 64, 178
Traill, Catherine Parr, 177
transcendence of God, 53
trustees, 186
Tyndale, William, 166, 267
Tyndale University College & Seminary, 142, 213, 221

unitarianism, 148, 216, 220, *see also* Socinianism
United Brethren in Christ, 140
United Church of Canada, 17, 140, 142, 172, 181, 206–207, 213
United Empire Loyalists, 174, 175
United Methodist Church, 203, 205, 211
University of Toronto, 141, 177
Upper Canada Academy, 177
Upper Canada Gazette, 176
"Upon Our Lord's Sermon on the Mount" (Wesley), 63

viaticum, 262
Victoria (Queen), 241
Victoria College/University, 141, 177, 179
Vincent of Lérins, 207
Vincentian Canon, 35, 268
virtue, 62, 74–75, 76, 235–236

War of 1812, 171
War of Independence, 155
Watts, Isaac, 168
Wednesbury riots, 277
Wesley, Charles, 12 12, 27, 30, 61, 62, 103, 107, 120–121, 130–131, 139, 153–170, 196, 198, 215k 219, 231, 232, 238, 249, 262, 273
Wesley, Hetty, 159–160
Wesley, Kezia, 156, 229, 230
Wesley, Samuel (father of JW), 29, 137, 155–156, 159–160, 227–228, 230
Wesley, Samuel Sebastian, 158

Wesley, Susannah, 29–30, 137, 143–144, 155–156, 225–232
Wesley's Chapel, 187
Wesleyan Church, 142
Wesleyan Methodist Church in Canada, 139, 142
Wesleyan Methodist Conference of Eastern British America, 139
Wesleyan Methodists, 47, 139–140, 174
Wesleyan Reformers, 189
Wesleyanism/Wesleyan theology, 12–13, 23, 64, 94, 106–107, 197, 207, 209–210, 211–212, 213–216
Western church, 21, 38–39, 93, 128–129, 204–205, 209
Whitefield, George, 143, 154–155, 157, 197–198, 266
William of Orange, 29, 228
Williams, William Carlos, 93–94
witness/testimony, of our spirit, 49–56; of the Spirit, 47–57, 105, 112, 114, 237–238
"Witness of the Spirt (I and II), The" (Wesley), 46, 48, 54, 55
women preachers, 199–201
Women's Missionary Society, 140
Woodsworth, James S. 17, 141
Wordsworth, William, 153, 198
works righteousness, *see* righteousness
worship, 26–27, 78, 80, 126, 138, 185, 190, 197, 208, 210, 213, 215, 216, 218, 226, *see also* liturgy

Yonge Street Circuit, 172

Zinzendorf, Count, 104, 105
Zwingli, Ulrich, 21, 147

www.ingramcontent.com/pod-product-compliance
Lightning Source LLC
Chambersburg PA
CBHW022106150426
43195CB00008B/296